Inequality, Power a

This volume highlights issues of power, inequality, and resistance for Asian, African American, and Latino/a students in distinct U.S. and international contexts. Through a collection of case studies it links universal issues relating to inequality in education, such as Asian, Latino, and African American males in the inner-city neighborhoods, Latina teachers and single mothers in California, undocumented youth from Mexico and El Salvador, immigrant Morrocan youth in Spain, and immigrant Afro-Caribbean and Indian teenagers in New York and in London. The volume explores the processes that keep students thriving academically and socially, and outlines the patterns that exist among individuals—students, teachers, parents—to resist the hegemony of the dominant class and school failure. With emphasis on racial formation theory, this volume fundamentally argues that education, despite inequality, remains the best hope of achieving the American dream.

Gilberto Q. Conchas is professor of education policy and social context at the University of California, Irvine. Conchas' research focuses on inequality with an emphasis on urban communities and schools. He is the author of *The Color of Success: Race and High-Achieving Urban Youth* (2006), *Small Schools and Urban Youth: Using the Power of School Culture to Engage Youth* (2008), and *StreetSmart SchoolSmart: Urban Poverty and the Education of Adolescent Boys* (2012).

Michael A. Gottfried is an assistant professor in the department of education at the Gevirtz School at the University of California, Santa Barbara. Dr. Gottfried's research focuses on the economics of education and education policy. Using the analytic tools from these disciplines, he has examined issues pertaining to peer effects, classroom context, and STEM. Dr. Gottfried has published numerous articles in these areas and won multiple scholarly awards for his research, including the AERA's Outstanding Publication in Methodology Award (2010 and 2012) and the Highest Reviewed Paper Award (2013).

Routledge Research in Educational Equality and Diversity

Books in the series include:

Identity, Neoliberalism and Aspiration
Educating white working-class boys
Garth Stahl

Faces of Discrimination in Higher Education in India
Quota Policy, Social Justice and the Dalits
Samson K. Ovichegan

Inequality, Power and School Success
Case Studies on Racial Disparity and Opportunity in Education
Edited by Gilberto Q. Conchas and Michael A. Gottfried with Briana M. Hinga

Inequality, Power and School Success

Case Studies on Racial Disparity
and Opportunity in Education

**Edited by Gilberto Q. Conchas
and Michael A. Gottfried
with Briana M. Hinga**

Routledge
Taylor & Francis Group

LONDON AND NEW YORK

First published 2015 by Routledge

2 Park Square, Milton Park, Abingdon, Oxon OX14 4RN
711 Third Avenue, New York, NY 10017, USA

Routledge is an imprint of the Taylor & Francis Group, an informa business

First issued in paperback 2016

Library of Congress Cataloging-in-Publication Data

Inequality, power and school success : case studies on racial disparity
and opportunity in education / edited by Gilberto Q. Conchas and Michael A.
Gottfried with Briana M. Hinga.
    pages cm. — (Routledge research in educational equality and diversity)
    Includes index.
  1. Educational equalization—United States—Case studies.   2. Minorities—
Education—United States.   3. Children of minorities—Education—
United States.   4. Children of immigrants—Education.   5. Racism
in education—United States.   6. Discrimination in education—United
States.   7. Educational sociology.   I. Conchas, Gilberto Q.
  LC213.2.I44 2015
  379.2'6—dc23
  2014047172

ISBN: 978-1-138-83788-1 (hbk)
ISBN: 978-1-138-71915-6 (pbk)

Typeset in Sabon
by Apex CoVantage, LLC

To research that makes a difference.

Contents

PART III
Gender, Self-Identity, and the Cultivation
of Sociopolitical Resistance

PART IV
Immigrant Global Communities, Disparity,
and the Struggle for Legitimacy

Introduction

Sean Drake, Gilberto Q. Conchas,
Briana M. Hinga, and Michael A. Gottfried

> I sit with Shakespeare and he winces not. Across the color-line
> I move arm in arm with Balzac and Dumas . . . I summon Aristotle
> and Aurelius and what soul I will, and they come all graciously with
> no scorn nor condescension. So, wed with Truth, I dwell above the
> Veil. Is this the life you grudge us, O knightly America?
>
> —W.E.B. Du Bois, 1903

Education is universally a powerful vehicle of social mobility—facilitating employment, economic freedom and stability, and contributing to an improved quality of life for those who experience its opportunities. Indeed, many individuals, families, and communities have made tremendous intergenerational progress toward achieving their dreams on the strength of a quality education in the United States and abroad. But education systems are also fraught with systematic inequalities that both mirror and reproduce disparities in broader society as they ripple beyond school walls. Let us walk you through glaring disparities in education.

Gaps in educational attainment have remained stagnant or have grown large over time. For instance, let us consider U.S. high school completion rates. According to many educational scholars, high school graduation rates are supported as highly indicative measures of educational attainment and future economic success (Card and Krueger 1994; Evans and Schwab 1995; Levy and Murnane 1992). In fact, many deem high school completion as more indicative than test scores (Card and Krueger 1994). Data on high school completion from the U.S. Department of Education (2013) suggests that White students are now practically graduating at 100%. Whereas Black students have made progress to close completion gaps with Whites and Asians over the past 30 years, significant Black-White and Black-Asian high school completion gaps persist, as shown in Figure 0.1. Latino students also continue to struggle. In 1985, less than half of all Latino students completed high school. In 2013, less than 70% of Latino students completed high school, compared to 93% of White students and 90% of Asian students. Therefore, whereas we do see improvements in completion rates across all student groups, these improvements have certainly not closed the gaps.

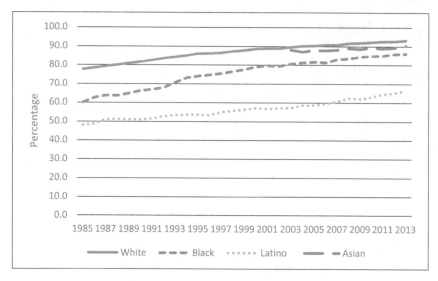

Figure 0.1   High School Completion Rates

A second key measure of both educational and economic success is post-secondary attainment (Card and Krueger 1994; Evans and Schwab 1995; Levy and Murnane 1992), and the patterns of disparity are even more glaring. Figure 0.2 shows that there has long been a persistent gap between White and Asian students, and Black and Latino students, when it comes to those who attain a bachelor's degree or higher in the U.S. The gaps were wide in 1985, and they remain so in recent years.

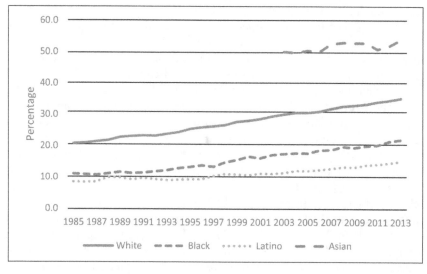

Figure 0.2   Postsecondary Attainment Rates

A major concern with postsecondary attainment is that the gaps have widened over time. For example, in 1985 the Black-White postsecondary gap was 9.7%, and the Latino-White gap was 12.3%. In 2013, the Black-White gap was 13.2%, and the Latino-White gap was 20.1%. This evidence suggests that patterns of educational inequality have, in fact, grown. Figure 0.3 below shows the growth of these postsecondary gaps.

Whereas these figures provide national data, educational gaps also persist at the state level. Figures 0.4 and 0.5 on the next page provide a sampling from various regions in the U.S., and they are representative of all 50 states. Here, we can see the glaring racial inequality.

These disparities are also common at the level of individual school districts. A recent *New York Times* article serves as a case in point, and it also sheds light on Asian Americans' position within the academic-racial hierarchy. The piece highlights tremendous ethnoracial disparities among New York city's top public high schools: of the 14,415 students enrolled in New York's eight specialized, elite public high schools for the 2011–2012 school year, 8,549 were Asian (59.3%). These numbers are staggering when we consider that Asians comprise just 14% of the city's overall population. The shift in the over- and underrepresentation of certain groups over time is equally striking: in 1971, Stuyvesant High School (one of the eight elite New York public schools) was roughly 80% White, 10% Black, 4% Latino, and 6% Asian; in 2012, Stuyvesant was 72% Asian, 24% White, and less than 4% Black or Latino. The various data illustrate that Asian students are riding on a tidal wave of academic success.

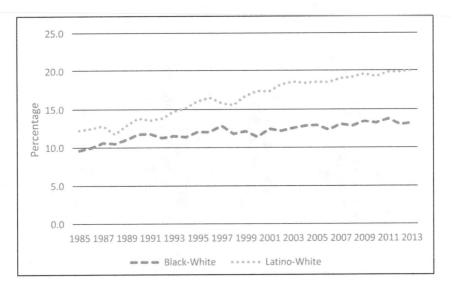

Figure 0.3   Postsecondary Gaps

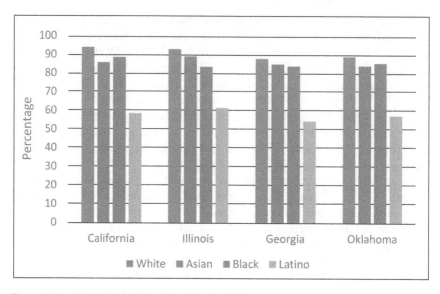

Figure 0.4   2011 High School Graduation Rates

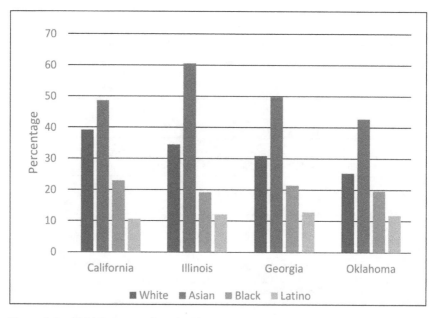

Figure 0.5   2011 Postsecondary Attainment Rates

In their book *The Triple Package,* Yale law professors Amy Chua and Jed Rubenfeld (2014) argue that certain ethnic groups (including Chinese and other East Asian groups) are more successful than others because of inherent cultural traits that predispose them to academic success and upward mobility. Commentary of this sort ignores the fact that Asians are not homogenous—whereas many do well in school, others do not. Most damaging is that this line of reasoning fundamentally ignores the structural disadvantages that underrepresented groups face, and thus reifies racial stereotypes and compounds ethnoracial inequality. It motivates, nonetheless, the need for counternarratives showing school success among underrepresented groups, despite these glaring levels of inequality. The chapters in this volume are filled with such counternarratives.

Moreover, the combination of persistent inequalities and the popular focus on the cultural deficits of certain groups demands that we shift our focus within American contexts, and broaden our focus to explore international cases. In this volume, we shift our focus away from expositions of achievement/opportunity gaps and spurious links between culture and educational outcomes, and toward examples of underrepresented groups achieving success despite their disadvantage. Additionally, we broaden our focus beyond the U.S. contexts to illuminate cases of educational inequality abroad. As such, these case studies represent an attempt to learn from the educational barriers, struggles, and triumphs of underrepresented groups on a global scale. This book paints a picture of systematic inequality within the context of history, policy, and structures of school and society. Within this picture, the bleak outlook of normative inequalities are contrasted and challenged by success stories within this system.

INEQUALITY, POWER, AND SCHOOL SUCCESS

This volume addresses one of the most important issues in modern social theory and policy: social inequality, power, and educational opportunity. More specifically, the book examines how education systems—in and out of schools—are contested spaces of power and resistance. The book interrogates and challenges popular discourses of educational achievement/ opportunity gaps—cultural explanations that rest on racial stereotypes— and illuminates the ways in which grassroots counterspaces can resist power relations and the status quo, empowering underrepresented, disadvantaged youth to engage and achieve academically.

This volume speaks to social transformation theories and critical theory in sociological thought. Critical theory posits that schools and other places where learning occurs are sites where power struggles between dominant and subordinate groups take place. A major theme of this line of research is an analysis of how schools are used to help dominant groups maintain their position of power, as well as how subordinate groups contest and resist domination to achieve success. On the macrostructural level, critical theorists view schools as places where a class-based, gender-based, and race-based society is reproduced through the use of the economic, cultural, hegemonic, and political capital of the dominant class. Therefore, this approach focuses on the construction of oppression and how individuals enact their agency to emancipate themselves from it. In so doing, the narratives in this book will focus on transformation—rather than transmission—of culture.

This book is a collection of original case studies in education that interrogate inequality and opportunity. Each case study highlights issues of power, inequality, and resistance in distinct U.S. and international contexts. The chapters in this volume range from in-school high school processes for Asian, Latino, and African American males in the inner-city neighborhoods, Latina teachers in Southern California, single mothers in Riverside, undocumented youth from Mexico, immigrant Moroccan youth in Spain, and immigrant Afro-Caribbean and Indian teenagers in New York and in London. The international cases provide a unique opportunity to compare features of educational inequality across national borders. Such comparisons broaden our understanding of educational inequity, and lend important insights on how we might create opportunities for groups that are disadvantaged through no fault of their own.

All told, the case studies presented forge a link between individual acts at the microlevel and social processes at the macrolevel as transformational counterspaces promoting school success. These counterspaces begin to fill the cracks in the opportunity structure that create disparity and failure. The case studies explore and interrogate three interrelated questions:

1. What processes operate within and outside of schools to limit opportunities for certain students, and what processes allow students to thrive academically and socially?
2. How do individuals and groups resist the hegemony of the dominant class and school failure, and what types of school structures and environments facilitate this resistance?
3. What does educational inequality and transformative resistance look like comparatively, on a global scale?

THEMATIC STRUCTURE AND CHAPTER SUMMARY

In Chapter 1, "Conceptualizing Disparity and Opportunity in Education as a Racial Project: A Comparative Perspective", Alex Lin, Sean Drake, and Gilberto Q. Conchas advocate for using the Racial Formation Framework (RFF)—advanced by Michael Omi and Howard Winant (2014)—to understand how schools are historically shaped by past policies and practices reflecting significant racial implications that seemingly produce unequal learning opportunities for nondominant students, nationally and globally. The highlight of this chapter is exploring how racial formation, in the form of inequality, passivity, and opportunity, has had a profound impact on distinct groups in various U.S. and international contexts. Lin, Drake, and Conchas offer critical implications to the study of RFF in a comparative and global perspective, and conclude by discussing the significance of racial formation in schools. The aim is to show how educational inequality can be viewed as a product of various racial projects at the school and community level.

Part II: Boys and Men of Color: Resilience and the Construction of Urban School Success

The case studies in this section focus on the unique barriers that boys and young men of color face in their pursuit of a quality education, and highlight school and community structures and practices that facilitate academic engagement and achievement for these students.

In Chapter 2, "The Problematization of Cambodian Male Youth in U.S. Schools: Beyond the Model Minority Stereotype of Asian American Youth", Vichet Chhuon calls attention to the misrepresentation and subsequent invisibility of Cambodian youth in terms of research, policy, and educational opportunities. Chhuon represents the complex and conflicting representations of this underserved population in U.S. schools—and effectively challenges the model minority typology. The inclusion of Cambodians within the insidious model minority stereotype leads to students' invisibility in research and policy, and difficulty in attaining proper academic support. He examines how Cambodian American adolescent boys are commonly perceived through a pervasive discourse of the Cambodian dropout, troublemaker, and gangster. Through a grounding in youth experiences, as well as larger political and social contexts, this chapter speaks to needs for improvements within the current system.

In Chapter 3, "'I Am Not the Stereotype': How an Academic Club in an Urban School Empowered Black Male Youth to Succeed", Sean Drake, Gilberto Q. Conchas, and Leticia Oseguera present the results of a qualitative case study that investigated (1) Black male students' perspectives on the salience and consequences of racial stereotypes perpetuated within an ethnoracially diverse high school, (2) these students' reactions to the racial stereotypes, and (3) the relationship between students' reactions to the stereotypes and an afterschool program (Male Academy) designed to increase their social and cultural capital. The findings indicate that Male Academy participation motivated students to respond to negative racial stereotypes with indignation and a focused resolve to achieve academic success in the face of adversity. These outcomes indicate that Black male youth in urban schools need not react in opposition to hostile educational environments, or education more generally, if they are given appropriate levels of institutional and social support. A supportive academic structure can function as a social buffer against the negative effects of racial stereotypes in schools.

In Chapter 4, "Dynamics of Urban Neighborhood Reciprocity: Latino Peer Ties, Violence, and the Navigation of Failure and Success", Maria G. Rendón addresses this issue by drawing on interviews with Latino male high school graduates and dropouts in Los Angeles. Her analysis reveals urban violence as the most salient feature of urban neighborhoods, and as a phenomenon detrimental to school completion. In an effort to avoid victimization, male youth exposed to urban violence draw on male peer ties for protection. Inherent in these social ties, as in other forms of social capital, are expectations and obligations. An orientation that privileges these expectations and obligations—and not specifically an anti-school orientation—gets male youth "caught up" in behavior counterproductive to school completion, such as truancy and fighting. However, family and school institutional factors limit some youths' time in the neighborhood, buffering them from urban violence. In turn, they avoid getting "caught up", and are more likely to graduate. Rendón argues that to understand the cultural orientation that guides behavior contributing to school dropout requires accounting for how the threat of violence punctuates and organizes the daily lives of male youth in urban neighborhoods.

Part III: Gender, Self-Identity, and the Cultivation of Sociopolitical Resistance

The case studies in this section privilege the experiences of girls and women of color as they struggle against a history of marginality within various educational contexts. These cases also reveal settings and cultural practices that engender educational success among girls and women of color.

In Chapter 5, "Beyond 'Warming Up' and 'Cooling Out': The Effects of Community College on a Diverse Group of Disadvantaged Young Women", Kelly Nielsen presents findings from a four-year qualitative case study with poor and working-class female community college students. The results indicate that narratives are a critical component of resisting pressures to lower one's ambition within the community college context. Using four waves of in-depth, semi-structured interviews to gather "social mobility narratives", Nielsen finds that lowering, raising, or maintaining aspirations requires narrative work, because these processes occur at the level of the self. In the process of setting goals and acting to achieve them, the women must tell stories that are convincing to themselves and others, both inside the community college and elsewhere. However, the cultural material for forming and transforming narratives is unevenly distributed throughout the community college, and the construction of personal narratives necessitates that these women draw on experiences with other institutions, such as welfare, work, religion, and rehab.

In Chapter 6, "Bicultural Myths, Rifts, and Scripts: A Case Study of Hidden Chicana/Latina Teacher's Cultural Pedagogy in Multiracial Schools", Glenda M. Flores reveals powerful ways Latina teachers are silently transforming processes within schools that value and foster Latino cultural resources. Flores situates this finding within the historical tradition of discrimination, segregation, and alienation faced by Latino students through policies. She highlights how Latina teachers are reshaping the way Latino students and their immigrant parents are received, engaged with, and incorporated into American ways of life. By serving as cultural liaisons, Latina teachers may facilitate the mobility patterns of Latino youth.

Often left out of popular and academic discussions of education are Latinas' specific raced and sexualized schooling experiences. In Chapter 7, "Gendered Expectations and Sexualized Policing: Latinas' Experiences in a Public High School", Gilda L. Ochoa draws on in-depth interviews with educators and Latina students collected over 18 months at a Southern California high school, and explicates the ways in which prevailing stereotypes of Latinas (as hypersexual teen mothers who are indifferent toward their education) intersect with school practices of curriculum tracking to reinforce gender, racial, and class hierarchies. Ochoa details processes of academic profiling and sexualized policing whereby many Latinas at the high school are funneled away from the school's top classes, and experience constant monitoring of their bodies and actions. Essential to this narrative is how Latinas resist such profiling by participating in social justice organizations.

Part IV: Immigrant Global Communities, Disparity, and the Struggle for Legitimacy

The case studies in this section address the unique educational plight of undocumented immigrant youth in America, and the ways in which prevailing stereotypes and stigmatizing labels affect immigrant youth in Spain and Britain.

In Chapter 8, "Difficult Transitions: Undocumented Immigrant Students Navigating Vulnerability and School Structures", Roberto G. Gonzales and Cynthia Nayeli Carvajal focus on undocumented immigrant students in high schools. They argue that upon exiting public school undocumented immigrant students find themselves at odds with their immigration status, especially as they transition to adulthood. Although a burgeoning line of research has focused on these transitions among high-achieving undocumented youth, very little is known about those who do not make successful transitions to college—the vast majority of the population. Drawing from a collection of studies carried out on the west coast, this chapter examines the ways in which schools shape undocumented students' social capital and how these relationships mediate the constraints of undocumented status. The findings suggest that students' ability to access trusting relationships with teachers and counselors is shaped by their position in the school curriculum hierarchy. Poor positioning within this hierarchy proved to be a double disadvantage for undocumented students. By being placed in the lower or middle curriculum tracks of their schools many of our respondents were not able to form trusting relationships with teachers or other school personnel. As a result, many of these young people were without the needed support and guidance to seek out information critical to making postsecondary transitions. The findings have important implications for school practices and their impact on their undocumented students' transition to illegality.

In Chapter 9, "The Diaspora Speaks Back: Youth of Migration Speaking Back to Discourses of Power and Empire", Anne Ríos-Rojas presents the results of an ethnographic case study of the experiences of immigrant youth in the "global city" of Barcelona. Ríos-Rojas devotes critical attention to the ways in which youth maneuver within a broader social field where the category of "immigrant" is at once intersected by dominant discourses of tolerance and integration, and dominant narratives that render immigrants' citizenship conditional and "delinquent". Ríos-Rojas privileges the voices and experiences of immigrant youth as they creatively maneuver between these polarizing discourses, and details the processes by which they cultivate a sense of belonging within a social landscape flooded with contradictory messages of what it means to belong. Moreover, this chapter explores the epistemological, theoretical, and pedagogical implications of paying attention to immigrant youths' perceptions of belonging and citizenship.

Segmented assimilation theory suggests that some children of immigrants in the U.S. adopt the oppositional culture of their disadvantaged African American peers, leading these second-generation youth to downward assimilation. In Chapter 10, "Global Urban Youth Culture: Peer Status and Orientations toward School among Children of Immigrants in New York and London", Natasha K. Warikoo assesses the utility of downward assimilation theory's cultural argument in multiethnic settings by analyzing the cultural lives of children of immigrants in diverse New York and London high schools. The London comparison sheds light on the degree to which the process of downward assimilation is unique to the urban American context. The strong similarities between second-generation youth cultures in London and New York suggest a global consumption pattern dominated by hip-hop culture, rather than the local influence of African American cultures that have previously been thought to lead to downward assimilation. The findings suggest that a thirst for peer status better explains the attitudes, behaviors, and taste preferences of the second generation in both cities.

Taken together, these chapters represent a new way forward in research on the sociology of education. For decades, social scientists have focused on educational achievement gaps between underrepresented minority groups and dominant groups, and brought to light the myriad obstacles that non-dominant groups face in their quest for a quality education. Whereas a continued focus on achievement/opportunity gaps unique to disadvantaged groups is still warranted, this volume takes the approach that the answers to the most vexing questions concerning educational inequality are right in front of us. To see these solutions, we need to focus on what is working for students, schools, and communities at home and abroad; we need to learn from examples in which individuals and groups succeed despite various structural disadvantages that stack the odds against them; we need to shift our attention toward these *achievement cases*, and adopt a comparative framework across cases to discern the features of each case that can be applied in other similar contexts with similarly situated groups. There is much progress to be made, which gives us belief in a brighter, more equitable future. We sincerely hope that this book represents a step in that direction.

REFERENCES

Aud, S., S. Wilkinson-Flicker, P. Kristapovich, A. Rathbun Xiaolei Wang, and J. Zhang. 2013. *The Condition of Education 2013 (NCES 2013–037)*. Washington, DC: U.S. Department of Education, National Center for Education Statistics. Retrieved January 2014 from http://nces.ed.gov/pubsearch.

Card, D., and A. B. Krueger. 1994. "Minimum Wages and Employment: A Case Study of the Fast-Food Industry in New Jersey and Pennsylvania: Reply." *American Economic Review* 84 (4): 1397–1420.

Chua, A., and J. Rubenfeld. 2014. *The Triple Package: How Three Unlikely Traits Explain the Rise and Fall of Cultural Groups in America*. New York: Penguin.

Du Bois, W.E.B. 1903. *The Souls of Black Folk*. Oxford: Oxford University Press.

Evans, W. N., and R. M. Schwab. 1995. "Finishing High School and Starting College: Do Catholic Schools Make a Difference?" *The Quarterly Journal of Economics* 110 (4): 941–974.

Levy, F., and R. J. Murnane. 1992. "U.S. Earnings Levels and Earning Inequality: A Review of Recent Trends and Proposed Explanations." *Journal of Economic Literature* 30 (3): 1333–1381.

Omi, M., and H. Winant. 2014. *Racial Formation in the United States*, 3rd ed. New York: Routledge.

Part I
Overview

1 Conceptualizing Disparity and Opportunity in Education as a Racial Project

A Comparative Perspective

Alex Romeo Lin, Sean Drake, and Gilberto Q. Conchas

On August 9, 2014, in Ferguson, Missouri, an unarmed Black male teenager was gunned down by a police officer in broad daylight. The shocking incident compelled the local community to mass protest and stoked the fire of an on-going national debate about the inextricable link between race and policing. But the full story runs deeper than the horrific events of that summer afternoon.

In a town where Blacks make up 63% of the population, Ferguson, Missouri is one of the most racially segregated neighborhoods in the country. The community suffers from a high poverty rate (22%) and decades of underinvestment in public schools and services. The mistrust between Ferguson residents and police officers is emblematic of racial tensions that exist in schools. In the wake of the Ferguson story, an *Education Weekly* article (Blad 2014) reports that Black students in the Ferguson-Florrisant school district were more likely than any other racial group to be suspended, expelled, or referred to the justice system (U.S. Department of Education 2012). These discipline patterns are consistent across the country. Despite the fact that Blacks make up roughly 16% of total school enrollment, they represent 33 and 34% of students who were suspended and expelled, respectively (McNeil and Blad 2014). The Ferguson story is a glaring reminder that race matters, especially in social settings involving youth and schools.

The opportunity gaps are glaring between dominant and nondominant students in school grades, standardized test scores, drop-out rates, and college completion rates (Editorial Projects in Education Research Center 2011). Our use of the term *nondominant students* refers to youth and young adults in school whose demographic characteristics and life circumstances jeopardize their ability to succeed academically (Aron and Zweig 2003; Stormont, Espinosa, Knipping, and McCathren 2003). Nondominant student populations must contend with in-school and out-of-school challenges—such as poverty, crime, and a lack of access to adequate housing or health care—that deleteriously affect the quality of education provided to these youth in distinct schooling contexts. Put differently, the educational issues faced by nondominant students are inextricably linked and related to issues and problems that are present within the urban environment marked by limited opportunity (Noguera 2003; Conchas 2006; Conchas, Lin, Oseguera, and Drake 2014). In this chapter, we focus on ethnic groups that have been historically marginalized and oppressed.

One major finding from the National Center for Education Statistics (NCES) report in 2009 and 2011 is that African American and Latino students trailed behind their White and Asian counterparts by more than 20 points on the National Assessment of Educational Progress (NAEP) 4th and 8th grade math and reading assessments—a difference of about two grade levels (NCES 2009 and 2011). Moreover, analysis of a national sample of the 2008 high school graduating class revealed racial disparities in graduation rates: 78% of White students graduated high school on time, whereas just 57% of African American and 54% of Latino students achieved the same result (Education Week 2011).

The schooling performance of Asian American students should not be ignored either; intraracial comparisons yield critical insights. Although students of Chinese, Korean, and Japanese descent tend to earn higher grades and test scores than Whites, students from Southeast Asian communities (e.g., Laotian, Cambodian, Hmong, and Vietnamese) continue to lag behind in school performance (Tang, Kim, and Haviland 2013). The 2011 U.S. Census reports that the college persistence and graduation rates for Southeast Asian students among Cambodian (16.0%), Hmong (14.8%), Laotian (13.2%), and Vietnamese (25.5%) remain far below the national average rate (U.S. Census Bureau 2011). In light of these achievement data, population growth of these subgroups of Asian Americans over the last 10 years (20% Vietnamese, 15% Khmer, 5% Cambodian) represent new challenges for school systems (Uy 2008). In addition, there is strong concern regarding students from American Indian/Alaska Native backgrounds. In 2007, Native American students were found to be 2.4 reading grade levels behind their White counterparts, as measured by the National Assessment of Education Progress (NAEP) assessment (NCES 2007). A 2003 report by the National Center for Education Statistics also indicates that Native American students had lower college completion rates (39%) than White (60%), Asian (65%), and Hispanic (46%) students (Ingels et al. 2007). Overall, these reports call for closer examination as to why nondominant groups lag behind their more racially privileged peers.

This chapter advocates for using the Racial Formation Framework (RFF)—advanced by Michael Omi and Howard Winant (2014)—to understand how schools are historically shaped by past policies and practices reflecting significant racial implications that seemingly produce unequal learning opportunities for nondominant students, nationally and globally. RFF shifts focus from the observed characteristics of the groups themselves to the sociocultural processes that impact the social mobility among youth and young adults in a racialized ecology. First, we explain the significance of race and why it is relevant in the education context. Then, we highlight structural factors that contribute to the often marginalized schooling experiences of nondominant students. The highlight of this chapter is exploring how racial formations in the form of inequality, passivity, and opportunity have had a profound impact on distinct groups in various U.S. and international contexts. We offer critical implications to the study of RFF in a comparative and global perspective and conclude by discussing the significance of racial formation in schools, as well as the theoretical contributions made to the relevant literature. The aim is to show how racial inequality in education—in schools and communities—can be viewed as a product of racial projects.

THE CONCEPTUAL POWER OF STRUCTURAL EXPLICATIONS OF SCHOOL SUCCESS

In trying to account for disparities in academic performance among students from different backgrounds, some researchers have focused on cultural differences to explain individual- and group-level school failure and success, whereas others have investigated the structural antecedents of racial educational inequality. Cultural explanations tend to focus on "the (human) product of beliefs, values, norms and socialization" shared among particular families and ethnic groups that shape the individuals' own actions (Noguera 2003, 439). In contrast, structural explanations view individuals as the product of external factors that shape their social realities (Noguera 2003). Class structure and social geography are external, structural factors that are particularly consequential for the educational opportunities and life chances of American youth (Massey and Denton 1993; Wilson 2012). More recently, empirical researchers have primarily shifted their focus from cultural to structural arguments to explain underrepresented minority students' schooling experiences, and ethnoracial disparities in academic engagement and achievement.

Structural Explanations on Schooling Inequalities

Bowles and Gintis's (1976) seminal study of schools—*Schooling on Capitalist America*—represents the most cited account of how structural factors explain educational disparities between dominant and nondominant student groups. The study considers how schools operate according to *correspondence theories*, whereby students experience varying levels of social interactions and individual rewards depending on their position for the workforce (Bowles and Giles 2002). Students are socialized differently depending on the class characteristics of their origins. The educational system prepares future blue-collar workers by subordinating lower-class children to external control related to conforming to the work place needs. According to Bowles and Giles (1976), schools may constrain these lower-class children from developing close interpersonal relationships with their peers. Students set for upper-class positions, however, are more likely to experience active peer involvement and opportunities to develop independent skills. Although the study shares useful insights on the possibility that schools have a social reproduction function, Oakes (1982) argues that the study fails to demonstrate actual classroom differences in students' peer relationships that reinforce differences in social class.

To address these concerns, Oakes (2005) studied the tracking phenomena and how it produces schooling experiences that vary for students from different backgrounds. In the groundbreaking book, *Keeping Track: How Schools Structure Inequality*, Oakes (2005) presents results from a comprehensive study on school tracking policies that analyzed data[1] from students, teachers, administrators, and parents in 25 middle and high schools. Oakes argued that *tracking*, as defined as the process of grouping students by ability, was related to students being assigned to academic (high track) and non-academic (low track) preparation. A major finding in her study was that curriculum content and instruction quality varied substantially between different tracks. Students in the higher track were enrolled in courses that stressed critical thinking and problem-solving skills conducive to raising their college entrance exam scores. In contrast, lower-tracked students were typically enrolled in remedial courses that focused on developing rote memorization skills. Oakes contends that poor and nondominant students were largely overrepresented in the lower track. Further, these students developed more negative attitudes about their future plans than their high-tracked counterparts. The implications of her study suggest that socioeconomic status (SES) is central to explaining why students from lower-class backgrounds were typically enrolled in the lower tracks. In considering these findings, Oakes emphasizes that more research is needed to understanding how race and ethnicity play a role in school tracking.

The strength of structuralist theories relates to understanding how certain school practices related to tracking and curriculum development may adversely influence students' educational opportunities. More specifically, schools provide different experiences for students from low and high socioeconomic backgrounds. Students from lower-class backgrounds are less likely to develop positive school experiences (Borman and Overman 2004). Theories that focus on structural factors are useful in considering why nondominant students may have limited success in school. However, one aspect that may be inadequate or weakly defined in structuralist theories relates to understanding the significance of race in school practices.

THE SIGNIFICANCE OF RACE AND RACISM

"Race" is a social construct that highlights differences in phenotype between broad groups of people. Historically, dominant groups have used race as a basis for human categorization and social organization, and to explain socioeconomic, educational, political, and labor market differences between groups (Bonilla-Silva 1997; Fields 1990; Loury 2002). Race is, by definition and praxis, about the creation and maintenance of human boundaries. As such, race is highly useful as an analytical tool to understand the structural, cultural, and agentic factors that perpetuate social inequality.

Students from different backgrounds attend schools in the hope of accessing equal education opportunities. Many researchers continue to be concerned about the ways that students' racial identity development is linked to their self-esteem (Altschul, Oyserman, and Bybee 2006), motivations (Bowman and Howard 1985), and efficacy (Witherspoon, Speight, and Thomas 1997). Yet despite this substantial body of research, less is known about how school practices reflect unequal distribution of educational opportunities for ethnic/racial minorities. Even though race plays a role in students' access to academic learning opportunities, it continues to be a powerful presence in other aspects of the school experience, such as friendship and peer groups, club membership (Steinberg, Brown, and Dornbusch 1997), and discipline (Meier, Stewart, and England 1989).

In considering these findings, we wanted to gain deeper knowledge of how nondominant students perceived and experienced racism at school. This required conducting in-depth interviews that enabled students to deliver honest accounts on how race manifested in the school setting. In considering this inquiry, Conchas, Lin, Oseguera, and Drake (2014) explored a sample of low- and high-achieving African American youth who were enrolled in a racially diverse high school[2] catered towards career preparation in the health, science, and technology fields. Students not only provided rich and detailed accounts on their schooling experience, but also their career aspirations. In general, our African American informants were acutely aware of racial discrimination at the school. These individuals perceived their teachers as having low academic expectations of them and other African American students, at the same time holding high academic expectations of their Asian and White peers. Such signals suggesting that African Americans were not compatible with academic achievement may explain why the participants were more likely to choose non-academic careers related to professional sports and entertainment. Although the respondents also expressed being exposed to racism through gang interactions in their neighborhoods and stereotypes portrayed in the media, they perceived these influences as aspects contributing to racial inequalities at school. It should be no surprise that these African American youths also wanted the school to make racial discourse transparent and an on-going process with administrators and teachers. The findings from this study suggest that nondominant students are not immune to experiencing certain forms of racism at school, and this threat can be detrimental to their perceptions of social mobility.

We argue that the significance of race is reflected in the structural aspects of schools. Race is constantly defined and interpreted in schools, which influences school climate (Ferguson 2001; Lewis 2003; Tatum 2003), curriculum (Banks 2006), and funding (Darling-Hammond 2010). The transparency of race varies considerably and manifests in various contexts from willful acts of hatred (race-based aggressions) to deliberate exclusion of race (colorblindness). Discussions of race, however, venture beyond actions or policy practices reflecting racial discrimination. Instinctively, students and teachers use race to read the world and make decisions on how to act (Lewis 2003). Race never stays static and continuously functions in a dynamic way. For these reasons, schools are often theorized as engaging in the "production of race" (Wacquant 2002), because it can provide lessons and practices that inform students on what it means to be White, Black, Asian, or Latino. Not only do schools ascribe racial meaning to ideas and identities (Almaguer and Jung 1999), but the institution may also draw racial lines on who receives benefits and privileges. Thus, schools are the product of a racialized institution and practices that produce unequal opportunities for students. The racial formation framework evolves from past structural theories to explain how past social policies reflecting racial discrimination continue to be relevant in race relationships between the students and school.

WHAT IS THE RACIAL FORMATION FRAMEWORK (RFF)?

In the trailblazing book, *Racial Formation in the United States*, Omi and Winant (2014) present an invaluable foundation for the discussion and analysis of racial dynamics in a *global* society. According to Omi and Winant (2014), racial formation refers to "the socio-historical process by which racial categories are created, lived out, transformed, and destroyed" (109). The RFF considers how the significance of racial categories are determined by historical, social, economic, and political forces, and that racial categories signify social conflicts that influence how society is structured. According to RFF, race is characterized by fluidity because racial meaning and status are constantly maintained, contested, and transformed through competing political projects. The RFF departs from the dominant notion of race as a fixed construct based on classifying human identities to an informed understanding of how race plays a fundamental role in constantly structuring and representing the social world.

Omi and Winant (2014) argue that the vast historical shift in the meaning and significance of race cannot be understood without considering how race operates in a variety of everyday social structures and practices. A *racial project* is "simultaneously an interpretation, representation, or explanation of racial identities and meanings, and an effort to organize and distribute resources (economic, political, cultural) along particular racial lines" (125). In other words, racial projects connect what race means in particular practices and can influence how everyday experiences are racially organized. Racial projects represent racial dynamics through certain practices, such as public action, state activities, and cultural artifacts. The authors argue that racial projects signify the "building blocks" of a racial formation at a particular time and place. From this perspective, every racial project serves to reproduce, extend, or challenge the broader constellation of race relations.

RFF has been applied in various research contexts, including studies on state formation and social structure (Almaguer 2008), evangelical movements (Alumkal 2004), schools (Rhee 2013; Riley and Ettlinger 2011), and language issues (Brock 2009). The strength of the racial formation framework is the perspective that racial projects, large and small, have structured society in many ways throughout history. Racial formation is always understood in its historical context and allows for a dynamic and changing perspective of race in modern times.

SOCIAL POLICY WITH RACIAL CONSEQUENCES IN EDUCATION

Macrolevel racial projects signify race relations on a larger scale by framing racial dimension within a social structure like state activity and policy (Leonardo 2013). These racial projects vary in their degree of direct influence on racial inequality in educational opportunities and outcomes. For example, sociologists have devoted several decades of scholarship to examining racial segregation and its effects on the spatial and social distance between different racial groups, and the disparate life chances and outcomes between these groups. In *American Apartheid: Segregation and the Making of the Underclass*, Douglas Massey and Nancy Denton (1993) present a thorough analysis of the persistence of Black residential segregation. Massey and Denton deftly delineate the historical legacy of Jim and Jane Crow segregation and the various institutional processes and public policies (e.g., overt and covert discrimination in the housing market), and private behaviors of citizens (e.g., White flight), that maintain surprisingly high levels of Black-White residential segregation in the United States. These structural forces confine large numbers of Blacks to urban ghetto environments, thus promoting the stubborn link between race and class in American society.

More recent scholarship on racial segregation has attempted to move the discussion beyond the Black and White divide. Results typically reveal marked intergroup differences. For instance, Charles (2003) finds that: (1) Black-White segregation has declined somewhat in recent decades but still remains quite high, (2) Latinos and Asians experience modest levels of residential segregation from Whites, but these levels are much lower than they are for Blacks, and (3) Asians are the racial group least segregated from Whites. Charles concludes that Blacks' high levels of segregation from Whites is made possible in large part by structural forces predicated on racial prejudice; Blacks express a desire to live in racially integrated neighborhoods but Whites do not want many Blacks living near them, especially not next door. In contrast, Whites are far more accepting of potential Latino and Asian neighbors.

Race scholars have also found that socioeconomic status facilitates integration for Latinos and Asians, but much less so for Blacks (Charles 2003; Iceland 2009). Furthermore, in his study of immigration and racial segregation, Iceland (2009) finds that length of U.S. residence is associated with less residential segregation among Latino and Asian immigrants; however, Black immigrants who have been in America for decades remain just as highly segregated as recent Black immigrants. Therefore, at least in terms of segregation, the boundaries separating Whites from Blacks are thicker than those separating Whites from Latinos and Asians—nonetheless, this is not to deny the negative aspects of inequality imposed upon Latinos and Asians.

The findings presented above contribute directly to the racial inequality in educational opportunities and outcomes that are so prevalent in our society. Residential racial segregation concentrates poverty, violence, and drug abuse among certain racial groups. Consequently, segregation works to produce and maintain educational inequality by systematically confining nondominant groups to underclass environments, and thus promoting the social isolation of these groups. This social isolation begins with children in schools. Education is a valuable resource, and access to quality education is highly contested. Middle-class parents often move their families to specific neighborhoods in specific cities due to a school district's reputation for academic excellence (Jimenez and Horowitz 2013).

In stark contrast, highly segregated Black and Brown communities are denied access to quality educational resources. Their neighborhood schools and surrounding communities typically lack the human or financial resources necessary to produce graduates who can compete in an increasingly competitive labor market (Goldin and Katz 2009). During the 1970s and 1980s, for example, many manufacturing industries relocated from central cities to suburbs, taking their low-skill jobs with them. Simultaneously, technological innovations in urban labor markets affected the number and types of jobs available by increasing the requisite education and skill level for many urban jobs. These changes were particularly devastating for poor Blacks living in these segregated urban areas. These macrostructural changes in the American economy effectively trapped inner-city Blacks in squalid ghettoes with few prospects for education and good jobs (Wilson 2012), a trap that these communities have yet to escape from.

Furthermore, it is no coincidence that segregation indices between Whites, Blacks, Latinos, and Asians are congruent with educational attainment figures between these groups (National Center for Education Statistics 2011). For non-White racial groups, a negative relationship exists between a group's level of societal segregation from Whites, and that group's educational opportunities and trajectory. In more specific terms, Asians outperform Latinos and Blacks in school partly due to lower levels of racial segregation from Whites. Less segregation amounts to greater access to coveted educational resources, and to the social and cultural capital necessary to navigate the education system. For example, most Black male youth living in segregated, inner-city ghetto communities spend more time and energy contending with the criminal justice system than they do with their formal education. Instead, their primary education takes place in the street (Goffman 2014). In the next sections we continue to elucidate racial formation framework and discuss how inequality, passivity, and opportunity structures contribute to differential schooling experiences and educational inequality for students of color.

Inequality

The Civil War ended the roughly 250 years of slavery endured by African Americans; however, it was not until the mid-1950s to late 1960s, during the Civil Rights era, that state policies reflected widespread efforts to reverse racial discrimination against African Americans. Guided by the spirit of *Brown v. Board of Education* (1954)—a landmark Supreme Court case and decision that challenged the segregationist racial projects that surfaced during reconstruction—busing and affirmative action policies emerged to promote educational opportunities for students of color. Omi and Winant (2014) argue, however, that the New Right represented an ideological movement focused on counteracting the growing threat of minorities and immigrants to the American identity, a threat stemming from significant achievements garnered during the Civil Rights era. This ideological movement was particularly appealing to those who mainly supported interests of the White, middle-class, and Protestant community. To strategically appeal to the public interest, the movement rearticulated its race-based cause by supporting an agenda based on restoring America's traditional morality and individual freedom. The New Right movement, which started in the middle 1970s, initiated a series of racial projects that eventually diminished significant progress made on the civil rights front. We present two cases that illustrate how the New Right movement influenced efforts to dismantle progress made to equalize opportunities for Black and Latino students: race-based busing in North Carolina and a critical ethnic studies program in Arizona schools.

Billings and his colleagues (2014) analyzed efforts and initiatives to desegregate the school systems in the Charlotte-Mecklenburg, North Carolina area. In 1971, the Supreme Court ordered race-based busing to improve African American youths' access to educational and social services, which helped increased academic achievement (Guryan 2014) and financial earnings (Ashenfelter, Collins, and Yoon 2006), while leading to decreased homicide and arrest rates (Weiner, Lutz, and Ludwig 2009). New Right activists argued that busing was problematic because it launched an "assault" on family values, and particularly faulted the government's unfair practice of depriving parents from deciding schools for their children. By advocating strong support for pro-family values, such as "community control" and "parental involvement", the New Right movement greatly slowed momentum of the school busing policies. The end of court-ordered busing, coupled with racialized redistricting of neighborhoods, led to sudden increases in school segregation almost immediately. The movement to dismantle school busing policies was pivotal to limiting educational opportunities for African American youth. By keeping schools and the community segregated, the New Right movement reestablished social structures that promote, maintain, and perpetuate White privilege. The next section demonstrates how conservative policymakers and New Right activists challenged an ethnic studies program designed to help Mexican-American students develop better understanding of their ethnic heritage.

A story that generated national headlines in 2012 was the controversial decision made by Tucson Unified School District (TUSD) to dismantle its Mexican-American Studies (MAS) program, a program used in schools serving predominately Mexican-American communities. Salinas (2011) reports that the decision was in response to a House bill passed in Arizona (HB2281 or currently A.R.S. § 115–12), which prohibits schools from teaching ethnic studies classes "designed primarily for pupils of a particular ethnic group or advocate ethnic solidarity instead of treatment of pupils as individuals" (304). The MAS program was popular among the high number of Latino youths enrolled in the school district because of the program's capacity to promote "high Latino academic identity and an enhanced level of academic proficiency"[3] (Romero and Arce 2009, 179). Dismantling the MAS program not only served to send a message about reinstituting meritocracy and individualism, but also reflected the state's staunch views against Latino immigration (Cabrera et al. 2013). Hundreds of students walked out of schools throughout the district in protest against the controversial decision. This incident is a prime example of youth interpreting the significance of a racial project that devalues and marginalizes their presence.

Orozco (2011) argues that Arizona's decision to eliminate the MAS and other similar programs across public schools reflects interest to maintain White hegemony in the K–12 school curriculum, in particular to allow students to challenge the "Whites' right to the disposition of curricular property" (829). The MAS curriculum was particularly relevant for Latino students because they examined the institutionalized barriers in the context of school and the larger United States from a Latino/Chicano perspective. Shaped in large part by the mass protesting from Tucson students and community, a federal court eventually ordered TUSD to reinstitute the MAS program (Robbins 2013). Nonetheless, the national attention paid to Arizona's attack on the ethnic studies program demonstrates the extent that conservatives in the predominantly White and middle-class community were willing to take to disempower minority youth.

The racial formation framework aids in our understanding of how various social and educational policies have significant racial implications. In the next section, we address the ways in which racial projects in the form of passivity can also be used to strengthen existing racial hierarchies.

Passivity

The racial formation framework informs how racial categories fit into social hierarchies that can be created, transformed, and preserved to maintain privilege. More important, the Whiteness category has been historically structured to maintain privilege over other non-White categories (Dwyer and Jones 2000; Staiger 2004). According to Leonardo (2009), the category of "White" and "American" falls into the background as the default category. More importantly, White is characteristically *unseen*, whereas non-Whites represent a category that is distinct and seen. The pervasiveness of Whiteness "neutrality" of the White perspective is neither challenged nor addressed in the education system (Tatum 2003). *Passivity* and inaction refer to a type of racial formation where schools fail to acknowledge that certain students do not have equal access to learning opportunities (Marx 2004). In failing to recognize racial discrimination, the default response for schools is to support the dominant racial formation that privileges students from a certain racial, cultural, and class backgrounds. Teachers and students are taught to see that everybody should be treated in the same manner with equal opportunities of succeeding (Ryan, Hunt, Weible, Peterson, and Casas 2007; Schofield 2001). Without problematizing the issue of race, schools fall in the trap of accepting the status quo that maintains unequal educational opportunities for students of color (Delpit 1988). From this perspective, Whiteness is seen as the large, invisible background against which non-Whites are seen and judged (McIntosh 1998). We discuss the racial formations of giftedness and colorblind ideologies that play a powerful role in maintaining racial inequalities in schools.

Staiger (2004) conducted a comprehensive study that documented White hegemony in an urban California high school. The rapid influx in the 1960s of African Americans and Latinos into the historically White neighborhood community sparked concern from White families about the school. These concerned families created and supported committees that eventually led the school to develop a special magnet program for "gifted" students. The magnet program featured a predominantly White student population, despite the fact that White students accounted for less than one fifth of the total school population. In other words, White students were markedly overrepresented in the magnet program. These historic racial projects that developed from the 1960s carried through the modern era in which the study took place. Teachers and students continued to construct a shared understanding that White students were gifted and required protection. For example, one administrator gave magnet students his contact information, but refrained from giving the same to non-magnet students. Language and discourse used by students and teachers also suggest common understanding that the White students naturally belonged to the magnet program. The director of the magnet program used special terms like "gifted" or "talented" to justify acceptance of the non-White students enrolled in the magnet program; however, these qualifying terms were not used to describe the White students enrolled in the magnet program (172). This particular finding suggests that the White students were assumed to be naturally qualified for the magnet program.

The RFF frameworks aids in our understanding of how the category of Whiteness was conflated with being "gifted" or academically successful. We continue to see the relevance of how the historical construction of gifted-ness and intelligence has been linked to a predominately White middle- and upper-class phenomenon (Herrnstein and Murray 1994). Schools can make the category of "Whiteness" disappear in its explicit support for meritoc-racy, which raises the possibility that giftedness can be institutionalized without supporting overt racial exclusion. Next we illustrate how passivity can be enacted through school policies that adapt colorblind ideologies.

Colorblind social policies are policies that ignore racial and cultural differ-ences (Crenshaw 1997). Without attention to structural factors that produced clear patterns of racial disadvantage for ethnic minority groups, colorblind ideologies strengthen existing racial hierarchies and limit efforts to develop equal opportunities for all students (Essed 1991). In *Race in the Schoolyard* (2003), Amanda Lewis examined the effect of colorblind ideology that was pervasive in a predominately White elementary school. She observed that there were many daily instances suggesting that race was downplayed or trivialized. One teacher ignored a Colombian student's concern when he was wrongly categorized as Mexican. The school not only downplayed the sig-nificance of race, but also denied the presence of race in a variety of ways. Many teachers simply did not acknowledge students' race or address race as topics of instruction. For example, social studies lessons about the genocide of Native Americans or subjugation of Chinese immigrants did not include critical examinations of racial discrimination. Colorblindness provoked school members to avoid facing their own racist presumptions and dealing with racist incidents. Colorblind policies have a race-neutral context, which "stigmatizes attempts to raise questions about redressing racial inequality in daily life" (33). For these reasons, students and teachers avoided attempts to address or problematize issues that were racial in nature. This relationship is rooted in avoiding race-based issues and preserving the status quo that downplays the contributions of students from ethnic minority backgrounds.

Similarly, Mica Pollock (2004) published three years of ethnographic research in a racially diverse high school in California to illuminate the dam-aging effects of colorblindness. Her book, *Colormute: Race Talk Dilemmas in an American School* (2004), is based on in-depth analyses of everyday race talk between students and teachers. Pollock argues that the school com-munity promoted colorblindness, or the "purposeful silencing of race words themselves" (3). Furthermore, the school was embroiled in a controversy regarding its ineptitude to address the widening achievement gap, especially between the Latino and African American students and their White peers. The district specified that the school must address the welfare of "targeted students", and paid specific attention to the academic struggles of the African American and Latino students. School documents and communication material, however, demonstrated the degree to which the school avoided using racial terms to address the achievement gap. Assessment data on African Americans and Latinos were buried in the back pages of documents. Although the district mandated that all schools target certain groups who were not succeeding academically and behaviorally, the school failed to directly identify African American and Latino students as a targeted demographic. The school site plans communicated a general interest to "enhance the academic achievement *of all* students, and thereby to improve teaching and learning for all" (91). This colorblind approach to addressing inequities prevented the school from understanding the relevance of race. These findings suggest that the school's use of colorblind discourse was ineffective because the staff were primarily concerned with a "group fix" approach that ignored ethnoracial differences and individual experiences.

Riley and Ettliger (2011), furthermore, used students' perspectives to understand how colorblind ideologies limited students from forming positive and healthy ethnic identities. The study focused on the significant enrollment disparities between White and non-White students in the honors program. The school itself had a nearly equal mix of White (55%) and non-White (30% Blacks and 15% Latino) students. Students acknowledged the wide enrollment disparities between White and non-White students in the honors program; however, they reasoned that merit determined access and qualification into the honors program. In reconciling these two observations, students pointed to individual motivation ("African American students are too lazy") rather than the apparent racial segregation found in the school. Students reasoned that there were no "unfairness" concerns regarding the school's merit system, and justified that non-White students must not be "trying that hard" in comparison with White students. The implications of these results suggest that students may harbor unhealthy racial identities when schools inadequately address the significance of race.

The reviewed studies provide insights on how schools that support passivity can strengthen racial hierarchies that privilege Whiteness. It is apparent that the racial formation framework informs understanding of how the meaning of Whiteness is constantly shaped, transformed, and supported through various racial projects. School policies that reflect colorblind ideologies can also serve as a powerful force in preserving the status quo and deflecting attention away from race-based discourse. In the next section, we discuss how racial formations can manifest in the form of opportunities for all students.

Opportunity

Much of the extant literature has focused on how racial formations in schools are constantly created and transformed that are particularly constraining for poor and racialized students. However, there are a few notable studies that inform how nondominant students can navigate competing racial projects and find success in school and their careers—herein, we illuminate a few (Conchas 2006; MacLeod 1995; Marinari 2005). In these specific cases, individuals have acknowledged and fought the dominant racial formation, then somehow forged alternative pathways to achieving school success.

In *Ain't No Makin' It*, MacLeod (1995) conducted an ethnographic account of two low-income male groups from a Boston neighborhood. MacLeod compared a Black male group (the Brothers) and a White male group (the Hallway Hangers). Although the Brothers and Hallway Hangers perceived having lower-status positions, the two groups attributed different reasons for their current circumstances. The Brothers blamed racial inequality, whereas the Hallway Hangers saw society and social institutions as circumstances limiting their social mobility. Although the Brothers acknowledged racism in their lives, the Brothers found that their ancestors experienced upward social mobility when they migrated from the rural South into the North during the Civil War. Knowledge and understanding of their ancestors' struggles inspired the Brothers to develop positive attitudes about their social mobility. These findings suggest that past historical struggles not only inform ethnic minorities about institutionalized racial hierarchies in society, but may also provide learning opportunities suggesting possibilities to challenge racial discrimination, and that minority groups can develop positive attitudes while challenging competing racial projects that preserve the racial status quo—although, in the end, the Brothers fared worse than the Hallway Hangers. We move to our next study that informs how African American and Latino students can develop resiliency in the context of a racially diverse school that was observed to make students feel vulnerable to various ethnic stereotypes by their peers and teachers.

In the book *The Color of Success*, Gilberto Conchas (2006) elucidates unique perspectives on how underrepresented ethnic minority students managed to attain academic success despite experiencing various levels of inequality—based on racial stereotypes influencing student-teacher interactions and segregation among White, Asian, African American, and Latino students. The comprehensive study focuses on a racially diverse high school composed of African American (65%), White (31%), Latino (22%), and Asian (15.2%) students. The school boasted the largest percentage of students passing Advanced Placement (AP) exams and attending postsecondary education at higher levels in some programs, compared to the best public school in the district; nonetheless, issues related to school safety and high drop-out rates continued to persist. Interviews with African American students revealed perceptions of racial hierarchies at school, in which they observed Asians enrolled in academic tracks and African Americans in mostly non-academic tracks. A student reported that teachers seemed to be uncaring towards African American and preferred Asian students.

In facing these challenging aspects at school, African American and Latino students developed a critical understanding of how race played a significant role in tracking. They also managed to find opportunities to be successful. An important factor explaining the success of these high-achieving students relates to developing positive ethnic identities and how the school's institutional processes contributed to positive youth formation. These students were determined to pursue an educated profession, rather than fall into the Black male stereotype of becoming professional entertainers and athletes. Similarly, Latino students at the school resisted dominant racial formations that expected their ethnic group to belong to non-professional careers. In these instances, students strived to combat perceptions of inequality by forging a positive Latino identity associated with being college bound. The findings in the study highlight circumstances where nondominant students resist dominant racial formations that expect them to fail by embracing a positive ethnic identity tied to school success. The next study highlights resistance to dominant racial formations from the unique perspectives of Korean students who represent a more recent wave of Asian immigrants.

Marinari's (2005) ethnographic study explored the relationships between racial formation and academic achievement among Korean students in a high school. High-achieving Korean students fought against competing racial projects of *neutrality* and *visibility* to contest the dominant White perspective of achieving academic success. As Asian American students, the students were measured against the "model minority" stereotype that "collectively labels Asian Americans as educationally and economically successful" (377). The dominant racial project of *neutrality* meant that students needed to adapt to the "unspoken" White norms in order to achieve school success. Certain Korean students embraced this racial project of neutrality at the expense of being ostracized by their Korean peers for being too "Americanized". The study's main highlight is a subgroup of Korean students who actively challenged the model minority discourse (majority) and relied upon their Korean identities (minority) to support new ways of developing social bonds. These particular students embraced the racial project of *visibility*, which involved accentuating their "Korean-ness" by actively displaying their cultural language and dress style. For these students, school success was not defined as excelling in academics or adapting to White norms, but being recognized by their peers as being true to their culture and maintaining positive peer bonds.

In sum, we have demonstrated how the racial formations framework can aid in our understanding of how nondominant students resist dominant racial formations by collectively engaging with others to forge their own paths to success. The significance of race is reinterpreted, and students collectively form their own racial project that serves to create opportunities to succeed. We also encourage future research to consider how students' experiences with racial formations cross over multiple identity contexts, including developmental, gender, social, economic, and geographic contexts. In the next section we briefly grapple with the implications of RFF on a comparative global context.

RFF IN A GLOBAL SOCIETY

Throughout this chapter we have summarized RFF in the American context. Now, we introduce studies that demonstrate racial formation in the global context. In *Racial Conditions*, Winant (1994) argues that racial formation is becoming globalized; that is, the rapid movement of capital and labor that transcends international borders constantly redefines racial lines. Not long after the Civil Rights Movement challenged *de jure* segregation and state-enforced Jim Crow laws (American apartheid), the South African apartheid system crumbled in 1994 (Omi and Winant 2014). Extending racial formation to a comparative approach enables researchers to understand the linkage between Black communities that experienced slavery and apartheid in Africa and America in order to more fully examine the global impact "of racially organized subjection" (Winant 1994, 116). The successful waves of these anti-imperialist and civil rights movements were instrumental in reshaping the global racial order. For these reasons, several theorists situate racial formations theory within the processes of globalization (Bhattacharyya, Gabriel, and Small 2001; Marable 2009; Winant 1994). This section highlights comparative ethnographies that illustrate how the racial formation framework can address a variety of racialized experiences, identities, and structures on an international scale.

In the book *Balancing Acts: Youth Culture in the Global City*, Natasha K. Warikoo (2011) presents a comparative ethnography of second-generation immigrant youth living in New York and London. Warikoo argues that the hip-hop culture, which has African American roots, is now a global phenomenon that carries high-status symbols for high-achieving West Indian, Afro-Caribbean, and British Indian (e.g., Gujarati Hindu) high school students living in London. Hip-hop culture in the United States is mainly seen as a form of nondominant cultural capital, or an orientation towards certain linguistic and dress styles used by lower-status group members to gain "cultural status positions" in their communities (Carter 2003). Students in the study regarded hip-hop culture, or "acting Black", as a way to acquire high-status culture among their peers, which would be important to developing positive school identities. Hip-hop culture served as an important way of authenticating students' racial heritage, even though it is heavily regarded as an American art form.

In contrast to the New York minorities who mainly perceived adults (e.g., teachers, administrators) as perpetrators of ethnic discrimination, the British Indian students were more concerned about their peers engaging in bullying and social exclusion because of their race. Essentially, these students were bullied because they were seen as "uncool" and not historically a part of the mainstream population; thus, youths saw the importance of embracing hip-hop culture to attain respect among their peers and challenging the predominate, White, middle-class status quo at school.

Moreover, although hip-hop culture is usually perceived as having negative associations with school orientation, especially in the United States (Anderson

1999; Binder 1993), its manifestation has a different meaning within other cultures. Youths from all over the world are easily connected to the racial formations of hip-hop culture because its widespread influence has been facilitated by the rapid innovations created by social media and technology. Thus, racial formation does not reside solely in the local, but also in the globalized, context.

In *Stubborn Roots: Race, Culture, and Inequality*, Prudence Carter (2012) extends a global perspective and presents a richly comparative analysis of students' experiences in eight schools located within four cities in the United States and South Africa. South Africa and the United States serve as interesting contrasts because, in the former, the Black majority seeks academic and economic advancement after several decades (1948–1994) of educational segregation and economic exploitation (Downing 2004).

Similar to the experiences of those in the United States, the South African Black students were greatly aware of policies that reflect strong ethnic discrimination. For example, many of the girls were concerned about the school's stringent policies that forbade students from wearing their hair in braids and twists, which are considered hairstyles for traditional African women. School leaders felt that ethnic hairstyles (e.g., braids and twists) were not considered "normal" or appropriate to academic culture. The school's dress code was contradictory because it allowed a Sikh boy to wear a turban and grow a beard due to an exception made for "religious diversity". Furthermore, the South African school placed English language learning at the forefront whereas greatly undervaluing the teaching of Afrikaan languages such as IsiZulu or IsiXhosa. Many students, including Whites, wanted to learn Afrikaan languages because of their practical utility in the local communities to become economically and socially independent. The study reveals dominance of the White minority's native language, and the school's willful ignorance of the linguistic background of more than 40% of its student body (Carter 2012).

Looking ahead, Manning (2009) argues that the biggest concern in the twenty-first century is the racialized division of resources and wealth that separate Europe and North America from the rest of the world. The patterns of unequal economic exchange persist in this new "global apartheid" that penalizes people from Africa, South Asia, and other developing regions— "predatory policies of structural adjustments and loan payments to multinational banks" (1). Thus, an important challenge for scholars, activists, and policymakers is addressing the variety of racialized experiences, identities, and social structures that can help solve the problem of global inequalities in educational access, and drawing on examples of racial equality that can be applied across cultural and national borders.

CONCLUSION

We discussed how the schooling experiences of nondominant students are best understood when the racial formation framework is used to explain how racial projects in the form of inequality, passivity, and opportunities provide different schooling experiences for students. We argue that structural factors at the school and societal levels serve to limit nondominant students from developing academic success. For example, differences in curricula are evident for students from lower- (e.g., remedial courses that stress rote memorization) and higher-class (e.g., college preparatory courses that emphasize critical thinking skills) backgrounds (Oakes 2005). Inequalities in curriculum development, discipline, and funding prevent students from experiencing equal opportunities (Banks 2006; Darling-Hammond 2010). Taking it a step further, the racial formation framework advances understanding of how ethnic minority students encounter structural inequalities rooted in past racial projects in a global context.

Using the racial formation framework, we discussed how the significance of race is constantly interpreted and transformed to produce unequal learning opportunities for ethnic minority students. Racial formations have historically produced inequalities and privilege among students from various racial backgrounds. The end of court-ordered busing policies served as a racial project to racially segregate schools and perpetuate unequal learning opportunities between Black and White students (Billings et al. 2014). Racial formation also informs how schools privilege White culture, which serves to undermine the success of minority students. Staiger (2004) found that a school privileged Whiteness by associating this concept as giftedness. Colorblind policies also seek to de-racialize interactions that may be racial in nature, which has the impact of trivializing the significance of race and the value of non-White students (Lewis 2003).

The racial formation framework reminds us that race plays a significant role in school policies and practices. Conservative movements have spearheaded various racial projects aimed to protect the interests of White, middle-class, and Protestant communities, which have not only reversed progress made from the Civil Rights Movement, but also supported colorblind policies that stigmatize efforts to address racial discrimination in schools. To fully understand why nondominant students are placed at an academic disadvantage requires knowing how current school inequalities are rooted in past racial formations.

Although dominant racial formation in schools can be detrimental to ethnic minority students, we highlight several instances where nondominant students find opportunities to forge their own success. Low-income Black males interpreted past racial struggles experienced by their ancestors during the Civil War as motivators to develop their own success (MacLeod 1995). High-achieving Korean students confronted expectations to conform to the model minority myth by developing positive ethnic identities associated with their Korean heritage (Marinari 2005). Schools can serve as racial projects that structure failure and success simultaneously, thus giving agency to the production of school success among Black, Latino, and Vietnamese youth (Conchas 2006).

Although both structural forces influence choices and actions, we acknowledge that individual agency can counteract these forces (Datnow, Hubbard, and Mehan 2005; Levinson, Foley, and Holland 1996). Certainly, in the face of adversity, students and teachers are not *passive*, as they are both reactive and proactive—"resisting, conforming, making decisions, forming beliefs and dispositions" (Martin 2000, 36). According to Wyn and Dwyer (1999), individual agency implies that the person carries "a degree of personal investment that looks forward to—even insists on—positive outcomes" (14). Oppressed people can act to resist and influence subsequent events (Shilling 1992). Nevertheless, this is not to suggest that people will always choose, or be able, to counteract these forces. Teachers and policymakers are unfairly portrayed as "intentional agents" who are purposefully committed to certain classroom practices that reflect gender and ethnic discrimination. The agency of teachers and principals, in particular, must be understood in the context of large and complex institutional forces shaped by social relations, politics, and the economy (Datnow et al. 2005). While acknowledging that these actors have individual agency to influence events, these agents regularly draw on social norms of behaviors because "not to do so would threaten their basic 'security system'" (Giddens 1979, 123). Rather than arguing that schools are intentionally trying to uphold racist beliefs and norms, it is more productive to conceptualize teachers as unwittingly complicit in the perpetuation of particular racial inequalities on the colorblind premise that these racial disparities are natural.

Lewis (2003) concludes her research with the profound point that schools can both "challenge and reproduce the contemporary racial formation" (190). Schools provide an important socializing function because they offer youths from diverse backgrounds opportunities to interact with others who are not normally encountered in their everyday context. At school, students learn about themselves in the context of our diverse society, and hopefully have the opportunity to learn and value differences. At their best, schools reinforce the universal principle that everyone has a chance to succeed. However, this "meritocracy" system also represents a paradox of the education system. As we have seen in racial formation education movements based on ideological conceptualizations supporting individual freedom and colorblindness, schools have reversed progress made to equalize learning opportunities for all students. In turn, these efforts resulted in directing high concentrations of nondominant students into inner-city schools that lack the requisite resources for consistent student engagement and academic achievement. The racial formation framework frames racially motivated school policies and practices in socio-historical context—as racial projects. This theoretical framework allows us to understand why race continues to play a significant role in the unequal distribution of learning opportunities for students in various contexts.

However, we have reason to be hopeful for a brighter, more equitable future. Immigration, particularly from Asian and Latin American countries, is changing the face of America and our education system. The general academic achievement of middle-class East and South Asian immigrants is a well-known phenomenon, but their counterparts from south of the U.S.-Mexico border have received mostly negative attention, and their success as U.S. inhabitants has been harshly questioned (Feliciano 2006; Huntington 2004). But we typically measure human success at an endpoint, rather than taking progress into account. A recent study of immigrant assimilation in Los Angeles revealed that, in terms of generation progress in educational attainment, Mexicans—not Chinese, Koreans, or Japanese—constitute the most successful immigrant group in Los Angeles (Lee 2014).

We as educational scholars are witnessing widespread transnational movements forging new racial projects that contest racial disparity and promote opportunities in education. This is the major theme of this volume.

NOTES

1. Oakes's (2005) research considered a comprehensive approach to study tracking by collecting and analyzing data from principal and teacher interviews, school documents, lengthy questionnaires to students, parents, teachers, principals, and school board members, as well as observations based on the daily events of classroom life in a random sample of classes in each school. The 25 sampled schools represent diverse communities across America that includes sparsely populated schools in the rural South, suburban communities close to the major cities, and middle-sized cities in the Northwest, Southwest, and the Midwest.
2. The high school featured a racially mixed population of White (38.8%), Hispanic (33%), African American (13.7%), and Asian (10.6%) students (Conchas et al. 2014).
3. From 2003 to 2009, MAS participants surpassed all other students on the state's graduation exam and graduated at a higher rate than their White peers (Romero and Arce 2009).

REFERENCES

Almaguer, T. 2008. *Racial Fault Lines: The Historical Origins of White Supremacy in California*. Berkeley: University of California Press.

Almaguer, T., and M.-K. Jung. 1999. "The Enduring Ambiguities of Race in the United States." In *Continuities and Cutting Edges: An Agenda for North American Sociology*, edited by Janet Abu-Lughod, 213–236. Chicago: University of Chicago Press.

Altschul, I., D. Oyserman, and D. Bybee. 2006. "Racial-Ethnic Identity in Mid-Adolescence: Content and Change as Predictors of Academic Achievement." *Child Development* 77 (5): 1155–1169.

Alumkal, A. W. 2004. "American Evangelicalism in the Post-Civil Rights Era: A Racial Formation Theory Analysis." *Sociology of Religion* 65 (3): 195–213.

Anderson, E. 1999. *Code of the Street: Decency, Violence, and the Moral Life of the Inner City*. New York: W. W. Norton.

Aron, L., and J. Zewig. 2003. *Educational Alternatives for Vulnerable Youth: Student Needs, Program Types, and Research Directions*. Washington, DC: The Urban Institute. Retrieved November 10, 2014, from http://www.urban.org/uploadedPDF/410898_vulnerable_youth.pdf.

Ashenfelter, O., W. J. Collins, and A. Yoon. 2006. "Evaluating the Role of Brown v. Board of Education in School Equalization, Desegregation, and the Income of African Americans." *American Law and Economics Review* 8 (2): 213–248.

Banks, J. 2006. *Race, Culture and Education*. New York: Routledge.

Bhattacharyya, G., J. Gabriel, and S. Small. 2001. *Race and Power: Global Racism in the Twenty-First Century*. New York: Routledge.

Billings, S. B., D. J. Deming, and J. Rockoff. 2014. "School Segregation, Educational Attainment, and Crime: Evidence from the End of Busing in Charlotte-Mecklenburg." *The Quarterly Journal of Economics* 129 (1): 435–476.

Binder, A. 1993. "Constructing Racial Rhetoric: Media Depictions of Harm in Heavy Metal and Rap Music." *American Sociological Review* 58 (6): 753–767.

Blad, E. 2014. "Schools in Ferguson, Mo., Suspend Black Students at Higher Rates Than Their Peers." *Education Weekly*, 21 August. Retrieved August 21, 2014, from http://blogs.edweek.org/edweek/rulesforengagement/2014/08/schools_in_ferguson_mo_suspend_black_students_at_higher_rates_than_their_peers.html.

Bonilla-Silva, E. 1997. "Rethinking Racism: Toward a Structural Interpretation." *American Sociological Review* 62 (3): 465–480.

Borman, G. D., and L. T. Overman. 2004. "Academic Resilience in Mathematics Among Poor and Minority Students." *The Elementary School Journal* 104 (3): 177–195.

Bowles, S., and H. Gintis. 1976. *Schooling on Capitalist America*. New York: Basic Books.

Bowles, S., and H. Gintis. 2002. "Schooling in Capitalist America Revisited." *Sociology of Education* 75 (1): 1–18.

Bowman, P., and C. Howard. 1985. "Race-Related Socialization, Motivation, and Academic Achievement: A Study of Black Youths in Three-Generation Families." *Journal of the American Academy of Child Psychiatry* 24 (2): 134–141.

Brock, A. 2009. "Life on the Wire." *Information, Communication and Society* 12 (3): 344–363.

Cabrera, N. L., E. L. Meza, A. J. Romero, and R. Cintli Rodríguez. 2013. "'If There Is No Struggle, There Is No Progress': Transformative Youth Activism and the School of Ethnic Studies." *The Urban Review* 45 (1): 7–22.

Carter, P. 2012. *Stubborn Roots: Race, Culture, and Inequality*. New York: Oxford University Press.

Carter, P. L. 2003. "'Black' Cultural Capital, Status Positioning, and Schooling Conflicts for Low-Income African American Youth." *Social Problems* 50 (1): 136–155.

Charles, C. Z. 2003. "The Dynamics of Racial Residential Segregation." *Annual Review of Sociology* 29: 167–207.

Conchas, G. 2006. *The Color of Success: Race and High-Achieving Urban Youth*. New York: Teachers College Press.

Conchas, G., A. Lin, L. Oseguera, and S. Drake. 2014. "Superstar or Scholar? African American Youth's Perceptions of Opportunity in a Time of Change." *Urban Education* 49: 1–29.

Crenshaw, K. 1997. "Color-Blind Dreams and Racial Nightmares: Reconfiguring Racism in the Post-Civil Rights Era." In *Birth of a Nationhood*, edited by Toni Morrison, 97–168. New York: Pantheon Books.

Darling-Hammond, L. 2010. *The Flat World and Education: How America's Commitment to Equity Will Determine Our Future*. New York: Teachers College Press.

Datnow, A., L. Hubbard, and H. Mehan. 2005. *Extending Educational Reform: From One School to Many*. New York: Routledge.

Delpit, L. 1988. "The Silenced Dialogue: Power and Pedagogy in Educating Other People's Children." *Harvard Educational Review* 58 (3): 280–299.

Downing, D. 2004. *Apartheid in South Africa*. Chicago, IL: Heinemann Library.

Dwyer, O. J., and J. P. Jones. 2000. "White Socio-Spatial Epistemology." *Social and Cultural Geography* 1 (2): 209–222.

Editorial Projects in Education Research Center. 2011. "Issues A-Z: Achievement Gap." *Education Week,* 7 July. Retrieved July 28, 2014, from http://www.edweek.org/ew/issues/achievement-gap/.

Education Week. 2011. "Beyond High School, Before Baccalaureate: Alternatives to a Four-Year Degree." *Diplomas Count 2011,* 9 June. Retrieved July 28, 2014, from http://www.edweek.org/ew/toc/2011/06/09/index.html.

Essed, P. 1991. *Understanding Everyday Racism: An Interdisciplinary Theory*. Newbury Park, CA: Sage.

Feliciano, C. 2006. "Beyond the Family: The Influence of Premigration Group Status on the Educational Expectations of Immigrants' Children." *Sociology of Education* 79 (4): 281–303.

Ferguson, A. A. 2001. *Bad Boys: Public Schools in the Making of Black Masculinity*. Ann Arbor: University of Michigan Press.

Fields, B. 1990. "Slavery, Race, and Ideology in the United States of America." *New Left Review* 181: 95–118.

Giddens, A. 1979. *Central Problems in Social Theory, Action, Structure, and Contradiction in Social Analysis*. London: Macmillan.

Goffman, A. 2014. *On the Run: Fugitive Life in an American City*. Chicago: University of Chicago Press.

Goldin, C. D., and L. F. Katz. 2009. *The Race Between Education and Technology*. Cambridge, MA: Harvard University Press.

Herrnstein, R., and C. Murray. 1994. *The Bell Curve: Intelligence and Class Structure in American Life*. New York: Free Press.

Huntington, S. P. 2004. *Who Are We?: The Challenges to America's National Identity*. New York: Simon and Schuster.

Iceland, J. 2009. *Where We Live Now: Immigration and Race in the United States*. London: University of California Press.

Ingels, S., D. Pratt, D. Wilson, L. Burns, D. Currivan, J. Rogers, and S. Hubbard-Bednasz. 2007. *Education Longitudinal Study of 2002: Base-Year to Second Follow-up Data File Documentation (NCES 2008–347)*. Washington, DC: National Center for Education Statistics, U.S. Department of Education.

Jiménez, T. R., and A. L. Horowitz. 2013. "When White is Just Alright How Immigrants Redefine Achievement and Reconfigure the Ethnoracial Hierarchy." *American Sociological Review* 78: 849–871.

Lee, J. 2014. "Don't Tell Amy Chua: Mexicans are the Most Successful Immigrants." *TIME.com,* 25 February. Retrieved February 25, 2014, from http://ideas.time.com/2014/02/25/dont-tell-amy-chua-mexicans-are-the-most- successful-immigrants/.

Leonardo, Z. 2009. *Race, Whiteness, and Education*. New York: Routledge.

Leonardo, Z. 2013. *Race Framework: A Multidimensional Theory of Racism and Education*. New York: Teachers College Press.

Levinson, B. A., D. E. Foley, and D. C. Holland. 1996. *The Cultural Production of the Educated Person: Critical Ethnographies of Schooling and Local Practice*. New York: SUNY Press.

Lewis, A. 2003. *Race in the Schoolyard: Negotiating the Color Line in Classrooms and Communities*. Piscataway, NJ: Rutgers University Press.

Loury, G. C. 2002. *The Anatomy of Racial Inequality*. Cambridge, MA: Harvard University Press.

MacLeod, J. 1995. *Ain't No Makin' It: Aspirations and Attainment in a Low-Income Neighborhood*, 2nd ed. Boulder, CO: Westview Press.

Marable, M. 2009. *Globalization and Racialization*. ZNet Classic Series. Retrieved October 17, 2014, from http://zcomm.org/znetarticle/globalization-and-racialization-by-manning-marable/.

Marinari, M. 2005. "Racial Formation and Success Among Korean High School Students." *The Urban Review* 37 (5): 375–398.

Martin, D. B. 2000. *Mathematics Success and Failure Among African-American Youth: The Roles of Sociohistorical Context, Community Forces, School Influence, and Individual Agency*. Mahwah, NJ: Routledge.

Marx, S. 2004. "Regarding Whiteness: Exploring and Intervening in the Effects of White Racism in Teacher Education." *Equity and Excellence in Education* 37 (1): 31–43.

Massey, D., and N. Denton. 1993. *American Apartheid: Segregation and the Making of the Underclass*. Cambridge, MA: Harvard University Press.

McIntosh, P. 1998. "White Privilege: Unpacking the Invisible Knapsack." In *Race, Class, and Gender in the United States: An Integrated Study*, edited by Paula Rothenberg, 31–36. New York: Worth Publishers.

McNeil, M., and E. Blad. 2014. "Nation Falls Far Short on Educational Equity, Data Show." *Education Weekly*, 21 August. Retrieved August 21, 2014, from http://www.edweek.org/ew/articles/2014/03/21/26ocr.h33.html.

Meier, K. J., J. Stewart, and R. E. England. 1989. *Race, Class, and Education: The Politics of Second-Generation Discrimination*. Madison: University of Wisconsin Press.

National Center for Education Statistics. 2007. *State Non-Fiscal Survey of Public Elementary/Secondary Education 2005–06*. Retrieved October 14, 2014, from http://nces.ed.gov/ccd/.

National Center for Education Statistics. 2009. *America's High School Graduates: Results of the 2009 NAEP High School Transcript Study*. Alexandria, VA: U.S. Department of Education. Retrieved July 31, 2014, from http://nces.ed.gov/nationsreportcard/pdf/studies/2011462.pdf.

National Center for Education Statistics. 2011. *The Condition of Education*. Alexandria, VA: U.S. Department of Education. Retrieved July 31, 2014, from http://nces.ed.gov/pubs2011/2011034.pdf.

Noguera, P. 2003. *City Schools and the American Dream: Reclaiming the Promise of Public Education*. New York: Teachers College Press.

Oakes, J. 1982. "Classroom Social Relationships: Exploring the Bowles and Gintis Hypothesis." *Sociology of Education* 55 (4): 197–212.

Oakes, J. 2005. *Keeping Track: How Schools Structure Inequality*, 2nd ed. New Haven, CT: Yale University Press.

Omi, M., and H. Winant. 2014. *Racial Formation in the United States*, 3rd ed. New York: Routledge.

Orozco, R. A. 2011. "'It is Certainly Strange . . .': Attacks on Ethnic Studies and Whiteness as Property." *Journal of Education Policy* 26 (6): 819–838.

Pollock, M. 2004. *Colormute: Race Talk Dilemmas in an American School*. Princeton, NJ: Princeton University Press.

Rhee, J. 2013. "The Neoliberal Racial Project: The Tiger Mother and Governmentality." *Educational Theory* 63 (6): 561–580.

Riley, C., and N. Ettlinger. 2011. "Interpreting Racial Formation and Multiculturalism in a High School: Towards a Constructive Deployment of Two Approaches to Critical Race Theory." *Antipode* 43 (4): 1250–1280.

Robbins, T. 2013. "Tucson Revives Mexican-American Studies Program." *NPR.org*, 24 July. Retrieved August 22, 2014, from http://www.npr.org/blogs/codeswitch/2013/07/24/205058168/Tucson-Revives-Mexican-American-Studies-Program.

Romero, A., and M. Arce. 2009. "Culture as a Resource: Critically Compassionate Intellectualism and Its Struggle Against Racism, Fascism, and Intellectual Apartheid in Arizona." *Hamline Journal of Public Law and Policy* 31: 179.

Ryan, C. S., J. S. Hunt, J. A. Weible, C. R. Peterson, and J. F. Casas. 2007. "Multicultural and Colorblind Ideology, Stereotypes, and Ethnocentrism Among Black and White Americans." *Group Processes and Intergroup Relations* 10 (4): 617–637.

Salinas, L. 2011. "Arizona's Desire to Eliminate Ethnic Studies Programs: A Time to Take the Pill and to Engage Latino Students in Critical Education about Their History." *Harvard Latino Law Review* 14: 301–323.

Schofield, J. 2001. "The Colorblind Perspective in School: Causes and Consequences." In *Multicultural Education: Issues and Perspectives*, edited by J. Banks and C. McGee, 4th ed., 247–267. New York: Wiley.

Shilling, C. 1992. "Reconceptualising Structure and Agency in the Sociology of Education: Structuration Theory and Schooling." *British Journal of Sociology of Education* 13 (1): 69–87.

Staiger, A. 2004. "Whiteness as Giftedness: Racial Formation at an Urban High School." *Social Problems* 51 (2): 161–181.

Steinberg, L., B. B. Brown, and S. M. Dornbusch. 1997. *Beyond the Classroom.* New York: Simon and Schuster.

Stormont, M., L. Espinosa, N. Knipping, and R. McCathren. 2003. "Supporting Vulnerable Learners in the Primary Grades: Strategies to Prevent Early School Failure." *Early Childhood Research & Practice* 5 (2): 1–13.

Tang, J., S. Kim, and D. Haviland. 2013. "Role of Family, Culture, and Peers in the Success of First-Generation Cambodian American College Students." *Journal of Southeast Asian American Education and Advancement* 8: 1–21.

Tatum, B. D. 2003. *"Why Are All the Black Kids Sitting Together in the Cafeteria?": And Other Conversations About Race.* New York: Basic Books.

U.S. Census Bureau. 2011. *Profile America Facts for Features: Asian/Pacific American Heritage Month: May 2011.* Retrieved October 14, 2014, from http://www.census.gov/newsroom/releases/archives/facts_for_features_special_editions/cb11-ff06.html.

U.S. Department of Education. 2012. *Discipline of Students without Disabilities—One Out-of-School Suspension (2011–12).* National Center for Education Statistics. Retrieved August 21, 2014, from http://ocrdata.ed.gov/Page?t=dandeid=27900andsyk=6andpid=886.

Uy, P. 2002. "Response—K–12 Education: How the American Community Survey Informs Our Understanding of the Southeast Asian Community: One Teacher's Perspective." *Journal of Southeast Asian American Education and Advancement* 3: 44–50.

Wacquant, L. 2002. "From Slavery to Mass Incarceration." *New Left Review* 13: 41–60.

Warikoo, N. 2011. *Balancing Acts: Youth Culture in the Global City.* Los Angeles, CA: University of California Press.

Weiner, D., B. Lutz, and J. Ludwig. 2009. *The Effects of School Desegregation on Crime.* NBER Working Paper. National Bureau of Economic Research. Retrieved from http://www.nber.org/papers/w15380.

Wilson, W. J. 2012. *The Truly Disadvantaged: The Inner City, the Underclass, and Public Policy.* Chicago: University of Chicago Press.

Winant, H. 1994. *Racial Conditions.* Minneapolis: University of Minnesota Press.

Witherspoon, K. M., S. L. Speight, and A. Jones Thomas. 1997. "Racial Identity Attitudes, School Achievement, and Academic Self-Efficacy Among African American High School Students." *Journal of Black Psychology* 23 (4): 344–357.

Wyn, J., and P. Dwyer. 1999. "New Directions in Research on Youth in Transition." *Journal of Youth Studies* 2 (1): 5–21.

Part II

Boys and Men of Color
Resilience and the Construction of Urban School Success

2 The Problematization of Cambodian Adolescent Boys in U.S. Schools

Beyond the Model Minority Stereotype of Asian American Youth

Vichet Chhuon

This chapter[1] explores the problematization of Cambodian high school boys in a Southern California community. Cambodian student experiences tend to be lumped into an aggregate racial category that is frequently misrepresented by the model minority perception of Asian American students (Ng, Pak, and Lee 2007). This inclusion of Cambodians within the insidious model minority stereotype leads to students' invisibility in research and policy, and difficulty in attaining proper academic support (Chhuon and Hudley 2008; Chhuon, Dosalmas, and Rinthapol 2010). For instance, the U.S. Census has reported that of Cambodians (age 25 and over) living in the U.S., 34% have less than a high school diploma and only 16% have a four-year degree, far below the national averages for Asian Americans and the overall U.S. population (Southern Asia Resource Action Center 2011). Yet, Cambodian students are critically underserved and overlooked by educators and policymakers. My research with Cambodian American youth over the past few years has tried to represent the complex and frequently conflicting representations of this underserved population in U.S. schools.

Some scholars have documented the ways in which many Southeast Asian youth, including Cambodians, are negatively read by local school personnel (Chhuon and Hudley 2010; Conchas and Vigil 2012; Lei 2003; Ngo 2009; Lee 2005). This study examines how Cambodian American adolescent boys, in particular, are commonly perceived through a pervasive discourse of the Cambodian dropout, troublemaker, and gangster at Comprehensive High School (CHS).[2] *Discourse* in this study refers to popular and often stereotypical images ascribed to individuals and groups (Gee 1999), including Cambodian adolescent males. My aim is to understand not only what individuals say, but how their statements and attitudes about Cambodian American male youth are nested within a larger sociopolitical context of immigration, ethnicity, gender, education, and U.S. society (Fairclough 1989). I describe how these ideologies influence how Cambodian American students see themselves and approach schooling. As well, I show how educators at CHS utilize particular discourses of Cambodian male youth to deflect attention from larger school and institutional inequities. I conclude with a discussion of the significance of understanding these discourses for improving the education of Cambodian students and other immigrant and urban youth of color in U.S. schools.

RACE, GENDER, AND IMMIGRANT ACCULTURATION

A helpful framework for understanding the diverse educational experiences of immigrant children has been segmented assimilation (Portes and Rumbaut 2006). Under this perspective, the translation of attitudes and academic aspirations into actual achievement is contingent upon where families come from, as well as the context that youth are incorporated into, including quality schools and the presence of racial discrimination. Research has documented that immigrant children of color from lower-class backgrounds, including Cambodians, are especially vulnerable to assimilating into an underclass strata in U.S. society and develop oppositional identities toward schooling (Zhou 1997). The environments that less economically advantaged groups (including many Cambodian immigrants) settled in, combined with their pre-migration characteristics, shape the academic outlooks for their children (Portes and Rumbaut 2006). Ong (2003) has argued that newer, non-White immigrants, such as Cambodians, eventually undergo an assimilation process characterized by the ideological racial Whitening (e.g., Asian Americans as model minorities) and Blackening (e.g., Cambodians as academic strugglers) of their ethnic groups in the U.S. This racialization can have important implications for how Cambodian adolescent youth negotiate messages related to their racial and ethnic backgrounds, and influences overall adjustment into U.S. society.

Other research has indicated that gender can be a significant variable for understanding the school experiences and acculturation of many immigrant youths. For example, females from immigrant families, when compared to males, are likely more protected from certain risk factors such as negative ethnic stereotypes and hostile school environments, particularly during adolescence (Qin-Hilliard 2003). Ethnographic data suggest that daughters from immigrant families tend to endure stricter parental monitoring that contributes to better grades and fewer problems in school (Zhou and Bankston 1998; Waters 1999). Sons, however, may encounter different expectations for behavior and school achievement. Cammarota (2004) examined the gender socialization that many immigrant children of color experience in urban schools and observed that second-generation female students from West Indian and Mexican backgrounds defied common racial and gender expectations by working hard and achieving in school. In contrast, second-generation males from West Indian and Mexican backgrounds tend to express their resistance by avoiding class and defying school adults. Further, research has consistently revealed that immigrant daughters consistently reported higher aspirations and grades than sons throughout their schooling (Kao and Tienda 1998; Stepick et al. 2001; Zhou and Bankston 2001).

Relatively few studies have examined the educational struggles of Asian American male youth. Exceptions include some research that has observed that Asian American boys do not transition seamlessly through the K–12 pipeline, contrary to the model minority stereotype (Kumashiro 1999; Lei 2003; Ngo 2009). For instance, the representation of Asian American boys as small and weak has often resulted in their perceived emasculation in school (Kumashiro 1999; Lei 2003; Lee 2005). This image has led to verbal and physical harassment from peers. At the same time, studies of Southeast Asian American male students found that they are often rumored to be dangerous and gang involved. For example, Lei's (2003) ethnography of Hmong, Lao, and Cambodian high school boys show that whereas these students were often seen as quiet and docile, they were simultaneously represented as "bad Asians" because of their suspected gang involvement. Given the lack of what Connell (1996) termed "hegemonic masculinity" (i.e., not being White, middle class, and male), combined with a racist school context, marginalized Asian American boys are pushed to negotiate alternative ways of expressing themselves as tough urban males. Ngo's investigation into the experiences of Lao high schoolers found that Lao males created and reshaped identities in ways that confused educators. One of her male participants for example, an honor student, defied these categories by professing a dedication to education and being a "good Christian", while dressing in baggy, urban, "hip hop" style, including "a rag hanging out of his pocket" (Ngo 2009, 215). His good grades and college aspirations notwithstanding, teachers perceived this young man as "gangster-fronting" and possibly dangerous.

The school experiences of Cambodian adolescent males resonate with other literature documenting the discrimination and racialization of male youth of color (Chhuon and Hudley 2010). Some Cambodian male students are socialized to resist certain aspects of mainstream school norms, including doing well academically and holding college aspirations. Other scholars have argued that hostile institutional practices are generally designed to contain and marginalize young men of color (Garbarino 1999; Giroux 2009; Noguera 2003). Negative social and cultural beliefs are often funneled through social institutions to shape the way some ethnic minority males learn about belonging in school and broader society. The negative messages communicated to these young men—often that they are dangerous and menacing—shape their perceptions of schooling and academic achievement.

CRITICAL DISCOURSE ANALYSIS

Gee's (1999) conception of d/Discourses served as an analytical lens to make sense of the social practices linked to the popular discourse about being

Cambodian and male at CHS. In general, critical discourse analysis represents an effective means for looking beyond words and sentences to examine the relationships between people, ideologies, and power (Fairclough 1989; Foucault 1972; Gee 1999). For Gee, little "d" discourse refers to a specific set of images, sentences, and conversations that are routinely shared and experienced. These may be the literal quotes and images that are stated by individual actors, and circulated in regular conversations across varied contexts. In contrast, big "D" Discourse refers to the broader ideology from which these conversations, images, and beliefs are embedded and understood. Discourses (with a capital D) move beyond language and text to include the values and identities that are instantiated within institutions. Ostensibly for youths, one such important institution is the school they attend. As Gee (1999) put it, "big D discourses are always language plus other stuff" (17). This *other stuff* relates to the recognition of the larger identities asserted and sustained through talk and other social practices within institutions.

In schools, big D is often circulated and maintained through normalized, small d discourses related to class assignments, academic tracking, and explanations for student achievement. Although seemingly mundane, these *common sense* explanations and beliefs about students have within them powerful ideological messages that are maintained through language and texts. These norms are often part of a larger, dominant discourse of education in the U.S. centering on ideas of equal opportunity and meritocracy (Fairclough 1989; McGinnis 2009). It is big D's status as a dominant discourse that leads to its normalization in everyday practices. Fairclough (1989) asserted that whereas the ideologies associated with a dominant discourse "control both the actions of members of a society and their interpretation of the action of others", these assumptions are "rarely explicitly formulated or examined or questioned" (64).

BACKGROUND TO THE CASE STUDY

Community and School Context

The school and neighborhood setting for the study[3] is home to a large Cambodian enclave that is situated in an impoverished, diverse community. Whereas White American residents comprise approximately half of the population in this city, the inner-city community in which this study takes place is largely made up of Southeast Asian, African American, and Latino families. This particular community has also struggled for over two decades with the presence of gangs from various racial and ethnic groups, including Cambodian gangs. Comprehensive High School (CHS) is a racially and economically diverse school, and its surrounding neighborhood is home to many Cambodian families. During the 2006–2007 school year, the reported student enrollment was approximately 4,700 and 60% were eligible for the free/reduced lunch program. The school's ethnic breakdown was as follows: 27% African American, 33% Asian (including Cambodian), 26% Latino, 12% White, and 2% Pacific Islander. This district, like most other school districts in the U.S., could not provide disaggregated data on how many Cambodian students it enrolled. Thus, I relied on a CHS Khmer home language list that contained approximately 900 student names. Whereas the majority of Cambodian students were born in the U.S., their parents tended to be born abroad and so Khmer is still often the home language in this immigrant community.

Data and Interpretation

Eight months of participant observation during the 2007–2008 school year at CHS informed this research. During the first month I spent approximately four hours on campus two to three days a week, which was valuable for familiarizing myself with the school's layout, including the library, the college center, and extracurricular activities office. Classroom observations focused on core academic classes (English, math, and social studies) across CHS's various programs.[4] Of the 52 Cambodian students individually interviewed for the study, 24 were male and their voices form the basis of this article.[5] As well, I conducted formal individual interviews with various teachers, counselors, and other CHS staff. Purposeful snowball sampling techniques were used to recruit the appropriate range of participants. Teachers and students often nominated other individuals who they thought would be helpful for this research. All of the student informants in this study were familiar with me prior to the formal interview, having already met me in class or during lunch through their friends.

Data analysis was on-going and recursive (Marshall and Rossman 1995) throughout the study where concepts that emerged during analysis informed subsequent aspects of other data collection. After field notes and interviews were transcribed, these data were open coded to allow themes to aggregate themselves into common domains (Spradley 1979). Spradley describes domains as categories of objects, ideas, feelings, and events, as understood and perceived by individuals. During analysis, a consistent, albeit troubling, theme that surfaced was the way in which Cambodian boys were essentialized and critically viewed by CHS faculty, staff, and students. I looked to unpack some of the dominant Discourses about Cambodian boys in school. Therefore, in this study, I read these data with these specific questions in mind: How were Cambodian male youth talked about by adults and students at CHS? How did Cambodian male youth interpret these messages? In addition to these questions, I continually asked myself during the analysis and writing of this chapter about the possible different meanings of the words and discourses spoken across various formal and informal conversations with informants regarding their beliefs about Cambodian boys

and girls and the significance attached to racial, ethnic and gender categories. Instances of big D discourses are denoted with a capital "D" (e.g.,
Discourse/Discourses).

"You Know What I'm Talking About":
My Insider Identities at CHS

Some of my own identities are worth mentioning here. I am a product
of the U.S. public school system, a Cambodian male, and former urban
high school teacher. It should not be surprising that this research has been
shaped by these experiences. It was important for me to reflect on my multiple positionalities (e.g., ethnic, gender, class, age, and community outsider
status) to understand how these subjectivities were embedded within this
research. The literature has encouraged qualitative researchers, especially
scholars of color, to consider their subjectivities as potential strengths in
the research process (see Foley, Levinson, and Hurtig 2001). Though we
differed in age and educational background, I was able to build rapport
with youth based on cultural commonalities. Some students referred to
me as "bong" (big brother) or "pu" (uncle) and used Khmer/Cambodian[6]
terms to share anecdotes about growing up in an immigrant Cambodian
household.

Further, my presence at CHS contrasted with many adults' assumptions
of Cambodian male youth in particular. Teachers, counselors, and administrators were aware of my Cambodian heritage and my graduate student
status situated me in their minds as fitting the successful, high-achieving
Asian American stereotype. One administrator, for instance, who had
taught at CHS for many years prior, attempted to guess that my home experiences were guided by supportive, "Asian" cultural values. She commented,
"I know you're Cambodian but you're getting your PhD so I bet you know
what I'm talking about. Like, your parents probably put education as a
priority for all of you [me and my siblings]. I don't see that with our Cambodians here really." Whereas this administrator believed that she was offering a compliment by speculating that my own family placed education in
high regard, her comment points toward the larger Discourse that suggests
Cambodian youth largely do not come from academically supportive home
environments. The discrepancy between what was guessed to be my home
experience and her popular understanding of Cambodian families helped
rationalize Cambodian students' low school achievement. She assumed that
I knew what she was "talking about" because I represented an exception to
what was a popular conception about Cambodian students. As Gee (1999)
put it, "the key to Discourses is 'recognition'" (18), and she clearly recognized me to be part of the Discourse about being Cambodian in a U.S. high
school. I recognize that in some ways, my own status as a successful Cambodian male student may have unwittingly reified the popular perceptions
of Cambodian boys[7].

ETHNIC STEREOTYPES AT CHS

> Well, I think we feel that Asian students are good students. I do
> know that there are Cambodian gangs that people should be aware
> of. There is a lot of that going on around this area between the
> Blacks, Hispanics, and *these* Asians. So it's not like the Japanese and
> Chinese, you know?
>
> (Mrs. Jamison, administrator)

Recognizing the focus on my study, Mrs. Jamison openly explained how
Cambodians fit within CHS's larger student body. Similar to most staff
members interviewed, Mrs. Jamison differentiated Cambodians from other
Asian American students at the school. The model minority Discourse of
Asian Americans was a pervasive feature of Cambodian students' experiences at CHS, as consistent with previous works on Asian American
students in U.S. schools (Ng et al. 2007). This was evident in regular conversations with a number of students, teachers, and other school adults.
This *positive* generalization, however, seems constructed at the expense
of Cambodian youth at CHS. Whereas Asians as a racial group are stereotyped as high academic achievers, a less flattering image of Cambodians at CHS was consistently communicated. Cambodian students were
frequently described as poor, welfare dependent, and involved in gangs.
Mrs. Jamison's inclusion of Cambodians ("these Asians") with African
American and Latino gangs in the area suggested that Cambodian students
were not *genuinely* Asian, at least not in the vein of the "Japanese and Chinese" students mentioned.

Moreover, a firm hierarchy was suggested to be in place at CHS.[8] When
asked about how others saw them at school, Cambodian students themselves invoked "ghetto" to describe both place and behavior, and to differ-
entiate Cambodians from "other Asians". In her interview, Brenda stated,
"we're used to living in the ghetto. Well most of the Cambodians here [in
this city] and most of us, like especially guys and stuff they're like poor and
into crime and stuff like that. But then it's different from other Asians". As
Brenda explained, another popular and related Discourse (though one used
primarily by youth) was that Cambodians were "ghetto". It was used to
describe where Cambodians lived and "how they acted" in the community.
Both comments from Mrs. Jamison and Brenda support that Cambodian
and East Asian students were dialectically situated at opposite ends of the
racialized Discourse at CHS. Unlike Chinese, Japanese, and Korean students,
identifying as Cambodian at school and in the community often meant that
one would be racialized as poor and low achieving. Whereas the images of
Cambodian students often centered upon being troublemakers and gang
members, these representations were unevenly applied to Cambodian youth
by gender. For Asian Americans at CHS, negative Discourses centering on
crime, gangs, and "living in the ghetto" clearly meant Cambodian *boys*.

GANGSTER BOYS AND MODEL MINORITY GIRLS

> People are mostly scared of Cambodians I think. Like because us guys dress all ghetto and walk cool (laughter). If a White dude did that they would just laugh. Maybe not laugh, but they're not going to get all scared . . . Cambodian girls? People like the girls better probably. Like no one says nothing about them really. Like if a group of guys and group of girls get caught doing something they'll let the girls go.
>
> (Derek, 11th grade Cambodian male)

The "ghetto" dress and "cool" walk Derek mentions refer to his Cambodian peers, whose clothing choices and swagger was associated with African American urban youth culture. As others have documented, Asian American boys who dressed this way and listened to hip-hop music, including the Cambodian youth in this study, were frequently identified as "acting ghetto" (Lei 2003; Ngo 2009). Though they rarely hung out with African American peers, Cambodian boys' embrace of hip-hop fashion and music represented an affinity with perceived African American struggles against a dominant White culture. Consequently, Cambodian youth were "ideologically blackened" (Ong 2003) in the eyes of staff and peers, and profiled as "gangsters" or "wannabes". Either way, they were problem students.

It was not surprising that clothing choice appeared to be a common way for CHS adults to categorize students. What was poignant was the ways in which fashion was a proxy to discuss Cambodian male youth as trouble students. For example, in discussing the problems with gangs in the community, Cambodian and otherwise, one teacher remarked,

> . . . if we had a strong dress code then I think the problem here would be better. At least at [CHS] these kids want to be hoodlums and gangsters and really they're allowed to dress like gangsters. *(What do you consider gang-style dress?)* What I consider? Just walk around sometime . . . Pants that are falling down. Big shirts, jerseys, you know? Not having rules about this, or anything enforced, all that does is encourage the gang culture.

Though this teacher does not make mention of any specific group of students, his excerpt ostensibly references the Discourse surrounding CHS's male students of color. These young men, including Cambodian students (the subject of our conversation), are either gang involved or they aspire to be, and their ability to dress in this way allows them to practice this "gang culture". Whereas some were indeed gang members, most of the young men I spoke with who fit this image were not gang affiliated. Their manner of dress, they explained, was consistent with an urban youth culture that is glamorized on mainstream television and movies, as well as in popular press like *Rolling Stone* and *Vibe* magazines. When asked about this style, Ken, a Cambodian tenth grader, responded, "that's just how we look. It ain't just the gangsters. No one says nothin about how preppies and pretty boys dress. For real what's wrong with this? I look clean, right"? As he pointed to his feet, Ken clearly took pride in the pristine white tennis shoes he wore. Also obvious was that certain styles of dress were privileged at CHS, including those favored by the "preppies" and "pretty boys". As Ken and his friends quickly pointed out, the preppies and pretty boys tend to be White and East Asian students who usually wore brand name collared shirts and designer jeans or khaki pants. The preppies tend to be the higher-achieving students, whereas the pretty boys spanned a range of academic identities. The latter group was nevertheless neatly dressed. Cambodian boys felt that the negative attention their wardrobe choices generated was unfairly targeted by CHS staff. However, adopting hip-hop fashion, as linked to the styles of urban African American youth, represented a way for Cambodian boys to express an alternative form of masculinity, given that more mainstream aspects of manhood (White, tall, and involved in school sports) were generally unavailable to them (Lei 2003; Lee 2005).

My time spent with one young man, Johnny, revealed further how clothing choices helped frame how Cambodian male youth would be treated inside and outside of class. At the time, Johnny was a ninth grade student who was struggling academically, as evidenced by his four failing grades on his last report card. After being asked to tutor him in the spring by his English teacher, I shadowed Johnny for two months and spent time with him in his classes, during lunch, and after school.[9] I hung out with him, played basketball with him, and helped him with his school work. Interestingly, teachers rarely spoke with Johnny directly. When I was present, they often communicated things to him and about him through me. Like many other Cambodian boys at CHS, Johnny's preferred style of dress included sagging, baggy pants and oversized shirts, consistent with hip-hop youth fashion. Sure enough, my conversations with some of Johnny's teachers frequently centered upon his suspected gang involvement. Johnny stated that, despite his dress and "livin' in the hood", he was not involved with gangs, though his wardrobe convinced many CHS adults otherwise. His teachers were adamant that his "joining a gang" was why Johnny was not doing well in school. In her study of Hmong American high school boys in the Midwest, Lee (2005) noted that the "mysterious Asian American gang member represents the dominant group's fears about Asian American masculinity" (92). Johnny stated that his teachers rarely took the opportunity to know him or ask why he was "really doing bad". Johnny's academic struggles were significantly influenced by an unstable home life. He explained that his family moved about every four months and that his apartment was often too noisy to sleep. Further, his older brother was attending college two hours away and could not help him regularly with his school work, as he had done when Johnny was in middle school. Perhaps more importantly, his brother's emotional support was much less available to Johnny during a tough social and academic transition into high school. During one interview, Johnny sarcastically remarked, "it's like we're all involved in gangs. They can say that because my neighborhood has them. But I don't do that stuff. I don't bang. I know I'm absent a lot but they don't have to look at me like that. They don't know me". For Johnny, the "look" frequently received from teachers communicated to him that he was unworthy of their time and resources.

A number of teachers, counselors, administrators, and other school adults I spoke with made negative remarks about Cambodian male youth at CHS. Alternatively, there were markedly different Discourses about Cambodian female students. Whereas Cambodian boys often had to tip toe between student and gang member perceptions of themselves, these concerns were less relevant for Cambodian girls at CHS. Generally, Cambodian girls were perceived by students and school staff as fitting into CHS's version of the "good" student, consistent with the model minority image. Whereas the reflections that were mirrored back at Cambodian boys often communicated messages associated with academic apathy and/or gang ties, the general Discourses around Cambodian girls were that they were studious and quiet in class. One counselor explained,

> we have a lot of different kinds of students here. The Cambodians are generally split. Actually, I don't hear much bad about the Cambodian girls here. They're actually fairly decent students in my opinion. They come, they do their work, stay out of trouble, for the most part. You know? They're pretty good. Sometimes it's like night and day really. Because then you got the real hard, "you can't reach me" gang bangers. The gang kids are usually the ones hanging out together, all dressed the same, hanging around even after the bell rings.

Whereas the counselor does not refer to male students explicitly, it was understood that the "gang kids" in this case were Cambodian boys. Like other CHS adults, the counselor discusses Cambodian boys and girls mostly in dichotomous terms (e.g., "night and day"). Girls were largely discussed as "decent" and "pretty good" students, whereas boys were depicted as "hard", with troubling "you can't reach me" attitudes. However, I met a number of Cambodian female students who struggled and were disengaged in their school work, and there were many Cambodian boys who were high achievers. Just as conversations about Cambodians centered being "ghetto" in relation to East Asian students' positioning as "good Asians", Cambodian girls were situated as "hard workers" so that Cambodian boys at CHS could be positioned as "lazy". These assumptions and fears were often circulated and sustained through common sense understandings about the causes of Cambodian boys' disengagement from school. The identities and labels associated with such Discourses were constructed through everyday, normalized small "d" discourses. At CHS, how students were talked about and situated with respect to race, gender, and achievement inherently privileged some and marginalized others. This interplay between race, ethnicity, and gender significantly shaped how Cambodian boys behaved and how they were discussed and treated.

For example, a key informant throughout this study was Ms. Chim, one of two ethnic Cambodian teachers at CHS at this time. Ms. Chim is also a CHS alumnus. She was pleased to hear that a study about Cambodian students was being conducted. In my two interviews with Ms. Chim, she often discussed the gendered perceptions of Cambodian males vis-à-vis their female peers:

> like in here in my fourth period class, the two Asian girls, well the Cambodian girls, you know them? The kids perceive them as being smart like "Oh you're smart, you know you can answer that" . . . But it's also the Cambodian guys, the boys that are there they just find dumb. And the Cambodian guys are also like probably "Like oh my god I'm so dumb".

My observations of Ms. Chim's fourth period math class supported these different perceptions. I noticed, for instance, that Cambodian males in her fourth period class were often rowdy and frequently inattentive during instruction. Their female peers, however, tended to be on task and well behaved. However, these perceptions did not always reflect a student's actual achievement. Most of these young women shared with me that, contrary to what their peers and teachers might think, they did not see themselves as "good in math". A number of female students stated that they struggled in their other classes as well. I do not share this example from Ms. Chim's class to show that she was careless or an unconscientious teacher. On the contrary, Ms. Chim was a deeply committed professional whose decision to return to her high school was driven by a desire to be a positive role model to Cambodian youth. Rather, this example is provided to support that the Discourses about Cambodian boys and girls at CHS were often moderated by gender, easily described, and considered *commonsensical* by teachers and other significant adults at CHS, even from the perspective of an ethnic insider.

Finally, I show these examples to illuminate further how Cambodian youth were represented at CHS via problematic Discourses of Cambodians boys as gangsters (whether they were actually gang involved or not), and Cambodian girls as model minorities (whether they were doing well academically or not). In other studies, the pattern of female students of color outperforming their male peers within the same ethnic group has been attributed to (at least in part) teachers' perceptions of males as intimidating and females as generally more approachable (Lopez 2003; Valenzuela 1999; Zhou and Bankston 1998). Adapting Winnicott's (1967) earlier work in social psychology, Suarez-Orozco and Suarez Orozco (2001) argue that children of color are profoundly shaped by the reflections mirrored back at them by significant individuals in their lives. Such social mirroring takes on a greater importance when the child belongs to a stigmatized group. Hence, many Cambodian boys were keenly aware of these reflections, and over time, some learned to read these messages well and internalized the negative reflections received from significant individuals in their school lives.

NEGOTIATING NEGATIVE REFLECTIONS

> I tell other people I got 3.7 [grade point average] and they get all surprised and stuff. That's real annoying but to tell you the truth I like it too because it's like proving them wrong.
>
> (Saron, 17 years old)

> If the people around us treat us that way [ghetto] then that's how we're going to be.
>
> (Arun, 16 years old)

Like other Cambodian boys at CHS, Saron and Arun above were aware of how they were perceived at CHS by adults and peers. Still, some of these students discussed pride in their ethnic background. There were, however, differences in how Cambodian boys negotiated the negative reflections of their group. For some, their academic drive was influenced by a desire to disrupt the popular Discourses of Cambodian youth at school and in the community. These youth tend to be those that also described advantages to being Cambodian. One young man that I came to know over this school year was Saron, who explained that

> knowing how to speak Khmer is really good here because we can talk about people and laugh about stuff . . . Sometimes, the teachers want to know more about my culture and ask me to talk about Cambodia. I tell them I never went there but I think it's cool that they even ask. I showed [the teacher] a picture of my cousin's wedding and she looked real interested.

Of the 24 Cambodian boys interviewed, seven discussed explicitly some positive experiences related to their Cambodian background. At the same time, they acknowledged that Cambodians are often seen in negative ways at CHS. Saron shared with me that he received negative messages about Cambodians on a regular basis at school. He explained that Cambodian students often struggled with the negative stereotypes of their ethnic group, including poverty and low achievement, but that for males this involved assumptions related to criminality and gang involvement. Saron described the reaction that some non-Cambodian peers would have after learning he was "smart":

> some kids here don't want to be seen as Cambodian. They want to be seen as something else, like Chinese or Thai or something. Something better. But I don't see it like them. I'm Khmer and I'm not a gangster! We're not all bad and dumb, and stealing. . . . I feel like sometimes people got their mind made up about who's smart and who's going to go to college. It's like they say "we know you're smart so you're going, and you're smart and you're going." Whatever. I mean not everyone is like that. Some teachers don't care, true, but some actually do, believe or not. Some say like "you have to go to college" and you know they're just saying that because it's their job. They know damn well that some kids in their class aren't even going to make it to junior year. But then some [teachers] do mean it. I can tell . . .

Saron's satisfaction from the "surprised" look of others upon hearing that he was a high achiever was related to his desire to disrupt the popular Discourses around Cambodian students, particularly male youth. Knowing that he was "proving them wrong" counterbalanced the annoyance he felt. What was different about Saron and a few other boys I spoke with was that they felt support from teachers in school, though they conceded that most teachers were simply there "because it's their job".

Cambodian male students like Saron were relatively few at CHS. Unlike Saron, many young men hardly mentioned positive aspects of their Cambodian background. Instead, their sense-making of their ethnic group membership associated ethnic pride with school disengagement and low school achievement (Fordham and Ogbu 1986). I spent a good chunk of my lunch periods during the year with a group of Cambodian boys who hung out in front of the library. Proud of their Cambodian identity, these young men regularly pointed to the ways that they felt school personnel unfairly targeted them. A number of young men (e.g., Arun, quoted above) frequently shared that not all Cambodian students were discriminated against. Rather, some Cambodian students received favorable treatment because they were "white-washed". There weren't many Cambodians students at CHS that fell into this peer category. Accusations of being "white-washed" levied at peers hanging out with White American and other Asian American students represented some students' dissatisfaction with Cambodian peers who, in their minds, were not proud of their Cambodian background, as well as those in honors and Advanced Placement (AP) courses. Particularly troubling was that this frequently meant the same thing for Cambodian youth at CHS.

Unfortunately, many boys appeared to have accepted these lowered expectations, though many also questioned them and shared with me their critiques of these negative Discourses. My conversations with a number of Cambodian boys found many internalized, negative assumptions. Some admitted to themselves circulating negative stereotypes. A few of my participants stated that they attended school only to hang out with their friends. A general feeling among these young men was that if they could work they would leave school to earn money, because the prospects of doing well academically appeared slim. Aware of the negative Discourses associated with their group, these boys also linked their Cambodian identities to a negative lens they felt that others saw them through. Jason, for instance, explained to me the difference between Cambodian students and the "rich kids". He stated, "the rich kids are the White kids and the other Asian kids who think they're better than us. A lot of people think that. Maybe they are. Whatever. But they get paid attention to here. By teachers, by whoever. I mean, we get attention too. But the bad kind [*laughter*]". The rich kids these Cambodian boys referenced were certainly those students from higher socioeconomic backgrounds, but included all those they felt were part of the school's more accepted, mainstream community.

Furthermore, to better navigate the social worlds of their school and make sense of their families' lower economic circumstances, these young men seem to adopt the negative representations of Cambodians at CHS. Being an honor student and/or a popular athlete, for example, provided access to certain types of attention and social capital that was unavailable to Jason and his friends. Still, these Cambodian boys linked being rich to certain racial and ethnic categories. While they called these peers the "rich kids", they were clearly referring to East Asian and White American peers at school. These students predominately took the "hardest" classes at CHS. That is, East Asian and White American students represented a disproportionate number of enrolled students in Advanced Placement and honors courses. For many Cambodian boys, significant individuals, including their teachers and counselors, communicated a clear understanding of the meanings and expectations associated with their ethnicity and gender to them.

Moreover, Cambodian boys often stated that disciplinary policies, including "tardy sweeps", unfairly targeted them as a group. Those students that staff perceived as "good" students were often let off with a warning. James shared with me his frustration after missing an important quiz, which attributed in part to this unofficial policy:

> I've seen them let those kids go. *(Who are you talking about exactly?)* The White kids. The Asians who take the bus. Last week, me and my sister, we get dropped off late and they sent me to a detention office or something. I'm just saying . . . damn, why can't you do the rules for everybody the same. Like, I want to go to my first period too. Trust me. If I was one of the other kids, security would just let me go to class.

Many of the White and "other Asian" students that arrive by school bus, as referenced above, do not live in the neighborhood but participate in selective magnet programs at CHS. What was identified as preferential treatment for some students supported the notion that in place were inherently mistrustful institutional practices when it came to Cambodian boys. These practices resulted in students' further disengagement. For many Cambodian boys like James, significant factors related to race, class, gender, and academic program status all accounted for the differential disciplinary treatment they experienced from teachers and other school staff, including security personnel.

For the most part, a number of young men shared a general feeling that most school adults rely on who they *think* these young people are, which are often negative portraits, rather than recognize positive qualities and possibilities in their students. Research has found that when students perceive school discipline as fair, they are much more likely to follow rules and demonstrate higher academic achievement than those who perceive discipline as unfair (Arum 2003). I found that Cambodian youth perceived these differing standards of discipline as blatant and normalized. Thus, how Cambodian male students at CHS saw themselves was shaped by a Discourse that understood Cambodian boys as largely absent in AP and honors classes, but easily found in detention.

WHAT DOES THIS ALL MEAN?

The ways in which race, class, and gender collided in this study helps shed light onto the segmented pathways that Cambodian youth experience in school and U.S. society. This chapter demonstrates how the exalting of Asian American students as the model minority reinforces racist Discourses that adversely impact the lives of students. The negative school experiences for Cambodian boys especially manifested themselves in troubling representations that deflected attention away from the school's failure to teach these young men. For these negative representations to work, it was necessary to position Cambodian boys in contrast to more positive depictions of other students' racial (Whites and "East Asians"), class (non-"ghetto"), and gender ("good Cambodian girls") categories. By situating Cambodian boys as inherently disinterested in learning, significant adults at CHS were able to rationalize the school's structural inequities and shortcomings for educating these youth. Some teachers were keenly aware of how educational resources were inequitably distributed at CHS. The fact that the school's "hyper tracking" shaped—as one teacher put it—the ways relationships at CHS are constructed cannot be understated. Certainly not all Cambodian boys were mistreated and neglected at CHS. Some of the young men I spoke with enjoyed school; many did quite well and were high academic performers. These instances, unfortunately, were exceptions to a general Discourse of lowered expectations and underachievement pervading the school experiences of Cambodian boys at CHS. However, I don't contend that Cambodian boys were unique in this respect. For instance, this group was not necessarily mistreated or neglected more than other students of color. Their African American and Latino peers endured equal and often more severe mistreatment at the hands of some complacent educators. What I do argue is that Cambodian boys, often aggregated within a broad Asian American category, tend to be an overlooked and underserved group, both at CHS and in the larger conversations of educational equity, research, and reform.

In this work, critical discourse analysis was an important interpretive lens for increasing awareness of how Discourses are created, maintained, and significant for individuals' lived experiences (Gee 1999). These findings encourage educators to examine the extent to which Discourses shape opportunities and futures for students. An important goal of this study is to press educators to question the assumptions that they hold of the youth they teach in order to counteract the troubling Discourses that characterize many students' lives. Foucault (1972) contends that discourses contribute to particular social practices, as intertwined with power relations, and serve as a rationalizing mechanism for upholding those norms. Across routine, everyday discourses, individual educators, through their words and actions, defended their treatment of Cambodian students, particularly in conversation with a Cambodian interviewer. This was expected; but what also happened is that individuals perpetuated a Discourse that defended the systems and institutions that promote policies and practices that neglect Cambodian boys. They sometimes did this through the ubiquitous American dream discourse, which suggests that hard work will automatically translate into success, a notion circulated to poor immigrant children and other marginalized youth in the U.S. with little attention to the institutional barriers that characterize students' lived experiences (McGinnis 2009; Portes and Rumbaut 2006). This belief is rarely interrogated in schools.

It is critical that I—and other educators and scholars (including persons of color working within communities of color)—challenge the Discourse of meritocracy each step of the way in our work and in our careers. The power behind discourse(s) rest in their potential to negotiate change and to maintain or transform the status quo (Fairclough 1989). Schools represent a potentially powerful site for challenging those Discourses which link students' academic promise to race, class, and gender (Giroux 2009; Lopez 2003).

CONCLUSION AND EDUCATIONAL IMPLICATIONS

The purpose of this case study was to highlight the particular experiences of Cambodian male youth and describe how these young men were problematized in their school. This research also points to the idea that male youth of color are required to negotiate a complex web of (lowered) academic expectations and (negative) assumptions related to race, gender, and class on a daily basis. During the process of writing this chapter for the edited volume, Michael Brown, an 18-year-old African American male, was shot and killed by a police officer in Ferguson, Missouri.[10] Brown was unarmed and walking with his friends when he was stopped by a White police officer for jaywalking. This tragedy occurred outside of school and speaks powerfully of the problematization of male youth of color in U.S. society. Due to the enduring and insidious nature of racialization and racism in U.S. communities, many young men of color, like Brown (who had just graduated from high school weeks earlier), are likely viewed by police as dangerous and expendable youth.

The young Cambodian men in this study shared similar descriptions of how they were perceived in school and in their own community. The Brown tragedy represents one of many examples in which young men of color are institutionally problematized and criminalized. How might school adults better adopt dispositions that are supportive of their students, so that a pervasive Discourse of care and hope is more normalized for male youth of color, including Cambodian boys? Certainly, one place to start is with the educators themselves. Teacher education as a field has been slow to engage in the necessary and often uncomfortable conversations that center on both individual and institutional racism within schools and broader society (Duncan-Andrade 2011). Hence, a significant step for interrupting these Discourses is by moving current and future educators to identify and analyze the layers of oppression that shape their work and characterize their students' lives.

A number of my Cambodian male participants embraced hip-hop culture as an alternative masculinity to White hegemonic masculinity. They also adopted this mode in part to demonstrate affinity with African Americans, who were also marginalized at CHS. Educators would do well to develop authentic lessons about the cultural, and perhaps political, meanings of students' linguistic, music, and clothing preferences. Teachers are likely to find that hip-hop includes considerably more than the misogyny and violence that dominates the airwaves and popular music videos. Whereas some aspects of this youth culture indeed center on materialistic bravado, some literature has demonstrated ways that hip-hop culture provides educational and empowerment resources for marginalized youth (Irizarry 2009; Prior and Beachum 2008; Stovall 2006). I found in my own teaching that much can come from exploring the unique sociocultural histories of Cambodian families in the U.S. This is a powerful way to teach young Cambodian men who feel disconnected in school. Their families are part of an incredibly resilient community whose pre-immigration experience with political upheaval, genocide, and survival provide rich topics for classroom discussion across various subjects (Chhuon 2010).

It is such concern and attention to students' diverse backgrounds that can express to Cambodian youth the type of care and attention to support positive student relationships with their teachers, and teachers with their students, as a way to disrupt the negative Discourses surrounding Cambodian boys. Thus, educators must consider ways to engage youth through pedagogy that is critical of institutional inequities, as well as offer curricula that honors students' home values, strengths, and diverse backgrounds. These identity affirming, pedagogical moves can lead to students' increased feelings of being known by teachers, enhance teacher-student interactions, and promote critical dialogue about what it means to be a male Cambodian youth, among other important identities in school (Wallace and Chhuon 2014). With this awareness in hand, perhaps teachers and other significant school adults can begin contributing to Discourses about Cambodian male youth that emphasize genuine care and hope, rather than fear and apathy emanating from damaging racialization contexts.

NOTES

1. A version of this chapter was previously published in the *International Journal of Qualitative Studies in Education* 27, no. 2 (2014): 233–250.
2. All names and places in this study are pseudonyms.
3. The data from this article comes from a larger study of the social and educational experiences of Cambodian urban youth in a Southern California community. I moved to this neighborhood in the fall of 2007 to better ground myself in the community where Cambodian students and the adults they routinely had contact with were accessible.
4. I observed courses approximately twice a week and in a number of cases, I played multiple roles in these classrooms. Some teachers asked me to contribute to discussion, help pass out paper, and other routine classroom tasks. Observations were conducted almost daily during the second semester. I found it easy to blend in with most of the staff. Many of the students assumed that I was a paraprofessional. Others who had met me already regularly referred to me as the "guy writing the book".
5. Most students selected their own pseudonym. In other cases, Khmer pseudonyms are used to describe those with actual Khmer names, and western American pseudonyms are used to describe those with actual western American names.
6. Participants often used the terms *Cambodian* and *Khmer* interchangeably to discuss language, community, and identity. Khmer refers to the ethnic group and language of individuals that live within the political boundaries of modern-day Cambodia. In this article, these terms will be used in a manner consistent with participants' usage.
7. For some, it may be that I embodied the "American dream", the idea that we live in a true egalitarian meritocracy where those who work hard will succeed (McGinnis 2009). It was important that I recognized this throughout the study and that CHS adults probably looked to me, a successful, older, male Cambodian student, as a potential role model for adolescent Cambodian boys whose lives, through their eyes, might be relegated to leaving school and/or gang activity.

8. This ethnic hierarchy at CHS is largely reflective of a perceived ethnic hierarchy within the Asian American community, particularly between East Asian and newer Southeast Asian populations. This discussion is taken up elsewhere (Chhuon and Hudley 2010).
9. Many of his teachers assumed that I was a youth worker or teaching assistant assigned to Johnny. For unknown reasons, Johnny transferred to another school two months after I met him.
10. Brown was shot multiple times, and several eye witness accounts reported that Brown held his hands up in an attempt to surrender (Robles and Bosman 2014). I do not bring up this issue to equate the systematic violence that is perpetuated against African American male youth with the experiences of my Cambodian youth participants. Rather, I raise the issue here to highlight the racialized interactions that urban male youth of color must confront and navigate in everyday life.

REFERENCES

Arum, R. 2003. *Judging School Discipline: The Crisis of Moral Authority.* Cambridge, MA: Harvard University Press.

Cammarota, Julio. 2004. "The Gendered and Racialized Pathways of Latina and Latino Youth: Different Struggles, Different Resistances in the Urban Context." *Anthropology & Education Quarterly* 35 (1): 53–74.

Chhuon, V. 2010. "The Education of Cambodian Students in the United States: Future Directions and Implications for Practice." In *Cambodian American Experiences: Histories, Communities, Cultures, and Identities,* edited by Jonathan Lee, 126–144. Dubuque, IA: Kendall Hunt Publishing Company.

Chhuon, V., A. Dosalmas, and N. Rinthapol. 2010. "Factors Supporting Academic Engagement among Cambodian American High School Youth." *Journal of Southeast Asian American Education and Advancement* 5: 1–14.

Chhuon, V., and C. Hudley. 2008. "Factors Supporting Cambodian American Students' Successful Adjustment into the University." *Journal of College Student Development* 49 (1): 15–30.

Chhuon, V., and C. Hudley. 2010. "Asian American Ethnic Options." *Anthropology and Education Quarterly* 41 (4): 341–359.

Conchas, G.Q., and J. D. Vigil. 2012. *Streetsmart Schoolsmart: Urban Poverty and the Education of Adolescent Boys.* New York: Teachers College Press.

Connell, R.W. 1996. "Teaching the Boys: New Research on Masculinity, and Gender Strategies for School." *Teachers College Record* 98 (2): 206–235.

Duncan-Andrade, J. 2011. "The Principal Facts: New Directions for Teacher Education." In *Studying Diversity in Teacher Education,* edited by A.F. Ball and C.A. Tyson, 309–326. New York: Rowman & Littlefield.

Fairclough, N. 1989. *Language and Power.* Harlow, UK: Pearson Education.

Foley, D., B. Levinson, and J. Hurtig. 2001. "Anthropology Goes Inside: The New Educational Ethnography of Ethnicity and Gender." *Review of Research in Education* 25: 37–98.

Fordham, S., and J. U. Ogbu. 1986. "Black Students' School Success: Coping with the Burden of 'Acting White.'" *The Urban Review* 18 (3): 176–206.

Foucault, M. 1972. *The Archeology of Knowledge.* London: Tavistock.

Garbarino, J. 1999. *Lost Boys: Why Our Sons Turn Violent and How We Can Save Them.* New York: The Free Press.

Gee, J. 1999. *An Introduction to Discourse Analysis: Theory and Methods.* New York: Routledge.

Giroux, H. 2009. *Youth in a Suspect Society.* New York: Palgrave.

Irizarry, J. 2009. "Representin': Drawing from Hip-Hop and Urban Youth Culture to Inform Teacher Education." *Urban Education* 41 (4): 489–515.

Kao, Grace, & Marta Tienda. 1998. "Educational Aspirations of Minority Youth." *American Journal of Education* 106: 349–384.

Kumashiro, K. 1999. "Supplemental Normalcy and Otherness: Queer Asian American Men Reflect on Stereotypes, Identity, and Oppression." *Qualitative Studies in Education* 12 (5): 491–508.

Lee, S. 2005. "Learning About Race, Learning About 'America': Hmong American High School Students." In *Beyond Silenced Voices: Class, Race, and Gender in United States Schools*, edited by Lois Weis and Michelle Fine, 133–146. New York: SUNY Press.

Lei, J. 2003. "(Un)Necessary Toughness?: Those 'Loud Black Girls' and Those 'Quiet Asian Boys.'" *Anthropology and Education Quarterly* 34 (2): 158–181.

Lopez, N. 2003. *Hopeful Girls, Troubled Boys: Race and Gender Disparity in Urban Education*. New York: Routledge.

Marshall, C., and G. Rossman. 1995. *Designing Qualitative Research*, 2nd ed. Thousand Oaks, CA: Sage Publications.

McGinnis, T. 2009. "Seeing Possible Futures: Khmer Youth and the Discourses of the American Dream." *Anthropology and Education Quarterly* 40 (1): 62–81.

Ng, J.C., S.S. Lee, and Y. K. Pak. "Contesting the Model Minority and Perpetual Foreigner Stereotypes: A Critical Review of Literature on Asian Americans in Education." *Review of Research in Education* 31 (2007): 95–130.

Ngo, B. 2009. "Ambivalent Urban, Immigrant Identities: The Incompleteness of Lao American Student Identities." *International Journal of Qualitative Studies in Education* 22 (2): 201–220.

Noguera, P. 2003. "The Trouble with Black Boys: The Role and Influence of Environmental and Cultural Factors on the Academic Achievement of African American Males." *Urban Education* 38 (4): 431–459.

Ong, A. 2003. "Cultural Citizenship as Subject Making: Immigrants Negotiate Racial and Cultural Boundaries in the United States." In *Race, Identity, and Citizenship: A Reader*, edited by R. D. Torres, L. F. Miron, and J. X. Inda, 262–293. Malden, MA: Blackwell Publishing.

Portes, A., and R. Rumbaut. 2006. *Immigrant America: A Portrait*. Berkeley: University of California Press.

Prior, D., and F. Beachum. 2008. "Conceptualizing a Critical Discourse Around Hip-Hop Culture and Black Male Youth in Educational Scholarship and Research." *International Journal of Qualitative Studies in Education* 21 (5): 519–535.

Qin-Hilliard, D. B. 2003. "Gendered Expectations and Gendered Experiences: Immigrant Students' Adaptation in Schools." *New Directions Youth Development* 100: 91–109.

Robles, F., and J. Bosman. 2014. "Autopsy Shows Michael Brown was Struck at Least 6 Times." *The New York Times,* 17 August. Retrieved August 18, 2014, from http://www.nytimes.com/2014/08/18/us/michael-brown-autopsy-shows-he-was-shot-at-least-6-times.html.

Southeast Asia Resource Action Center. 2011. Statistics on Southeast Asians adapted from the American Community Survey (Report from the Southeast Asia Resource Action Center). Washington, DC: SEARAC.

Spradley, J. 1979. *The Ethnographic Interview.* New York: Holt, Rinehart and Winston.

Stepick, A., C. Dutton Stepick, E. Eugene, D. Teed, and Y. Labissiere. 2001. "Shifting Identities and Inter-generational Conflict: Growing up Haitian in Miami." In *Ethnicities: Children of Immigrants in America*, edited by R. Rumabut and A. Portes, 229–266. Berkeley: University of California Press, Russell Sage Press.

Stovall, D. 2006. "We Can Relate: Hip Hop Culture, Critical Pedagogy, and the Secondary Classroom." *Urban Education* 41 (6): 585–602.

Suarez-Orozco, C., and M. Suarez-Orozco. 2001. *Children of Immigration*. Cambridge, MA: Harvard University Press.

Valenzuela, A. 1999. "Gender Roles and Settlement Activities Among Children and Their Immigrant Families." *American Behavioral Scientists* 42 (4): 720–742.

Wallace, T. W., and V. Chhuon. 2014. "Proximal Processes in Urban Classrooms: Engagement and Disaffecton in Urban Youth of Color." *American Educational Research Journal* 51 (5): 937–973.

Waters, Mary. 1999. *Black Identities: West Indian Immigrant Dreams and American Realities*. Cambridge, MA: Harvard University Press.

Winnicott, D.W. 1967. "Mirror-Role of Mother and Family in Child Development." In *The Predicament of the Family*, edited by P. Lomas, 26–33. New York City: International University Press.

Zhou, M. 1997. "Growing Up American: The Challenge Confronting Immigrant Children and Children of Immigrants." *Annual Review of Sociology* 23: 3–95.

Zhou, M., and C. Bankston. 1998. *Growing Up American: How Vietnamese Children Adapt to Life in the United States*. New York: Russell Sage.

3 "I Am Not the Stereotype"

How an Academic Club in an Urban School Empowered Black Male Youth to Succeed

Sean Drake, Gilberto Q. Conchas, and Leticia Oseguera

Black male youth are in deep trouble in America. When compared to other ethnoracial and gender groups, Black males lag behind in terms of school attendance, grade point average, and standardized test scores (Anderson 2008; Belfanz and Legters 2004; Blanchett 2006; Jencks and Phillips 2011; Ladson-Billings 2011; Noguera 2003b, 2008). Black males also demonstrate a greater likelihood to be suspended or expelled from school (Tienda and Wilson 2002), classified as mentally retarded or suffering from a learning disability (Harry et al. 2000), and tracked into remedial curricular tracks devoid of any Advanced Placement or honors courses (Conchas 2006; Howard 2008; Oakes 2005). Thus, a deeper understanding of the unique struggles faced by this population, and the identification of potential solutions, remain critical for scholars of race and education.

In this chapter, we present the results of a qualitative case study that investigated (1) Black male students' perspectives on the salience and consequences of racial stereotypes perpetuated within an ethnoracially diverse high school, (2) these students' reactions to the racial stereotypes, and (3) the relationship between students' reactions to the stereotypes and an afterschool program designed to increase their social and cultural capital. Our findings indicate that Black male students wage a constant struggle against a variety of racial stereotypes within high school and popular media contexts that systematically criminalize them, and that a supportive academic structure can function as a social buffer against the negative effects of racial stereotypes in schools.

RACE AND EDUCATIONAL ACHIEVEMENT GAPS: OPPOSITIONAL CULTURE AS AN INSTITUTIONAL PHENOMENON

Scholars of race and education have argued that the differences in school achievement between Blacks and Whites rest upon Black youths' perceptions of the American opportunity structure. The "oppositional culture" thesis contends that Black youth are not as successful as their White peers because Black youth have internalized their group's subordinate position in society and do not expect much academic or labor market success. The perception of a limited opportunity structure for Blacks in schools and broader society leads to the development of an oppositional identity and oppositional cultural frame of reference among Black youth in U.S. schools. Through this process, Black students associate academic engagement and achievement with White students and Whiteness; thus, they disengage academically as a form of resistance and to avoid "acting white" (Fordham and Ogbu 1986). Essentially, many Black youth learn to behave as if they are too cool for school. Other scholars have subsequently supported this position (Farkas et al. 2002).

But another body of literature argues against the oppositional culture paradigm by focusing on the academic structures and cultures within schools that work to produce racial disparities in academic performance (Ainsworth-Darnell and Downey 1998; Carter 2005; Conchas 2001; Harris 2006; Howard 2010, 2013). For instance, curricular tracking policies in many urban public schools disproportionately assign Black students to general or remedial education classes that are ill equipped to prepare them for the rigors of college. Students in these lower tracks are often treated as second-class citizens within their schools, whereas White and Asian students benefit from the wealth of social and cultural capital available to them in higher academic tracks and Advanced Placement (AP) classes (Noguera 2003a, 2008; Oakes 2005). Thus, the oppositional culture framework can be reinterpreted to understand the ways in which dominant cultures and institutional practices particularly stand in opposition to Black male students.

SCHOOL STRUCTURES THAT PROMOTE ACADEMIC ACHIEVEMENT FOR STUDENTS OF COLOR

Schools are cites of frequent social interaction and cultural transmission. As such, schools have a unique opportunity to serve as sources of social and cultural capital for students. In this chapter, we employ the concept of *social capital* as developed by sociologist James Coleman. According to Coleman, social capital consists of the opportunities and benefits that one receives from one's social ties. Social capital is embedded with specific social relationships and networks that enable an individual to garner achievements that would be impossible if she or he were not a part of the relationship or network (Coleman 1988). *Cultural capital* has been defined in part as "long-lasting dispositions of the mind and body" that are valued by affluent and/or dominant members of society (Bourdieu 1984, 47). According to Bourdieu, the most significant component of cultural capital is characterized by a "diffuse, continuous transmission within the family [that] escapes observation and control so that the educational system seems to award its honors solely to natural qualities" (Bourdieu 1984, 55).

Social and cultural capital can function as vital educational resources. In fact, cultural capital and high school grades share a positive relationship (an increase in cultural capital is often followed by an increase in grade point average) and are highly correlated (DiMaggio 1982). Accordingly, scholars have successfully worked to identify school policies, cultural practices, and structures that foster academic engagement and achievement among under-represented minority student groups by marshaling these forms of capital. For example, in an ethnographic study of Latino high school students, Stanton-Salazar (1997) explores mechanisms that make school "work" for some of these youths. He finds that students' grades and occupational expectations are influenced by relationships with "institutional agents" such as peers, teachers, and school counselors, who introduce students to academic achievement and the college-going process. Thus, the microprocess of information networks can function as a source of social and cultural capital and eventual school success for underrepresented minority (URM) students.

Other scholars have assessed the effectiveness of school programs geared toward boosting the academic engagement and achievement of URM students. Mehan and colleagues (1996) found that schools could significantly increase the college enrollment rates of Black and Latino students by untracking them—that is, by placing them in college preparatory courses regardless of their academic preparation and achievement to date. However, and most importantly, Mehan and his associates also found that untracking only worked when the policy was combined with explicit, individualized academic and social support (Mehan et al. 1996).

In a similar vein, scholars have found that the most successful school programs for URM students are those that work to

> build trusting relationships between teachers and students, to create a sense of belonging for all students and not just those from the dominant group, to structure peer relationships that support rather than undermine academic achievement, and to provide access to the social capital and institutional support that students need in order to prepare for college and careers.
>
> (Gibson 2005, 599)

Furthermore, high schools can foster the academic engagement of underrepresented students of color by instituting cooperative learning communities characterized by curricular programming that makes overt links between coursework and subsequent educational and career opportunities (Conchas 2001, 2006). In this chapter, we continue this thread of research by showing how school programs can create and transmit social and cultural capital among student members, thereby increasing students' academic engagement and achievement, and thus countering the harmful presence of racial stereotypes at school.

Scholars have found that Black male students are likely to frame their educational goals in accordance with the most prevalent racial stereotypes associated with their racial group. Therefore, Blacks tend to profess educational goals focused on avoiding failure instead of achieving success (Kao 2000). Furthermore, past research has found that Black male youth are apt to disengage academically and display a "willful laziness" when they encounter negative and criminalizing racial and gender stereotypes at school (Lopez 2003). These findings have important implications for the current study because they suggest that the Black males in our sample should hold low educational expectations of themselves and react to their racially stigmatizing school climate by adopting an oppositional stance toward education. However, our informants react by markedly *increasing* their level of academic commitment in an effort to challenge prevailing stereotypes and prove them false. Why do our respondents react in a manner contrary to that predicted by prior research? We will provide an answer to this question.

THE RESEARCH SETTING

Smith High School (SHS or Smith) is a large public high school and magnet school serving over 4,000 students. SHS offers an expansive curriculum ranging from a general education program to an Advanced Placement curriculum track. SHS is located in a large and ethnoracially diverse city in California.[1] According to the 2010 U.S. Census Bureau, the city's racial and ethnic composition is 46.1% White, 40.8% Hispanic or Latino, 13.5% Black, and 12.9% Asian (including Filipino). All ethnoracial group percentages are close to the statewide percentages of each group, with the exception of Blacks, whose percentage in this city is roughly twice the statewide figure. The median household income in this city for the period 2007–2011 was $52,945.

During the 2007–2008 academic year, 4,364 students were enrolled, and the average class size ranged from 27 to 30 students. Together, White and Hispanic students constitute 71.8% of the school population (38.8 and 33%, respectively). Blacks represent 13.7% of the student population and Asians are 10.6%. The number of SHS students who qualify for free or reduced lunch is lower than the district average—48.4 and 67% for SHS and the district, respectively. Only 9.8% of SHS students are English Language Learners, compared to a 24.7% district average. And although located in a middle-class community, SHS also draws students from affluent and working-class neighborhoods. Thus, the student body is quite diverse socioeconomically, ethnoracially, and in terms of academic preparation.

METHODOLOGY

We employed qualitative case study methods during data collection and analysis because such methods facilitate the in-depth exploration, understanding, and rendering of a phenomenon by embedding the research within a particular sociocultural context. Case study research yields data from multiple sources and over an extended period of time—features that stimulate a comprehensive analysis of social structures. Moreover, situating research within a specific sociocultural context and over a sustained period of time allows for the analysis of potential changes in the social systems and life courses of those studied (Faegin et al. 1991; Yin 2013).

The data that we present here are derived from a yearlong (2008–2009) qualitative case study of Black high school males involved in an afterschool, academic Male Academy (MA). 24 Black students were involved in the program during the research period. The MA program endeavored to cultivate a sense of academic engagement in students through a collaborative "brotherhood" atmosphere of positive teacher-student interaction and peer culture, as well as to provide valuable social and cultural capital to students as they planned their futures. The goal of the research project was to determine the effectiveness of the Male Academy implementation in terms of its ability to positively alter the academic engagement, aspirations, expectations, and achievement of Black male youth. As such, interview questions probed students' experiences in the general school community, and a comparison of those experiences with participation in the Male Academy.[2]

THE SAMPLE

We present data gleaned from 23 semi-structured interviews with Black male high school students (11th and 12th graders). The interviews elucidated students' perceptions of racial stereotypes and the racial-academic hierarchy both within Smith High School and in broader society, students' reactions to the negative stereotypes attributed to them in the school environment, and the ways in which the Male Academy provided its members with social support and knowledge specific to their academic engagement, aspirations, expectations, and achievement. We recruited all subjects from the Male Academy using a combination of purposive and snowball sampling, and interviewed all who volunteered and/or consented.[3] This sampling strategy yielded a subject pool that was diverse both in terms of socioeconomic status[4] and educational achievement.[5]

RACIAL STEREOTYPES IN THE SMITH
HIGH SCHOOL ENVIRONMENT

Common Stereotypes

Black male students at Smith High School were keenly aware of the negative academic racial stereotypes about Blacks that circulated freely within the school community. When asked whether certain racial groups held stereotypes about which groups do well or poorly in school, Darnell responded, "yeah, supposedly Asians are the smartest and Blacks are always good in athletics and White guys are just good in everything overall. Mexicans are always good in soccer". Brandon, a biracial student of Black and Filipino decent, shared Darnell's perceptions of academic racial stereotypes in the school. Consider his response when asked about the academic reputation of his co-ethnics:

INTERVIEWER: Do people of your same ethnicity have a reputation for doing well or poor at this school?
BRANDON: Well, I'm half, so one side yes, we would be successful and the other side no, generically speaking.
INTERVIEWER: Why do you think that would be?
BRANDON: Because of the stereotypes that everybody puts against other people. They say like, "oh, they are Black, they can't be—they don't succeed too often and the percentage is not that high". Or like, "oh, they are Asian, they must know everything, they must be good at math and science".

Pinpointing the origin of a stereotype can be difficult once that belief is well established in a particular context. One might suspect that negative academic racial stereotypes are rooted in data; people know what the education statistics are on race and achievement, and they attribute those data to all members of a certain racial group. However, Black male students at Smith had other ideas about the antecedents of academic racial stereotypes. Myles perceived the stereotypes as visually based:

INTERVIEWER: Where do you think people get their ideas about which type of kids do best or worst in school?
MYLES: Probably just stereotypes.
INTERVIEWER: Where do those stereotypes come from?
MYLES: Most people it's just based on what you see everyday. So, if I see a Caucasian male everyday, you know, with his pants all the way up and a nice shirt on and maybe a tie, so I'm thinking, "OK, this guy is successful". Whereas, if he sees me everyday and sees me dressed the way I am, he's probably thinking, "OK, he goes to school but you can tell he doesn't do anything there. You can tell he's always in detention or something like that". So I think that really the ideas, they start in the back of your mind, but you know you can't say it, but you just see it so much then it gets all the way in your mind so whenever you see a person that's when you start getting those thoughts.

Myles's comments highlight the ways in which ability stereotyping can be rooted in the perception of another's culture (in this case, clothing and style of dress). In Myles's example, the White male with his pants pulled up, wearing a nice shirt and tie, could be a high school dropout and gang member who is dressed in business-professional attire to attend a wedding, and Myles could be an academically engaged student who is on track to attend a four-year college (which he happens to be). Another student, Darnell, also felt that negative racial stereotypes about Blacks were based upon speculative inferences laced with racial bias and detached from reality:

> *INTERVIEWER:*   How does society view you?
> *DARNELL:*   A gangster, a gang member, or someone who's not gonna be successful.
> *INTERVIEWER:*   Why?
> *DARNELL:*   Just because of the way I carry myself, other times my appearance, and just other times the first impression. They think because I'm Black and live in Long Beach, I got to be a gang member.

Like Myles, Darnell is cognizant of the way that others stereotypically perceive him. He knows that his mannerisms, clothing style, race, and even the city that he is from send signals to other people that he is probably a criminal without a chance to succeed in the labor market. (In fact, Darnell had already been admitted to a local community college and had plans to transfer to a four-year university.)

Teachers and Stereotypes

Ostensibly, schools are institutions that nurture the intellectual development of students, but our respondents often felt like intellectual outsiders within their school community because of the negative racial stereotypes about Blacks that hounded them from the street to the classroom. And, for these students, the stereotypes were more than a burden without a clear source; students implicated those most firmly in charge of fostering their intellectual development—their teachers—in the practice of racial stereotyping:

> *INTERVIEWER:*   Do you think that the way the teacher perceives the student also plays an important part in the successful student?
> *MELVIN:*   I've heard of instances where teachers are, like, stereotyping students and treating some students certain ways and treating other students a different way because of how they think they are gonna perform.
> *INTERVIEWER:*   Do you think the stereotype is more tied into finances or race or both?

MELVIN: Well, I think race would have to be the first factor because the teacher would have no idea if they were low or high financed.

Elijah commented on teachers' racial stereotypes and the consequences of those views:

INTERVIEWER: You mentioned that society has these stereotypes. Do you think that teachers ever hold these stereotypes of students?

ELIJAH: Some teachers—some teachers and administrators hold stereotypes.

INTERVIEWER: How do you think that affects the learning that that student's gonna receive then?

ELIJAH: They're not gonna teach as good. They're not gonna teach 'em [their students] as hard. They're not gonna give them as much information. They don't expect them to know certain information so they're not gonna give it to 'em.

INTERVIEWER: Do you think that sentiment is expressed by teachers on this campus?

ELIJAH: There's definitely some.

Some students experienced teacher bias directly. Consider Jamal's remarks on the issue:

INTERVIEWER: Where do you think people get their ideas about which kids are going to do better or worse in school?

JAMAL: Just probably stereotyping them I guess. Seeing how they act and their personality. Some of my teachers didn't expect me to do good. They didn't verbally say it but I could see how their actions were. They didn't expect me to be the one answering questions in class and actually doing my homework and trying to go to tutoring and get a better grade.

Carter also experienced classroom environments in which teachers acted as if they did not care about student learning. This perpetuated a stubborn cycle of student and teacher disengagement:

CARTER: I've seen as I'm in class there's a lot of student that do not like certain teachers so they wouldn't perform at their highest levels. And there's a lot of teachers that they just go over the work. They don't really explain it and then students get frustrated at that and they just give up right then and there. I've experience that many times.

Similarly, Joe said, "when I was messing up, my teachers, it's like they didn't even pull me to the side or tell me that I'm failing". These insights regarding the prevalence of racial stereotypes and student-teacher relationships in the Smith High School community and culture are representative of the Black male students interviewed for this study. Many students felt that teachers stereotyped them strictly based upon their appearance as young, Black male students in an urban environment, and that these stereotypic views affected teacher commitment and efficacy.

THE RACIAL HIERARCHY OUTSIDE OF SCHOOL

Black male students at Smith High School demonstrated an acute awareness of the racial stereotypes and resulting racial academic hierarchies within their school. They also perceived many links between their racially stratified school environment and the racial order in society. Students spoke about societal expectations for different races. Carter's perception of the expectations for Black students is representative of all students we interviewed: "for most Blacks, most people expect us to not even make it out of high school". When asked whether he felt society held different expectations for different races, Joe responded, "yeah. Like people may say Asians are smarter than a lot of other people". When asked how society views Blacks, Joe succinctly states, "troublemakers". The implication here is that society expects more out of Asians (who are deemed "model minorities") because they are smarter than Blacks, and thus more capable of achieving both in school and once schooling is finished. At the other end of the spectrum, not much success is expected from Black "troublemakers" in any academic endeavor or job that requires the human capital gained through education. Melvin offered a similar, yet more detailed, view:

> *INTERVIEWER:*   If you had to give me an example of three positions that you typically think successful White men or women hold, what three positions would they be?
>
> *MELVIN:*   Well the president is one of them, it's typical—and not just the President of the United States, but presidents like the CEOs. President, CEOs, and, like, whatever usually the person at the top is.
>
> *INTERVIEWER:*   Is White?
>
> *MELVIN:*   Yeah.
>
> *INTERVIEWER:*   What about a successful position for a Black man?

MELVIN: Well that will probably be more—when you talk about that you think more the sports aspects like maybe NBA or NFL type.

Melvin's perceptions of society's expectation for successful White and Black adults are aligned with prevailing racial stereotypes that construct Whites as labor market leaders and Blacks as athletic specimens. Melvin perceives an American society that does not expect Blacks to be successful in professions that require a moderate or high educational pedigree. Myles offered a similar perspective. When asked how he thought society views Blacks, he said:

MYLES: Slowly it's starting to change, but I still think that society looks at my race as solely just athletes really. They don't think we can do anything in the business world. They just think, "OK, when they grow up they're just going to play in the NFL or the NBA" or one of those . . . we're not going to do anything other than that and they still think that all we are is just hip-hop music and baggy pants and a lot of that stuff.

Myles's comments underscore the limited professional opportunities, aspirations, and expectations that many low-income Black youth have. In short, there is a dearth of attractive options for many of these youth outside of a career as a professional athlete or entertainer. Furthermore, for athletes, the odds of reaching the National Football League (NFL) or National Basketball Association (NBA) are extremely long, rendering the career opportunities and life chances of these youth extremely grim in many cases (Conchas et al. 2014).

These perceptions of success for different racial groups are especially noteworthy because all interviews took place either during Barack Obama's 2008 presidential campaign or after he had won the election. Barack Obama provided a highly visible alternative to the negative racial stereotypes so often attributed to Black males. However, according to these students, the societal opportunity structure remains firmly supported by racial stereotypes perpetuated in popular media, stereotypes that—despite Barack Obama's ascendancy—continue to portray Black males as athletic, uneducated, and potential menaces to society.

Students also perceived congruency between common racial stereotypes in and out of school. For example, when asked whether or not the same racial hierarchies that marginalized Blacks in schools were present outside of school, Myles responded:

MYLES: If you really look at maybe an office you just always see— you rarely see a Black or Latino boss. You always see a Caucasian man and it's in everywhere. It's in TV; it's in movies, magazines, wherever you look, and you always see either the Black or Latino—they're at a little desk working and the boss is always coming in to check on them. So I think that really it's not just at school; it's really everywhere . . .

His response identifies popular media as a mechanism through which stereotypes operate to both construct and maintain dominant racial ideologies and hierarchies within the labor market. In fact, several of our respondents identified the media as an outlet for prevailing racial stereotypes. Popular media is flooded with depictions of heavily muscled Black athletes and profligate Black rap stars.

In sum, these Black male youth perceived direct links between the racial academic hierarchy in their high school and the societal opportunity structure that exists beyond school walls. Thus, Obama's meteoric rise appears to exert little effect on these students' conceptions of a successful Black man, the career opportunities available to Black youth, and the salience of baleful racial stereotypes in their daily lives.

CHALLENGING THE STEREOTYPES

Racial stereotypes created a disconcerting environment for this sample of Black students, and nearly all of them felt a need to dispel the damaging stereotypes about their race. For instance, when asked how it felt to know that society expects Blacks to be troublemakers, Joe responded, "I try to avoid all that type of stuff so when I meet new people I try not to come to that expectation". Many students expressed similar views and sought to forge an identity in opposition to the negative extant stereotypes about Blacks. For instance, Elijah felt that "sometimes people might just look at me and not think that I'm a smart person or, like, wonder why I'm taking these certain [AP] classes that other smart people are in, and like look at me like I'm just the stereotype, which I'm not". Myles also worried that people would view him only in terms of a negative stereotype: "I don't want somebody just to look at me and, you know, just think I'm just another Black guy and going to turn out to be a criminal, so I work hard every day so that maybe one day they can say, 'oh, well, he's a doctor', or maybe, 'he's a dentist', or something like that".

All Black male students in our sample were well aware of racial stereotypes about their racial group and the racial academic hierarchy within Smith High School and broader society that placed them at the bottom. Our respondents found pervasive negative ideas about Blacks' educational and socioeconomic abilities and culture disconcerting, and nearly all expressed a strong desire to ameliorate the unseemly perceptions of their racial group. But why did these Black males react to pernicious academic racial stereotypes in this fashion? An elucidation of their experiences in the Smith High School Male Academy yields critical insights.

THE MALE ACADEMY AS SOCIAL BUFFER: ENGENDERING ACADEMIC ENGAGEMENT AND STEREOTYPE RESISTANCE

As noted previously, all students in this sample were members of the Male Academy at Smith High School, an afterschool club that met twice each month. Sessions alternated between group meetings, guest speaker presentations, and fieldtrips to local colleges. The Male Academy directors were determined to give students practice as group leaders. As such, most meetings were led by a smaller group of two to four members. This group of student leaders changed from meeting to meeting, giving all members an opportunity to lead group discussions. The directors worked with students to identify talking points and help prepare each presentation. Students also came up with titles for their presentations, such as "Creating Positive Labels", "Hope is not a Plan", and "Holding Ourselves Accountable to the Group". This student-based structure strengthened each member's commitment to the academy by explicitly facilitating and valuing the contributions of each member.

The academy endeavored to bolster male students' interests in pursing academically oriented career options via a college education. Nearly all of the students interviewed spoke openly about the profound effect that their participation in the MA had on their academic motivation, confidence, aspirations, expectations, and engagement. Consider Carter's experience with the MA: "to be honest, if I wasn't a part of the Male Academy I'm quite sure I would have ditched at least 2 to 3 times already [this semester]. I'm quite sure of that". Likewise, Joe also felt that the Male Academy motivated him to engage academically:

INTERVIEWER: How do you think your junior year [of high school] would have been different had you not joined the Male Academy?

JOE: I think if I had not joined the Male Academy I would be doing the same thing I did last year—not getting any help, not doing anything, and getting frustrated, and I probably would have dropped out [of high school].

Another student, Darnell, offered a candid and compelling testament to the positive effect that his participation in the Male Academy had on his life trajectory:

INTERVIEWER: If you weren't in the Male Academy, what do you think would have happened [to you at this school]?

DARNELL: I would have either been a drug dealer or a dropout or in jail for killing someone or in jail for almost killing someone.

Myles felt that if he weren't in the MA, his "grades would drop . . .
I would probably just really just give up in school. I'd probably be still
with my old friends in my neighborhood doing bad things". Thus, the Male
Academy had an unequivocal positive effect upon the academic engagement, aspirations, and expectations of these youth. And, as we will soon
see, the Male Academy also boosted academic achievement.

Why was the Male Academy so successful for these students? Because
the program altered students' academic and life trajectories by providing
them with cultural capital (Bourdieu 1984; DiMaggio 1982; Heath 1983)
and social capital (Coleman 1988; McDonough 1997), which shifted their
dominant educational "frames" (Goffman 1974; Snow et al. 1986). In other
words, by supporting students academically, socially, and emotionally, the
Male Academy impelled students to view college as a viable option, and
their high school education as a critical step on the path to college. For
instance, Joe commented, "before [joining the Male Academy], I hated
school. It [the Male Academy] has changed my whole mindset. Before the
Male Academy, I didn't even *want* to go to college". Such a mindset may
have given the MA members an alternative script to the one predicted for
Black males by racial stereotypes.

Social Capital

The Male Academy was successful because the program structure generated
a tremendous amount of social capital—the intangible resources one gains
through supportive social networks and relationships. Academy members
benefitted from these social ties. Several respondents described the Male
Academy as a "brotherhood" that instilled a sense of pride and self-esteem
in its members. According to Carter,

> the Male Academy is a brotherhood and it's something that most of us,
> if not all of us, in the Male Academy cherish. It's something that we're
> proud to be in. Being part of the Male Academy, it gives you a sense that
> you're somebody, not just a random student.

Furthermore, Black male students in the Male Academy were in agreement that their "brothers" (peers) in the academy held high expectations
of them. For instance, Myles felt that "they [brothers] expect improvement
no matter how well or how bad you are doing. They expect now that he's
a member, I know that he's going to work that much harder. Even if he had
a 4.0 [GPA], OK, he's a brother now. That means by working with us he's
going to have a 4.2".

The Male Academy engendered this culture of high expectations through
program activities that relied on social interaction. For instance, a portion
of each meeting was devoted to a group discussion of all members' grades
and attendance records. Students were praised for good work and held

responsible for mediocrity. According to Walter, the MA "forces them [student members] to be accountable for what they do. If we're missing class then when we have a meeting it's like a peer thing and we sit there and talk about the attendance". Walter then explained how the MA structure promotes positive student behavior:

> I had to apologize to the whole group when I did something I wasn't suppose to do. I got into a fight with a gang member. I let the group down so I had to apologize to them because I know as a brother and in this brotherhood I wasn't suppose to do that.

Thus, the highly cohesive social network of Black male youth provided a tremendous amount of social capital for group members, so much so that participants changed their cultural disposition towards their schooling.

The Smith Academy also fostered student accountability by building a communicative relationship between student members and lead teachers. Consider Myles's comments on teacher involvement:

> what's really great is they [the head teachers] know about all of us. They know about all our grades all our classes, our conduct, they know about everything. If they see that somebody is having problems they're going to call you in and you're going to talk about it. They're going to figure out something for you to where you can fix it. The Male Academy has been great for me because in the times that I do slack off I know as soon as I come to school I'm going to have to see one of them and they're going to come talk to me about it, and that gets me right back on track.

Likewise, David felt that the MA compelled him to stop cutting class and increase his attendance record, because "they're [the head teachers] gonna be checking, monitoring—monitoring your progress and stuff". These statements reflect the importance of caring teachers in a student's academic experience. Overall, the student-teacher relationships in the Male Academy were quite different from the student-teacher relationships that these students experienced in the typical class at Smith High School. Whereas students often felt that their relationships with teachers in their regular classes were complicated and strained by the racial stereotypes that teachers relied upon, students consistently praised the Male Academy teachers for believing in them and holding them to high academic standards.

In addition to dedicated teachers, the MA gave students access to encouraging guidance counselors. Carter explained the positive impression that these counselors made on him and his Academy brothers, and how he even used the counselors' messages to help struggling peers:

> it [the Male Academy] gives you the sense that you're gonna do it. That's the type of messages that they [the counselors] send. There's something

that Mr. Davis [a counselor] told me—he said, "you go through certain things but you just gotta suck it up and deal with it because the world isn't gonna care about the things you go through; the world is gonna care about the progress that you make". One of my friends, he was going through something, and I remembered what Mr. Davis said and I said the same thing to him and I helped him out.

Furthermore, the Male Academy's provision of college knowledge, and its social support structure, may have helped these students deal with the omnipresence of racial stereotypes that these students experienced at SHS. In fact, one student made a direct link between the MA and his desire to challenge harmful stereotypes about Black males:

> INTERVIEWER: Has the Male Academy influenced your ability to focus in school?
>
> MYLES: Yes, because I want to change my stereotype so bad. I don't want people to see me like that anymore. I'm going to sit in the front [of the classroom]. I even see my teachers look at me different like, "why is he up here? He must be about to do something [bad]". I sit in the front of all my classes, so now all the teachers expect that of me. I really changed their opinion, which is great for me.

Thus, the Male Academy's most powerful impact may be in its ability to inspire students to challenge and resist negative racial stereotypes by increasing their academic engagement and cultural dispositions toward school success.

Cultural Capital

Male Academy members were treated to field trips to local colleges where they met college students and administrators, and received valuable information about college applications and financial aid packages. Academy meetings hosted guest speakers who were able to further convey valuable information about pursuing higher education. Rodney expressed a sentiment that was common among all respondents: "I've always wanted to go to college, so it's helped open my eyes to like see how we can get—I didn't know there was so much financial aid out there" Similarly, Myles said,

> they've talked about financial aid and really I never heard about that before, because it's always been in my mind, "ok, maybe I don't get a scholarship—how am I going to pay for college". Then we met and we talked about financial aid one meeting and I thought, "ok, I can still get there".

Rodney and Myles underscore how important valuable application information can be to a student's decision to enroll in college. Simply having college ambitions is not enough; students must also have access to information about the proper courses to take while in high school in order to be eligible, the college application process, and college student life. The Smith Male Academy was a resource for this critical knowledge.

Information about college can alter perceptions of the utility of education and engender a college-going culture. Consider Darnell's astute perception of the MA's impact: "before [joining the Male Academy], college was always that dream, like that 'one day, I'm gonna be a superhero' dream. Now, it's just college; before, it was a joke". Likewise, Carter felt that the Male Academy had a profound influence on him, because "before, I didn't know the steps . . . now I have some knowledge that it takes in order to get those long term goals since being a part of the Male Academy, so its influenced a lot". Darnell and Carter eloquently convey a common sentiment among our respondents—how the MA changed their college frame from an unattainable dream to a realistic goal.

Moreover, the MA structured some of the meeting to simulate a college lecture environment, with presentations made by one of the head teachers or a guest speaker. Guest speakers were usually representatives from local colleges. These sessions were coupled with note-taking tutorials and other tips for studying, and nearly all respondents felt that their study habits had improved since joining the MA. In essence, academy members learned *how* to think and perform like successful, college-bound high school students, and this new knowledge changed students' cultural dispositions towards education. This impact is reflected in students' academic achievement.

THE MALE ACADEMY AND ACADEMIC ACHIEVEMENT

The Male Academy increased students' academic engagement and enhanced their pursuit of higher education. Additionally, the academy increased students' academic achievement. Many students in the MA reported that their grades had risen since joining the program, and they credited the MA for this improvement. For Rodney, the MA culture of accountability inspired him to improve his grades:

> I saw that a lot of people had improved their grades, so I didn't want to be, like, one of the people that everyone's improving their grades and I don't improve mine, so that's what pushed me to, like, get my grades up even more.

The MA peer culture of academic excellence inspired members to invest more time in their studies in an effort to improve their grades. Simply put, the academic engagement fostered in the group setting was contagious for academy members—being part of the MA meant showing up to class, paying attention during the lesson, and studying outside of school (often with peers from the MA).

Ultimately, most students hinged their assessment of the MA's effectiveness on its ability to raise their grades and their peers' grades. For instance, when asked whether or not the Male Academy was a success, Scott replied, "I think it [the MA] has been successful. I think there was like 30 something guys that raised their GPA". Melvin also measured the program's success in terms of members' academic achievements. According to Melvin, "something like 38 of the 45, or however many members we have, improved their GPA. Like, half of the kids were under a 2.0 and almost every one of them raised it at least above a 2.0". Darnell remarked, "one of my friends went from a 1.1 to a 3.5 in a semester of being in the Male Academy". Clearly, the Male Academy had a profound effect on the academic achievement of its members.[6] This is important because achievement metrics such as grade point averages are used to rank college and job applicants.

In sum, the Male Academy provided its Black male youth with an invaluable academic resource. Through the provision of critical information about the college application process (cultural capital) and a tight-knit system of both peer and adult support (social capital), the MA positively impacted its members by shifting their educational frames and, consequently, altering their academic and life trajectories. The Male Academy boosted academic engagement and achievement among its members. The Male Academy gave students the knowledge and social support to resist and overcome the negative racial stereotypes that these students were confronted with in and out of school.

THE MALE ACADEMY AS AN EDUCATIONAL MODEL: THE UTILITY OF AN ACHIEVEMENT CASE

In America, we are often figuratively warned not to judge books by their covers, but society readily encourages us to judge each other by our colors. Black students at Smith High School perceived a school culture that held low academic expectations for them, but high academic expectations for White and Asian students. Respondents also felt that the general climate of racial stereotypes ossified a racial academic hierarchy in which they were relegated and confined to the lowest-ranking strata. Moreover, these Black male students felt negatively and falsely judged by their school community, regardless of individual academic ability or class status, such that those who reported good grades and middle-class backgrounds still felt heavily and negatively stereotyped based on their race, style of dress, and mannerisms. Thus, neither middle-class status nor a competitive academic record were enough to inoculate these Black males from direct experiences with injurious racial stereotypes.

Furthermore, students perceived direct links between the racial academic hierarchy in their high school and the societal opportunity structure that exists beyond school walls. According to these students, the societal opportunity structure is supported by racial stereotypes perpetuated in popular media. These stereotypes frame Blacks as violent offenders or intellectually dull athletes and entertainers. Thus, the stereotypes that students perceived within their high school were congruent to those they perceived in society at large.

According to oppositional culture theory (Fordham and Ogbu 1986), the climate of negative racial stereotypes that these Black male youth experienced both in and out of school should have caused them to rebel by disengaging academically (Lopez 2003). Contrarily, the Black males in this study responded to a general climate of rigid racial stereotypes in their high school by devoting *more* time to their studies in an effort to overcome and disprove these stereotypes. Moreover, past research has found that adolescents tend to frame their educational goals in accordance with the most prevalent racial stereotypes associated with their racial group. Therefore, Blacks tend to profess educational goals focused on avoiding failure instead of achieving success (Kao 2000). The Black males in this sample perceived a climate of academic racial stereotypes similar to that conveyed by Kao's (2000) respondents. However, these stereotypes had a different effect upon the students in our sample: despite these stereotypes, Black males in our sample expressed educational goals that were achievement oriented and included strong college aspirations. Why the divergence from previous findings?

The Male Academy provides a compelling answer to this question. The MA provided its members with a tremendous amount of valuable cultural capital and social capital. The program fostered different forms of capital through a series of college fieldtrips, guest speakers, and student-led presentations on a host of pertinent academic issues. The MA was purposely structured to provide its members with valuable "college knowledge" that turned college enrollment from a distant dream to a realistic and practical possibility.

Due to its structure as a largely student-led afterschool club with clearly designated membership, the MA represents a closed social network within James Coleman's social capital framework. A closed social network is a social group in which each member of the group has a direct relationship with every other member, and closed networks represent the most efficient spaces for the transmission of social capital. According to Coleman (1988), a high degree of closure exists among peers who see each other daily, have consistent expectations of one another, and establish norms about group and individual behavior. The Smith Male Academy members saw each other daily as students at Smith High School and, through their participation in the MA, held high expectations for one another and developed pro-academic and college-going norms about each other's behavior. The high degree of closure provided by the Male Academy structure encouraged members to monitor their peers and, in so doing, maintain a high level of academic engagement. The Male Academy increased students' academic engagement, boosted their academic aspirations and expectations, and increased students' achievement levels. The program functioned as an effective social buffer for the Black males in this case study—a buffer against a pervasive culture of racial stereotypes in their general high school environment. Male Academy participation motivated students to respond to negative racial stereotypes with indignation and a focused resolve to achieve academic success in the face of adversity. These outcomes indicate that Black male youth in urban schools need not react in opposition to hostile educational environments, or education more generally, if they are given appropriate levels of institutional and social support.

The prevalence of racial stereotypes that these students perceived within the school and society underscores the importance of programs like the Male Academy. And the overwhelming success of the Male Academy for these Black male students' educational trajectories speaks to the *utility of achievement cases*—the benefit that scholars, educators, and policymakers gain from focusing on what works and attempting to replicate successful structures and practices, rather than concentrating solely on fixing systems, programs, and students that are perceived as broken. *Achievement cases* offer a trustworthy way forward. In this case, teachers, administrators, and policymakers would be wise to consider implementing similarly structured student academies in similar school contexts, and with various underrepresented minority populations.

NOTES

1. Smith High School and all program and student names are pseudonyms.
2. Interviews lasted between 45 and 90 minutes, and were conducted during "free periods" within the school day, or directly after school.
3. Study participants are representative of MA members, because nearly all members consented to participate and were interviewed.
4. All student informants are from working- or middle-class backgrounds. We obtained this information during interviews with students and program directors. Students were asked questions about their parents' level of education and occupation and their own neighborhoods, and directors were asked to describe the demographics of the program participants.
5. We use grade point average (GPA) as a measure of academic achievement. Our informants' GPAs in the semester directly preceding involvement in the Male Academy ranged from a low of .11 to a high of 3.71, with a mean of 1.94.
6. In the semester directly preceding their involvement in the Male Academy, our informants collectively held a mean GPA of 1.94. However, during the three semesters in which our informants were part of the Male Academy, their mean GPA was 2.26—an average increase in GPA of .32 points per student. Furthermore, Male Academy members experienced GPA gains regardless of their achievement level prior to entering the program. For example, the highest GPA of all academy members in the semester directly preceding

enrollment in the academy was a 3.71, and that student maintained an average GPA of 3.80 during his first three semesters in the Male Academy. The lowest GPA of all academy members in the semester directly preceding enrollment in the Male Academy was a .11, and that student maintained an average GPA of 1.14 during his first three semesters in the Male Academy. Thus, in terms of GPA, the Male Academy was beneficial for both the highest and lowest of prior achievers.

REFERENCES

Ainsworth-Darnell, J. W., and D. B. Downey. 1998. "Assessing the Oppositional Culture Explanation for Racial/Ethnic Differences in School Performance." *American Sociological Review* 63 (4): 536–553.

Anderson, E., ed. 2008. *Against the Wall: Poor, Young, Black, and Male.* Philadelphia: University of Pennsylvania Press.

Balfanz, R., and N. Legters. 2004. *Locating the Dropout Crisis. Which High Schools Produce the Nation's Dropouts? Where Are They Located? Who Attends Them? Report 70.* Center for Research on the Education of Students Placed at Risk (CRESPAR).

Blanchett, W. J. 2006. "Disproportionate Representation of African American Students in Special Education: Acknowledging the Role of White Privilege and Racism." *Educational Researcher* 35 (6): 24–28.

Bourdieu, P. 1984. *Distinction: A Social Critique of the Judgement of Taste.* Cambridge, MA: Harvard University Press.

Carter, P. L. 2005. *Keepin' It Real: School Success Beyond Black and White.* New York: Oxford University Press.

Coleman, J. S. 1988. "Social Capital in the Creation of Human Capital." *American Journal of Sociology* 94: S95–S120.

Conchas, G. Q. 2001. "Structuring Failure and Success: Understanding the Variability in Latino School Engagement." *Harvard Educational Review* 71 (3): 475–505.

Conchas, G. Q. 2006. *The Color of Success: Race and High-Achieving Urban Youth.* New York: Teachers College Press.

Conchas, G. Q., A. R. Lin, L. Oseguera, and S. J. Drake. 2014. "Superstar or Scholar? African American Youth's Perceptions of Opportunity in a Time of Change." *Urban Education* 29 (1): 0042085914528720.

DiMaggio, P. 1982. "Cultural Capital and School Success: The Impact of Status Culture Participation on the Grades of US High School Students." *American Sociological Review* 47 (2): 189–201.

Farkas, G., C. Lleras, and S. Maczuga. 2002. "Does Oppositional Culture Exist in Minority and Poverty Peer Groups?" *American Sociological Review* 67 (1): 148–155.

Feagin, J. R., A. M. Orum, and G. Sjoberg, eds. 1991. *A Case for the Case Study.* Chapel Hill, NC: UNC Press.

Fordham, S., and J. U. Ogbu. 1986. "Black Students' School Success: Coping with the 'Burden of Acting White.'" *The Urban Review* 18 (3): 176–206.

Gibson, M. A. 2005. "Promoting Academic Engagement Among Minority Youth: Implications from John Ogbu's Shaker Heights Ethnography." *International Journal of Qualitative Studies in Education* 18 (5): 581–603.

Goffman, E. 1974. *Frame Analysis: An Essay on the Organization of Experience.* Cambridge, MA: Harvard University Press.

Harris, A. L. 2006. "I (Don't) Hate School: Revisiting Oppositional Culture Theory of Blacks' Resistance to Schooling." *Social Forces* 85 (2): 797–834.

Harry, B., J. Kingner, and R. Moore. 2000. *Of Rocks and Soft Places: Using Qualitative Methods to Investigate the Processes that Result in Disproportionately.* Conference Paper presented at the Minority Issues in Special Education, Harvard University, November, vol. 17, p. 2000.

Heath, S. B. 1983. *Ways with Words: Language, Life and Work in Communities and Classrooms.* Cambridge: Cambridge University Press.

Howard, T. C. 2008. "Who Really Cares? The Disenfranchisement of African American Males in PreK-12 Schools: A Critical Race Theory Perspective." *The Teachers College Record* 110 (5): 954–985.

Howard, T. C. 2010. *Why Race and Culture Matter in Schools: Closing the Achievement Gap in America's Classrooms.* New York: Teachers College Press.

Howard, T. C. 2013. "How Does it Feel to be a Problem? Black Male Students, Schools, and Learning in Enhancing the Knowledge Base to Disrupt Deficit Frameworks." *Review of Research in Education* 37 (1): 54–86.

Jencks, C., and M. Phillips, eds. 2011. *The Black-White Test Score Gap.* Washington, DC: Brookings Institution Press.

Kao, G. 2000. "Group Images and Possible Selves Among Adolescents: Linking Stereotypes to Expectations by Race and Ethnicity." *Sociological Forum* 15 (3): 407–430.

Ladson Billings, G. 2011. "Boyz to Men? Teaching to Restore Black Boys' Childhood." *Race Ethnicity and Education* 14 (1): 7–15.

Lopez, N. 2003. *Hopeful Girls, Troubled Boys.* New York: Routledge.

McDonough, P. M. 1997. *Choosing Colleges: How Social Class and Schools Structure Opportunity.* Albany, NY: SUNY Press.

Mehan, H., ed. 1996. *Constructing School Success: The Consequences of Untracking Low Achieving Students.* Cambridge: Cambridge University Press.

Noguera, P. A. 2003a. *City Schools and the American Dream: Fulfilling the Promise of Public Education.* New York: Teachers College.

Noguera, P. A. 2003b. "The Trouble with Black Boys: The Role and Influence of Environmental and Cultural Factors on the Academic Performance of African American Males." *Urban Education* 38 (4): 431–459.

Noguera, P. A. 2008. *The Trouble with Black Boys: . . . And Other Reflections on Race, Equity, and the Future of Public Education.* San Francisco: Jossey-Bass.

Oakes, J. 2005. *Keeping Track: How Schools Structure Inequality,* 2nd ed. New Haven, CT: Yale University Press.

Snow, D. A., E. Burke Rochford Jr., S. K. Worden, and R. D. Benford. 1986. "Frame Alignment Processes, Micromobilization, and Movement Participation." *American Sociological Review* 51 (4): 464–481.

Stanton-Salazar, Ricardo D. 1997. "A Social Capital Framework for Understanding the Socialization of Racial Minority Children and Youths." *Harvard Educational Review* 67 (1): 1–41.

Tienda, M., and W. J. Wilson, eds. 2002. *Youth in Cities: A Cross-National Perspective.* Cambridge: Cambridge University Press.

Yin, R. K. 2013. *Case Study Research: Design and Methods.* Thousand Oaks, CA: Sage Publications.

4 Dynamics of Urban Neighborhood Reciprocity

Latino Peer Ties, Violence, and the Navigation of School Failure and Success

María G. Rendón

Youth who grow up in urban neighborhoods experience higher odds of high school non-completion (Harding 2003; Wodtke, Harding, and Elwert 2011). Whereas popular perception is that high rates of school failure reflect an "anti-school" orientation among urban youth, studies show urban youth vary widely in their cultural orientation towards education (Carter 2005; Flores-Gonzalez 2002; Harris 2011; Warikoo 2011). If an oppositional outlook does not explain why urban neighborhoods are so detrimental for school completion, then what does? I spent a year in two urban neighborhoods in Los Angeles meeting with 42 young Latino men to examine how the urban neighborhood influences educational outcomes. Ethnographic observations of these neighborhoods and multiple interviews with each of these young men—high school completers and non-completers alike—point to exposure to urban violence as a significant factor contributing to school failure among young urban men.

It was during one of my first interviews that the effects of urban violence came into focus. I sat with Simon, 21, at a local park one sunny weekday afternoon, learning about what it was like to grow up in his neighborhood. A couple feet from us were two mothers pushing their young children on swings. There was a homeless man in sight sleeping in one corner of the park and a small group of young men, one on a bicycle, in the opposite direction when our conversation was suddenly interrupted.

The three young men, who appeared to have gang attire, assaulted another young man, around 16 years old, who was walking through the park with a young female. The young man on the bike got off, the bike fell to the floor, and he proceeded to hit the victim on the head with a glass bottle, shattering it to pieces. The victim was then surrounded and jumped by all three young men. His female friend watched as the victim curled into a fetal position on the floor, covering his face for protection, while the group of young men simultaneously kicked and punched him for a couple of minutes. I looked around the park. The few people there passively watched on or simply turned around. The three young men left the scene calmly. The victim sprung up, his white t-shirt full of dirt, particularly his stomach where he was most hit, and, limping, he continued to walk in the original direction he was heading with his friend.

With a smirk and a chuckle, Simon explained, "it's always been this way". The incident triggered his memory and, as it happened with most young men in this study, outpoured the numerous acts of violence Simon witnessed or fell victim to growing up.

Exposure to urban violence profoundly impacts the well-being of urban residents and is a serious problem that permeates into and challenges urban schools. Yet only recently have scholars begun to examine if and how exposure to urban violence impacts youths' educational outcomes directly. In this chapter, I examine how this impacts school non-completion. The "dropout/ pushout" process involves failing courses, falling behind on course credits, getting retained in school, and experiencing interrupted schooling. I specifically draw attention to the social context that influences and constrains students' choices and decisions on a day-to-day basis. I argue that to understand the cultural orientation that guides behavior counterproductive to school completion—like skipping school and fighting—requires accounting for how the threat of violence *punctuates* and *organizes* the daily lives of male urban youth.

CAUGHT UP AND BUFFERED YOUTH

Research shows that to avoid victimization youth exposed to urban violence draw on male peer ties not only for friendship but for physical and symbolic protection and respect (Anderson 1999; Harding 2010; Jones 2009). I elaborate on this finding by calling attention to the *dynamics of reciprocity* embedded in such peer ties. Drawing on male peer ties to avoid victimization is an urban-specific kind of social capital (Anderson 1999), and inherent in these social networks are "obligations" and "expectations" (Coleman 1988, S102). Urban youth who fail to complete school often do so for being repeatedly truant *with*, and getting expelled *for*, peers. I find that behavior that contributes to school non-completion among urban, male, Latino youth is guided by an orientation to the obligations and expectations youth have towards peers—specifically those they draw on to navigate urban violence. These expectations include "kicking it", partying, and at times engaging in delinquent acts like "tagging" or "smoking out"—in and out of school. Obligations also involve providing "backup" to peers engaged in peer group conflicts. By drawing on male peer ties to navigate the threat of urban violence, male youth become "caught up" in male peer group dynamics—that of gangs and "crews"[1] in the Los Angeles context. Ultimately, these ties make "excess claims" (Portes 1998, 15), as the behaviors that enhance cohesion among these peers and urban-specific social capital jeopardize school completion.

Yet not all urban youth get "caught up", and there is much to learn about the way in which institutional arrangements and policies can either buffer or further expose young men to urban violence. Though Simon described being chased by gang youth all the way home several times in middle school, he did not seek male peer ties for protection or become entangled in conflicts like others. Studies find that young, inner-city men respond differently to their environment. Yet it is important to acknowledge that not all urban youths are similarly exposed to the neighborhood in the first place. In contrast to youth who had ample leisurely time to hang out in the neighborhood, Simon was buffered from the neighborhood and its violence in significant ways. In high school, Simon experienced few assaults, as his greatest threat came while waiting for the school bus that would take him out of the neighborhood. At 21 years old, he also remained embedded in a local youth organization where—strongly encouraged by his mother—he spent his adolescent years after school, taking refuge from his surroundings. Less exposed to urban violence with more structured time and peer ties in comparison to other young men, Simon bypassed the opportunity and need to draw on male peer ties for physical and symbolic protection. Not having to employ these "strategies of action" (Swidler 1986), he avoided getting "caught up" in "obligations" and "expectations" with other young men, and graduated from high school. A subset of youth in the inner city, the most vulnerable, takes the brunt of urban violence and faces the highest odds of school failure. Labeled as "oppositional", they experience zero-tolerance responses, like suspensions, expulsions (Bowditch 1993; Hirschfield 2008, 2009), and arrests (Kirk and Sampson 2012) known to increase school non-completion. I find these institutional practices reinforce youths' exposure to the neighborhood, urban violence, and the dynamics of male reciprocity, derailing them further from school completion.

THE LATINO PUSHOUT REALITY

Conservative estimates indicate Latinos have a high school non-completion rate *twice* the national average, and about a quarter of Latino young men never earn their high school diploma. Numerous factors account for this problem. Studies repeatedly find that socioeconomic background, family structure, poor academic achievement, being retained in school, absenteeism, and student mobility contribute to this issue (Rumberger 2011). For Latinos, this problem is particularly pronounced among the foreign born, in part due to their limited English proficiency (Rumberger 1991; Valencia 2002). Studies also find that the social composition of schools, their resources, social climate, and school practices impact high school non-completion. For example, suspensions, expulsions, and attending an alternative school increase the odds of dropping out (Rumberger 2004). Moreover, the hypersegregation of Latinos in schools (Orfield 2004) and the tendency for Latinos to be tracked in lower academic programs (Conchas 2006; Valenzuela 1999) increase the odds of school failure.

Social ties also factor prominently in Latinos' educational outcomes. Some studies consider the role teachers and other institutional agents have in creating social capital that facilitates school success (Croninger and Lee 2001; Stanton-Salazar 2001). Other studies focus on social capital among peer ties, which can be positively related to educational outcomes (Conchas 2006; Flores-Gonzalez 2002), as well as sources of "negative social capital" (Ellenbogen and Chamberland 1997; Ream and Rumberger 2008). Carbonaro (1998) finds that a lack of intergenerational closure—that is, a lack of ties among friends' parents—increases the odds of school non-completion.

Few studies examine how the neighborhood context contributes to the Latino pushout problem. This is a huge gap in the literature, as Latinos make up a sizeable portion of the U.S. population living in the most concentrated poor and segregated neighborhoods, where school non-completion is pronounced. Especially lacking are studies that aim to identify the neighborhood *social processes* that lead to poor educational attainment. Some scholars suggest that institutional resources are the driving force behind the poor educational outcomes of urban youth. The most disadvantaged children continue to attend the most underresourced public schools due to persistent high levels of school segregation by race (Orfield, Frankenberg, and Lee 2003) and class (Reardon 2011). However, with few empirical studies disentangling neighborhood from school effects (Goldsmith 2009; Owens 2010; Pong and Hao 2007; Rendón 2014), it remains unclear if and how schools and neighborhoods function independently or together to produce dismal educational outcomes.

Other researchers hypothesize that the social disorganization of urban neighborhoods, specifically the lack of social cohesion among neighbors and social capital, may possibly impact youth educational outcomes (Crowder and South 2003; Bowen, Bowen, and Ware 2002). Studies repeatedly find social disorganization in urban neighborhoods contributes to high rates of crime and violence (Sampson et al. 2002; Sampson, Raudenbush, and Earls 1997). This, then, may contribute to school non-completion indirectly through youth engagement in crime and delinquency, a function of communities struggling to monitor youth and enforce conventional norms. A lack of social cohesion may also impact educational outcomes by making it challenging for parents to exchange information and serve as resources for one another in promoting school success (Ainsworth 2002).

Given the lack of empirical research examining how urban neighborhoods matter has allowed for one dominant idea—that of an oppositional culture—to continue to influence how we think urban neighborhoods impact educational outcomes. Urban sociologists have long called attention to how social isolation and racial segregation leave urban youth with a lack of role models and allow for the development of a ghetto-specific culture that further contributes to poor youth outcomes (Anderson 1999; Massey and Denton 1993; Wilson 1987). These studies echo Ogbu's (1983) contention that a "reactive identity" and an oppositional culture of racial minority youth explain the achievement gap (Fordham and Ogbu 1986). Advocates of segmented assimilation follow this logic. They suggest that residential concentration in urban neighborhoods is devastating for children of immigrants who acculturate to an oppositional culture in these contexts and experience downward assimilation (Haller, Portes, and Lynch 2011; Portes and Fernandez-Kelly 2008). Nonetheless, these claims remain mostly speculative, as few studies empirically examine how neighborhoods impact school outcomes.

HOW URBAN VIOLENCE MATTERS

Findings in this study corroborate urban ethnographies that repeatedly find urban violence to be one of the most salient and impactful characteristics of urban neighborhoods (Anderson 1999; Briggs et al. 2010; Harding 2010; Jones 2009; Noguera 2003). Specifically, this study contributes to emerging research that examines the link between urban violence and educational outcomes (Harding 2010; Sharkey 2010). Scholars remain unclear through what mechanisms urban violence contributes to school failure. Some contend that exposure to violence is detrimental to educational achievement because it impacts mental health. Sharkey (2010) finds that exposure to a local homicide impacts children's cognitive performance, and he hypothesizes this occurs via various physiological, emotional, or social responses related to stress, fear, or trauma. Research documenting rates of post-traumatic stress disorder (PTSD) among urban youth finds that such is comparable or higher than it is for war veterans, and has captured national attention (Reese et al. 2012) and suggests a probable link between the impact of urban violence, mental health, and academic performance.

In his research, Harding (2010) considers how urban violence impacts social relations. He finds that exposure to urban violence encourages youth to establish ties with older youth to stay safe, and he argues that these ties prove detrimental for school completion. Harding contends that drawing on these ties with older young men for protection sways the younger generation away from the traditional or conventional education paths via the transmission of alternative and/or non-mainstream educational outlooks. For Harding (2010), older peer ties matter in shaping poor educational outcomes of inner-city youth because they influence youth cultural orientations.

I also find that the threat of violence leads youths to draw on peer ties for physical and symbolic protection and respect. However, I do not suggest high school non-completers are socialized into leaving school behind. I find those who fail to complete school express similar education outlooks as those who graduate—some express discontent with schooling, whereas others affirm their belief in education and attempt to earn their diploma by reenrolling in school. Instead, I find that high school non-completers fail to graduate because they engage in behavior counterproductive to school completion—like skipping school and fighting—which school officials penalize. An "anti-school" or "oppositional" orientation does not drive this behavior; rather, it is driven by youths' sense of obligation to peer ties that afford them urban-specific social capital—a cultural orientation that emerges *as a function of* the being exposed to urban violence. In this study, I highlight that not all youth receive the same "dose" of exposure. The extent to which the neighbor-hood influences youth outcomes depends on several other factors, like family background characteristics, the schools youth attend, or the amount of time spent in the neighborhood (Burton and Jarret 2000; Furstenberg 2000; Small and Feldman 2012). Not all urban youth get "caught up" because not all urban youth are similarly exposed to the neighborhood and urban violence. This implies that to promote school success for young Latino men, it is neces-sary to minimize their exposure to violence in their neighborhoods.

STUDY DESIGN AND METHODS

Data come from a yearlong case study designed to uncover the neigh-borhood mechanisms that explain *why* and *how* disadvantaged neigh-borhoods shape school and work outlooks and decisions of young adult, male children of Latino immigrants. The original study includes semi-structured interviews with 42 young men, between 17 to 23 years old, and their immigrant parents living in two high-poverty neighborhoods in Los Angeles. Ethnographic observations of these neighborhoods enhanced interview data.

Here, I draw primarily on the interviews conducted with young men. Two-thirds of the respondents are U.S. born and one-third is foreign born, having arrived in the United States at a very early age (between two and five years old). I purposefully sampled young men on different educational trajectories: one-third were high school "dropouts", one-third were on the college track or in a four-year college, and the rest were in between, usually having attained a high school degree when the study began. This sampling strategy allowed me to account for outlook and behavioral diversity within poor neighborhoods and to better leverage neighborhood mechanisms con-tributing to education- and work-related outcomes in young adulthood. Half of the young men were from a poor, predominantly Mexican, immi-grant neighborhood, Pueblo Viejo, and the other half were from a simi-larly disadvantaged Black and Latino neighborhood, Central City, in Los Angeles[2] (see Tables 4.1 and 4.2 in the Appendix).[3]

To gain entry into these two neighborhoods, I relied on help from personal networks who had contacts in the neighborhoods. These personal ties led me to specific families, teachers, and academic counselors in local schools and community organizations, such as Boys and Girls Clubs of America, churches, and organizations serving youth whose circumstances place them "at risk". These initial informants either linked me directly to youth or to others who then linked me to youth who fit my sampling criteria. Whereas some young men were connected to neighborhood institutions, others were not. Initial informants were particularly instrumental in putting me in contact with the hard-to-reach group—school dropouts not linked to any of these neighborhood institutions.

I met with the 42 young, male adults three times, on average, over the course of a year. I also interviewed one of their parents once, resulting in 160 interviews. Each interview visit explored different themes, including how the neighborhood mattered, their social relations, and their identity and outlooks and decisions regarding school and work. I conducted interviews at community organizations, churches, youths' homes, school campuses, local parks, and eateries. Each interview lasted between two and three hours, and these were recorded and transcribed. In between interviews, I conducted ethnographic observations of the neighborhood, local high schools, alternative schools, community organizations, and family life. Respondents also outlined their neighborhood boundaries and described where they spent most of their time and the places they avoided and why through the use of a map. The ethnographic field notes, cognitive maps, and parent interviews allowed me to triangulate the data, giving me greater confidence in my findings. Data were coded and analyzed using the Atlas.ti software. Having identified urban violence as a salient feature of the neighborhood, I then compared high school graduates and non-graduates to examine if urban violence mattered differently across these cases and how it factored into their educational trajectories.

NAVIGATING URBAN VIOLENCE

> Walking to school wasn't as bad as walking home. Walking home is when you thought alright, uhm . . . where is what's his name and what's his name? Because we wanted to walk, like, in a group. And yeah, we wouldn't walk home, say, me and my brother. We wouldn't walk all by ourselves.
>
> (Pedro, 22)

Despite national declines in violence over the past 20 years, the presence of gangs persists in Pueblo Viejo and Central City, both of which are among the most disadvantaged neighborhoods in Los Angeles and have a long history of urban gang violence. Like Pedro, young men in this study had to contend with this reality growing up. Substantial research exists on gang youth. I focus on the majority group, the bulk of young men in urban neigh-borhoods who do not join gangs, but who are nonetheless affected by urban violence in their neighborhoods on a day-to-day basis.

Most young men explained they first became exposed to violence in mid-dle school, often in two ways: by being "hit up"—asked to what gang they belong—or when "pocket checked"—assaulted, usually with a weapon. The threat of violence looms in these encounters, as David, a 20-year-old school non-completer, described:

> usually they ask me, "where you from"? I just look at them, like, "no, no where". . . . But, that one time . . . I looked back and they started running . . . getting closer . . . one of them pulled out a bat.

Most youths described having several incidents like these over the course of their adolescence. It led youth-like Eddie to express, "you can't walk the streets" (of his neighborhood). As a resident of one of the housing projects dominated by one local gang, Eddie, a non-gang youth, was careful not to walk through the local gang enemy territories. Not only was it likely he would be "hit up" but he explained,

> well I could (walk through those blocks) but then they will probably mistake you because they done a lot of drive-bys, people just shooting up, acting up . . . They are not going to be playing with me. That's why I don't be going over there because I know what I am going for . . . I am going over there just to get messed with or whatever.

Young men understood that the threat of violence walking through the neighborhood was real.

This led several young men to refer to the walk home from school as "a mission", because assaults by older youth usually came after school. Alfredo, an 18-year-old senior, began experiencing "pocket checks" in sev-enth grade. During these assaults, Alfredo and his brothers not only had to give up money, but on one occasion their jackets and sneakers as well. Another youth, Osvaldo, a 20-year-old college student, described two inci-dents when he was "jacked" (assaulted and robbed), once with a knife, after school. Genaro, a 20-year-old school non-completer, similarly expe-rienced repeated assaults by a gang member at the bus stop on his way to work and had to surrender money every time. When youths became victims of assaults, most felt they had to give up their belongings either because they were threatened with a weapon or because the assault involved several young men. Others, like Rigoberto, a 19-year-old high school graduate, put up fights throughout high school.

Early in adolescence boys in these neighborhoods learn *not* to navigate the urban context alone or risk being "caught slippin'"—caught off guard, unprotected, and vulnerable to victimization. As Pedro noted, youths in these two neighborhoods "always walked with two or three guys", a strategy they picked up after their first "pocket checks" or after "getting hit up". In these neighborhoods, peers become an important resource, a source of protection from victimization or getting "punked". These ties provide urban male youth with an urban-specific kind of social capital, whereas navigating the urban context *solo* can be a liability. Violence, therefore, impacts the way youth establish and maintain male peer ties in these communities, including youth who do not identify as gang members, but who must, nonetheless, learn to navigate the threat of violence in their neighborhoods characterized by gang dynamics.

One way non-gang youth tried to stay safe was by drawing on gang ties in their neighborhood or block. Whereas these young men were often critical of gang activities, several non-gang youth repeatedly expressed that they "kept it cool" with gang members. In a context characterized by gang rivalries and violence, non-gang youth had a strong incentive to maintain friendly ties to gang members in their immediate neighborhood. On the one hand, youth tried to avoid problems with their local gang. Eddie explained, "of course I'm going to keep it cool. I don't want any beef with them". On the other hand, young men explained how they benefited from their ties to the neighborhood gang. Joaquin shared that he was assaulted one day by a new gang youth in the local gang, a stranger to him. When the gang found out, they harshly reprimanded and beat the young gangster. Joaquin explained, "because they [the older gang members] know me for a while, they actually protect me somewhat". Joaquin's gang ties in the neighborhood made him feel he would not be "messed with".

In Central City, Latinos often felt they were targets of Black gang members. This perception contributed to minimal cross-racial ties between Latino youth and Black gang youth (Rendón forthcoming). Without a sense of protection from the local gang, youth like Pedro, who grew up in a predominantly Black public housing complex, spent very little time in the projects due to fear. Instead, Latino youth in Central City gravitated to co-ethnic peers, including Latino gang members. Pedro explained,

> I went over there [a predominantly Latino block in Central City] and I see Hispanic kids with their bikes, just riding and having fun, playing out in the street. . . . I guess that's why I went there a lot because you don't have to worry. . . . The guy that I used to hang with, his cousin . . . he was from a gang. . . . The older guys, they would look out for him.

In this case, Pedro relied on his friend's ties to the gang for a sense of safety in Central City.

Another way young men drew on male peer ties to stay safe was by joining a crew. Unlike neighborhood gangs who are long-standing, entrenched neighborhood institutions, most crews in Los Angeles tend to be short-lived, loose associations of male adolescents and form an identity around "party-ing" or "tagging".[4]

Gonzalo recalls that once he got into middle school, he no longer felt like he was a kid. He recalled, "everyone was fighting. There were people selling drugs in school". It was then that Gonzalo joined a tagging crew, though he was hesitant to call it such. He states, "it was just a crew. If something would happen, they [crew] would get in fights. That was pretty much it. They tagged, but it wasn't like an actual tagging crew". Rigo echoes these comments, confessing that he was scared in middle school because he felt small relative to other boys and he had no friends upon returning from Mexico after a two-year stay. He said he joined a tagging crew, "but just to fight". Efrain, 22, a school non-completer, formed a crew in middle school after being pocket checked and "jumped" (beaten up) several times. Efrain explained,

> after that [assault] I started . . . pumping up [lifting weights] and started getting confidence on my own. . . . I'm not going to let them punk me . . . 'cause I have brothers behind me that are going to come to the same school. I can't leave a reputation saying that "this fool used to be punked, then, we can punk the brothers". Oh, hell no. I'm going to get everybody that gets punked and start a crew, and that's the way we did it. . . .

Aside from providing physical protection, joining a crew allowed Efrain, Rigo, and Gonzalo to signal to others that they could not be "punked".

Crew members felt strongly about the importance of holding respect and believed it key to avoiding victimization. Jaime, 19, a school non-completer, joined a tagging crew early in high school. He explained the appeal of being a crew:

> people are like, yeah, I heard about you . . . I got all of that [reputa-tion and respect] cause of them [his crew]. 'Cause they were telling me, "don't ever be a punk because it's going to make us look bad". . . . See, if they come talking shit and you just let yourself [get victimized], that means . . . you're a punk; anybody can just come and step over you. . . .

Although they were willing to put up a fight and uphold "respect", crew members like Jaime distinguish themselves from gang youth. They echoed other non-gang youth views about gangs, in particular a disdain for the more serious forms of violence they associated with gang members. Eze-quiel, a 19-year-old school non-completer and crew member, described the fine line he walked with his gang peers: "if I had a party, I'd call them up, drinking together, smoking, but like *bust a mission* [engage in gang shooting] with them—no". Like youth who affiliated with gang mem-bers, young men revealed that, besides having an interest in the "party scene" or "tagging", youth in urban Los Angeles joined a crew because it offered important benefits in their neighborhoods—an identity with a peer group who could provide physical protection and allow the youth to claim respect, without having to join a gang or the gangster lifestyle. Yet, as young men found out, one of the consequences of drawing on gang and crew male peer ties for protection is that it increased their odds of school non-completion.

GETTING "CAUGHT UP" AND HIGH SCHOOL NON-COMPLETION

> If I go to community college I am still going to be in the streets. The homies are going be, "what's up, let's go kick it [hang out], let's go smoke" . . . That's how people don't make it. Yeah you are going to college but you are still *caught up* . . .
>
> (Sergio, 18, why he opted to join the U.S. Marines)

In this study, young men who failed to complete high school had engaged in certain behavior, like truancy and fighting, that set them behind academically and interrupted their schooling. In contrast to what some studies suggest, I did not find this behavior necessarily associated with anti-school attitudes. First, several high school graduates were as critical about "teachers who did not care" and the poor quality schooling they received as were school non-completers. For instance, Noel felt teachers treated him like a "dumb ass", and though academically disengaged, Noel graduated primarily to please his mother. Second, it was also the case that some high school non-completers expressed to value education, despite being disengaged. For Jaime, getting expelled from Central City High was a rude awakening. It was then he realized he should take school more seriously. He states, "that's when I really tried to get it through my head, that's when I realized all right, you really have to get this (diploma). I got to get my head in these books". High school non-completers like Jaime typically expressed deep regret for not having acquired their high school diploma.

Rather than anti-school attitudes, what set school non-completers apart from those who graduated was their counterproductive behavior—like skipping school and fighting—rooted in acts of reciprocity and a sense of commitment to male peer ties, which gave them, at least initially, a sense of protection and respect in their neighborhoods. These young men revealed they rarely skipped school alone or engaged in a conflict or a fight that did not involve male peer group dynamics. I found that in the process of drawing on gang and crew ties to navigate urban violence, these youth became "caught up" in group expectations and obligations, and this orientation towards male group dynamics factored into school non-completion in a number of ways.

Truancy, one of the biggest problems in both neighborhoods' schools, was central to not obtaining a high school diploma. Being perpetually truant resulted in an accumulation of "missing credits" and failed courses that put youth extensively behind in school. In some cases youth were retained a grade (or more), and in other cases youth were expelled to alternative schools where they could pursue a high school diploma or GED, but commonly failed to acquire either. For the most part, gang and crew ties pulled youth away from school for social reasons, such as parties, drinking, and smoking, which strengthened cohesion among these peers. Smiley, an ex-gang member and school non-completer, explained that right before he stopped attending school he "was taking care of business". He explained, "I was making sure I did my class work, but I was being sneaky . . . I was also getting drunk, smoking weed, and hanging with the boys". Whereas most youth in this study skipped school at some point (and some did so frequently), youth with gang ties or in a crew were more likely to report skipping school to be with their male peers. These ties made opportunities to hang out available. Furthermore, there was an incentive to maintain these ties due to the urban-specific social capital they provided.

Having ties to gangs and crews in adolescence not only fostered truancy in middle and high school, but as these young men explained, these peer ties ultimately introduced more conflict in their lives. "Keeping it cool" with gang members on the block proved risky for non-gang youth, because it sent the message that they were affiliated with the gang in substantive ways. Joaquin, who could draw on gang ties on his block to protect him because "they knew him for a while", went to the hospital for two days with bruises all over his body, a "messed up face", and three broken ribs. Members of a gang with a rivalry with the one in his neighborhood beat Joaquin after school as he walked home; they had "got the idea" Joaquin was from the local neighborhood gang because he hung out with some of the gangsters there. Eddie also ended up in the hospital when a bullet, aimed at a gang youth he was walking with to adult school, scraped his shoulder. Similarly, crews found themselves in conflict with other crews, as their members postured themselves to gain respect and were challenged in return. In a context riddled by gang dynamics, these crews often drew attention of local gangs, escalating the kinds of violence crew members then experienced. Ultimately, youth with ties to gang and crew peers described constantly "watching their back".

At a minimum these conflicts distracted youth from school. Yet often ties to gangs and crews absorbed youth into gang and crew behavior in direct and consequential ways that impacted school completion. For instance, youth with ties to gang members often felt they had to reciprocate protection and "back up" their gang peers in their neighborhoods, even when they were *not in* the gang. Despite not being a gang member and holding strong views against the gangster lifestyle, Sergio became involved in many gang fights:

> I had homies where I used to live in the apartments and you can say that
> they were gang related. They didn't try to get me in the gang . . . because

they were more the family type. "I'll respect you if you *don't* do this [join the gang]". They actually told me, "nah, don't do this . . . I already fucked up so you don't do this" . . . like family just looks out for you. But if something happened, if somebody did something to one of us, then we all got his back because we all kicked it together.

Sergio's strong ties got him in a lot of trouble, specifically fights, because he felt the need to "get their back"; i.e., support them, like they supported him when he was in need. These fights eventually led to his school expulsion. Though Sergio managed to graduate from high school, he enrolled in the military during a time of war specifically to remove himself from his neighborhood and its violence and break away from neighborhood ties.

Importantly, youth wrestled with their sense of obligation to their gang and crew peer ties. Ezequiel frequently found himself in the middle of fights, reluctantly providing "back up" to peers. Although feeling disinclined to help when his friends "started shit", Ezequiel did so anyway. He explained why:

I end up backing them up anyways . . . it's like having a minor. If he's out with you, he's under your responsibility. With my homies . . . if I'm out with them, they're not my responsibility, but I'm with them. So what kind of a friend am I to stand right there and let him get his ass kicked?

High school non-completers in urban Los Angeles were youth like Ezequiel who prioritized gang and crew ties at one point in their adolescence and became "caught up" in group behavior and dynamics that proved detrimental for school completion. Even though Ezequiel never joined a gang, his commitment to his gang and crew peers got him expelled four times from three different schools when he provided "back up", in one case punching a school police officer who was "manhandling" his friend.

Youth who failed to complete high school shared a distinct cultural orientation relative to most urban youth who graduated. Yet this distinction was not a difference in their orientation towards education or an oppositional or street orientation per se. Rather, the cultural distinction lies in how these youth privileged their male peer ties and, specifically, met the expectations and obligations that came with drawing on a social network that provided a type of social capital that they believed, at least initially, helped them better navigate the threat of violence. I found this orientation and ties to crews and gangs weakened over time for most youth as they reached their young adult years. The academic setbacks and greater exposure to conflict and violence taught most of the young men that the *sense* of safety they initially felt through gang and crew peer ties was illusive and came at a high cost. In some cases, breaking away from these ties occurred early enough in high school that youth were able to make up missing credits or failed classes in order to graduate. Such was the case with Sergio and Rigoberto, who scrambled their senior year to earn course credits and get rid of their demerits due to their history of truancy. Yet, whereas some managed to break away in time to graduate, others did not. Youth like Efrain who didn't meet the credit requirements to graduate had either turned away from these peer ties too late or were too far set behind academically when they did so to warrant graduation. For others, like Ezequiel and Jaime, a sense of obligation to gang and crew ties remained a feature of everyday life into their early adult years—and school success elusive.

WHY SOME DROP OUT AND OTHERS DON'T

> When I had extra time I would hang out in the street. Just walk up and down, talk to homies, homegirls, just kick it, do nothing. Just like that, when I had free time I would get home from school, have nothing to do, just walk around, ride my bike. Just kick it.
>
> (Ezequiel, 19, school non-completer)

To understand why urban violence contributes to school non-completion for some youth but not others, it is necessary to account for urban youths' *differential exposure* to the urban neighborhood and urban violence. Whereas no youth in these two communities could escape the reality of violence, some were exposed to it more than others. Where youth attend school and where and how youth spend their time after school, on weekends, and during school breaks (and school hours) influence their exposure to their neighborhood and to its violence. I found high school graduates had more limited exposure to the neighborhood and experienced the threat of violence to a lesser degree. By having less opportunity and feeling less of a need to draw on male peer ties for protection, they bypassed getting "caught up" and engaging in behavior that jeopardized school completion. Parents and schools had a pivotal role in moderating youths' exposure to the neighborhood and urban violence by structuring youths' time and peer connections.

Structured Time and Peer Connections

Parents reported that the threat of violence directed at them or their children influenced their decisions and behavior. Fearing the reputation of the local high school as violent, several parents sought to send their children to school elsewhere, including nearby high schools, charter schools, or busing them out. These approaches had mixed results, at times shielding youth from violence, but not always. For example, fearing the reputation of the neighborhood high school, Pedro's mom enrolled him and his brother at school in the next neighborhood. Yet, without a car, the youths had longer walks to and from school, and this increased their odds of assaults or victimization.

Ultimately, parents buffered youth most effectively from urban violence when they structured their sons' time and, by default, their peer ties. Parents did this in two main ways: by engaging them in extracurricular activities, such as sports, and by taking them to work. Leo's mother, a full-time, working, single parent of five boys, aggressively managed her sons' time in the neighborhood by enrolling them in various sports, beginning in their elementary school years and continuing throughout high school. Leo, 19, graduated from high school, and he recalled his family's commitment to the program and described how busy it kept them for several years. On Saturdays all five boys were up at 5:00 or 5:30 am to be ready at the park at 6 am. He explained,

> we'd line the field in the morning . . . set up the concession stand, cook, get ready for the game, play the game, and then after come back and cook some more and then clean. And we'll be back to school on Monday and just do the same routine over because we would practice during the week Tuesday, Wednesday, Thursday, and we were always involved . . .

Other parents engaged their children in extracurricular activities for their intrinsic value. Jose and Leonardo's parents began a soccer league when the twins were three years old because they felt it was good for "their mental health". 16 years later, these parents continued to run the league, now with 10 teams and 250 youths. Over time they learned to appreciate how sports could function to keep kids in the neighborhood "out of trouble".

Fathers, or father figures, played a critical role in encouraging time away from the streets for their sons. Youth who were consistently involved in sports throughout their childhood and adolescence—as opposed to trying a sport for one season—often had fathers who strongly encouraged these activities. Though Alfredo and his two brothers did not escape pocket checks growing up, they were also on the baseball and soccer teams in high school and as children had participated in numerous other activities, like taking piano lessons, karate, and swimming. Their father, Jorge, an undocumented, underemployed salesman, drove the boys to these different activities. Alfredo's parents expressed that Jorge's underemployment and flexible schedule allowed him to "dedicate time to [their] sons". They attributed the fact that their sons were not involved in gangs, like their cousins, to Jorge's constant involvement in their daily lives.

Moreover, several of the immigrant fathers were strong proponents of teaching their sons to work at an early age, some for the sake of instilling a strong work ethic and encouraging self-sufficiency and others as a strategy for keeping their sons out of trouble. Youth like Mauricio and Joaquin, who had extensive neighborhood ties, including gang ties, but who still completed high school, were kept busy by their fathers with work on weekends and occasionally during the week. Though neither sports nor work completely protected youth from violence—as stated earlier, Joaquin went to the hospital after a beating by gang members—these were alternatives to spending time in the neighborhood. Mauricio worked all day on weekends filming *quinceañeras* and weddings with his father, whereas Joaquin, who also played for the football team, joined his father in construction jobs on the side, sometimes even during school hours. Spending less time in the neighborhood, they avoided getting caught up in gang and crew peer dynamics, and, although not stellar students, Mauricio and Joaquin managed to graduate.

Not all parents were able to engage their sons in extracurricular activities or work. Jaime's father, Reynaldo, worked long hours. In an effort to keep an eye on his sons, he encouraged them to hang out with friends at home. Whereas Reynaldo got to know his son's friends well, his home became the "hangout" spot for Jaime's crew. The unstructured leisurely time spent by a group of young men on the block ultimately called attention from a nearby gang (and police), and during the study Jaime's house was "shot up". The lack of structured time and activities made the neighborhood context and its threat of violence persistently relevant in Jaime's life. It was after this incident that Jaime stopped attending school after getting expelled a second time for a fight.

Moreover, school institutional structures had a profound impact on the amount of time youth spent with peers in the neighborhood. Designed to desegregate schools, the magnet busing program in the Los Angeles Unified School District shuffles inner-city youth to non-neighborhoods. Whereas some of these host schools are racially mixed or in higher-income brackets, many are not. Often these youth are bused to other similarly disadvantaged schools. Regardless, being bused out of the neighborhood to other schools restricted these youths' exposure to their neighborhoods.[5]

Bused youth had to catch a bus at 6:00 or 6:30 in the morning to arrive at school on time. Because of the distance and Los Angeles traffic, these youth arrived home late in the evening in time for dinner and had very little time to spend in the neighborhood and draw on gang and crew ties. In general, youth whose parents picked them up at the bus stop bypassed getting "hit up" or "pocket checked" altogether. These youth tended to perceive and experience less violence in their neighborhoods, and therefore felt less need to establish or maintain gang or crew ties for protection and respect. Whereas other non-gang youth in the study were well informed about the gang dynamics that surrounded them, these youth expressed little knowledge about the local gang, their rivals, or gang conflicts in general.

Youth who were not picked up at the bus stop remained vulnerable to victimization. Federico, 19 and a college student, had been pocket checked five times and beaten up once during his way home from the bus stop in high school. Yet Federico had minimal opportunity to interact, much less form a close friendship, with any youth in his neighborhood because he'd been bused out since middle school. For these youth, drawing on gang and crew ties and getting "caught up" was simply harder to do and completing high school easier to achieve.

The structure of magnet programs buffered youth from the neighborhood and urban violence in other important ways. Attending the magnet program at the local neighborhood school shielded youth from urban violence to some extent. The program isolates students in separate classes from the larger student population. Forced to take the same courses in a cohort, the structure of magnet programs greatly influences who these youth spend time with and how. Magnet youth reported more close friendships with classmates than non-magnet youth or neighbors.

Less school and neighborhood peer overlap among youth attending magnet programs had two consequences. First, because classmates lived scattered throughout Los Angeles, magnet students gravitated to the after school magnet enrichment programs to socialize, and they spent less time with non-magnet students in and after school, or out in the neighborhood. Fernando, 22, a college student, explained:

> if I was in the regular track, I would have met all sorts of kids my age that lived around my block . . . and we would have hung out. I would have had friends that lived close by. . . . I didn't know anybody around my block. I didn't hang out with the neighborhood kids and till this day, the people that's my age around my block I don't know who they are.

Second, being isolated from the rest of the student population in magnet classrooms meant that the conflicts that flowed between the neighborhood and school rarely entered these classrooms. In this study, all young men who were on the college track had been in a magnet program, either bused out to another school or attended the magnet program in their neighborhood school with class peers from other neighborhoods. They were the youth most buffered from the neighborhood and urban violence and least likely to draw on gangs and crews to navigate their neighborhood and school.

In contrast, youth like Ezequiel who had "nothing to do, just walk around" encountered more threats of violence throughout their adolescence, and it was these youth who felt a stronger need—and had greater opportunity—to draw on gang and crew ties to navigate their neighborhood and schools safely. Unintentionally, school expulsion—a common policy enacted when a youth engages in a fight or other disorderly misconduct—often increased young men's exposure to urban violence, as these young men were forced to enroll in a new school in or near the neighborhood. After his third expulsion, Ezequiel enrolled in a high school in an adjacent neighborhood. Yet he attended this new school only for a week because a gang, TKB, was present at the school and he didn't "get along with them". Whereas he insisted conflict with members of TKB "was personal beef" and that "it had nothing to do with the [his friends'] gang", as a close friend to gang members rival to TKB, he had become entangled in some of their on-going conflicts. Knowing he was not safe, Ezequiel left the school. With more opportunity to hang out, his expulsion ultimately reinforced Ezequiel's exposure to the neighborhood and its violence, and the male peer dynamics that derailed him from school initially remained relevant in his life.

Given the volatile context, expulsion prompts some young men to opt out of school altogether. Yet those who are expelled often enroll in a continuation school, particularly when they have aged out of traditional high schools. Continuation schools are usually scattered throughout these neighborhoods, and I found that the social context in these institutions unintentionally promotes "acts of reciprocity" among male peers, increasing the likelihood they do not complete school. Whereas upholding respect and "having each other's back" became less relevant for most young men transitioning into adulthood, those in continuation schools continued to contend with violence and conflicts. These schools concentrated youth like Ezequiel with extensive truancy, tardiness, and a record of social disruption. It was at such a school that I met Jaime. Though expressing intent to earn his GED, he was expelled for fighting when one other young man "acted hard". Frustrated with this incident and his termination, Jaime was resigned to forget his diploma and focus only on work. He explained, "there are a lot of continuations around here but I don't feel safe around here . . . I just rather avoid them . . . people that I don't get along with". Though intended to reengage youth in education, these schools concentrate young men in gang and crew conflicts and unintentionally sustain young men's exposure to urban violence, reinforcing a cultural orientation to draw on male peer ties and make school completion hard to reach.

DISCUSSION AND CONCLUSION

Debate over the cultural orientation of urban youth has dominated current understanding of why such a large number perform poorly in school, including why so many of them drop out. Behavior associated with school failure, such as experiencing high levels of truancy and fights on campus that lead to suspensions and expulsions, is typically characterized as being "street" and not "school" oriented (Anderson 1999; Flores-Gonzalez 2002). Findings from this study suggest that it is important for scholars to shift attention away from educational norms presumed to figure prominently in educational outcomes and account for the everyday context that guides urban youths' choices and behavior.

Exposure to urban violence is an everyday feature in America's segregated, poor neighborhoods. This impacts young men in particular, and as I demonstrate in this study, exposure to violence has "collateral consequences". Urban violence impacts how young men navigate these neighborhoods. To avoid victimization, one natural response is to establish ties with individuals or a group of individuals who can offer protection. Yet these ties and the social resources they offer come at a cost.

In Los Angeles, youth draw on gang and/or crew ties to tap into an urban-specific social capital that assists them to get by in these neighborhoods. The downside to being embedded in these social networks is that, whereas seemingly useful for navigating violence, they actually expose youth to more violence over time and ultimately make "excess claims on group members", bringing about what Alejandro Portes (1998, 15) describes as "negative social capital". Research on gangs has documented that these acts of reciprocity and acts of retribution feed urban violence (Papachristos 2009; Papachristos, Hureau, and Braga 2013). Yet this study examines the youth who are at the periphery of these urban conflicts and who are often swept into their social dynamics in compromising ways. I argue that the cultural orientation and behavior counterproductive to school completion emerges out of a type of social organization that develops among urban youth exposed to urban violence. As others have found, the social cohesion that aids residents in navigating urban conditions can, at the same time, undermine the well-being of these communities (Pattillo 1998; Venkatesh 1997).

Through a multiple case study approach, this study helps identify "for whom" the neighborhood context matters. As Michelle Lamont and Mario Small (2008) explain, the strength of the qualitative research is in accurately depicting social processes or social mechanisms and describing "under what circumstances" two phenomena are associated with one another. By comparing cases of high school graduates and non-completers, this study draws logical inferences to explain "under what circumstances" high school non-completion occurs in urban neighborhoods. Two next door neighbors can experience the neighborhood quite differently, and the impact the neighborhood will have on their life outcomes will differ if one youth spends very little time on the block—because he's working, in extracurricular activities, or is bused out to school elsewhere—and the other spends ample, leisurely, unstructured time in the neighborhood. The negative impact of urban violence weighs heavier on youths lacking structured time and structured peer ties because they are more exposed to the context in the first place.

How urban parents can impact their children's educational outcomes should be assessed by taking into account their constrained information and resources. Research shows that the threat of violence weighs heavily on parenting practices in urban neighborhoods (Furstenberg et al. 1999). In this study, this concern underlined parents' decisions to send their children to different (though often similar quality) schools or encourage indoor activities (e.g., video games) or sons' friends to visit (and not the other way around). Yet most parents reported having minimal information to guide them in school selection. Most parents were unaware of busing or magnet programs. Further, parents who learned about these programs through a teacher, kin, or neighbor reported they enrolled their sons in large part to avoid the social disruption and violence in local schools. Ultimately, for most parents, engaging their sons in work and/or sports/extracurricular activities proved most effective in buffering their sons from urban violence. This strategy is distinct from Lareau's (2003) finding that middle-class parents encourage extracurricular activities to cultivate cultural capital, a means for upward mobility. In urban neighborhoods, parents turn to these activities often in response to gang activity and violence in their neighborhood, and to avoid "downward assimilation" of their children.

Future research should continue to examine how school structures and school processes function to expose or buffer young, inner-city men from urban violence. Whereas studies show that school institutional arrangements, like magnet programs, foster social and cultural capital that encourages academic engagement and achievement, it is less appreciated how these programs unintentionally minimize exposure to urban violence and curtail the opportunity and incentive to form "negative" ties. To the extent that urban violence remains an entrenched problem in our central cities, it is important that greater efforts are made to identify institutional arrangements that buffer young men in American's most disadvantaged environments to increase their odds of success. Findings in this study suggest educators and school administrators should be critical of practices like suspensions and expulsions that have the unintended consequence of further exposing young men to the urban conditions that prompt much of behavior that leads to school failure. Numerous studies find that expulsions and attending continuation schools increases the odds of high school non-completion. The experiences of the young men in this study help us understand why. The schools are situated in these neighborhoods and concentrate youth already amply exposed to the neighborhood and entangled in conflicts. Unintentionally, the social context sustains a normative orientation that encourages young men to seek other males for protection, to uphold "respect" and "get each other's back". Rather than buffering young men from urban violence, these institutional arrangements reinforce these dynamics that discourage school completion. The present study makes an important contribution for understanding why urban environments are detrimental for young men by highlighting the role urban violence plays in shaping their cultural orientation, behavior, and school outcomes.

NOTES

1. Crews in Los Angeles tend to be short-lived, loose associations of male adolescents. They form an identity around "partying" or "tagging" and differ from gangs in that they typically are not neighborhood bound, not linked to the drug market or prison gangs. These are discussed ahead.
2. The names of these informants and neighborhoods are pseudonyms. Communities were selected at the zip code level. The purpose for selecting this ecological space, as opposed to a census tract, was to allow greater freedom for respondents to designate their own neighborhood boundaries. I conducted the field research from 2006–2007, and the 2000 U.S. Census data was the most up-to-date neighborhood level data at the time.

3. I selected the two neighborhoods on theoretical grounds. The original study aimed to test underlying assumptions proposed by the segmented assimilation that exposure to U.S.-born native minorities (i.e., African Americans or third-generation Mexican Americans)—specifically their presumed embrace of an oppositional culture—contributes to downward assimilation.
4. In a party crew, young men "throw" parties on weekends and "ditching" (skip school) parties during the week. Tagging crews write non-gang-related graffiti on public property, and they gain status by spreading their "tags" (graffiti) throughout the city. Unlike Los Angeles gangs, crews typically lack neighborhood confines or links to the drug trade or prison gangs. Yet because of the vandalism, school officials and law enforcement often treat taggers as gang youth.
5. School busing and the magnet program may raise questions of selection. I found most parents were unaware of these programs and did not have the option to enroll their children. Parents who did hear about the program did so through a teacher who identified their son as a good candidate or through their personal networks, such as kin or a neighbor. While parents stated they bused out their children to receive a better education, parents' assessment of a "high quality" school typically centered on issues of social disruption and violence.

REFERENCES

Ainsworth, J. W. 2002. "Why Does It Take a Village? The Mediation of Neighborhood Effects on Educational Achievement." *Social Forces* 81 (1): 117–152.
Anderson, E. 1999. *Code of the Street: Decency, Violence, and the Moral Life of the Inner City.* New York: W.W. Norton.
Bowditch, C. 1993. "Getting Rid of Troublemakers: High School Disciplinary Procedures and the Production of Dropouts." *Social Problems* 40 (4): 493–509.
Bowen, N. K., G. L. Bowen, and W. B. Ware. 2002. "Neighborhood Social Disorganization, Families, and the Educational Behavior of Adolescents." *Journal of Adolescent Research* 17: 468–490.
Briggs, X. S., S. J. Popkin, and J. Goering. 2010. *Moving to Opportunity: The Story of an American Experiment to Fight Ghetto Poverty.* New York: Oxford University Press.
Burton, L. M., and R. L. Jarrett. 2000. "In the Mix, Yet in the Margins: The Place of Families in Urban Neighborhoods and Child Development Research." *Journal of Marriage and the Family* 62 (4): 1114–1135.
Carbonaro, W. J. 1998. "A Little Help from My Friend's Parents: Intergenerational Closure and Educational Outcomes." *Sociology of Education* 71 (4): 295–313.
Carter, P. L. 2005. *Keepin' It Real: School Success Beyond Black and White.* New York: Oxford University Press.
Coleman, J. S. 1988. "Social Capital in the Creation of Human Capital." *American Journal of Sociology* 94: S95–S120.
Conchas, G. Q. 2006. *The Color of Success: Race and High-Achieving Urban Youth.* New York: Teachers College Press.
Croninger, R. G., and V. E. Lee. 2001. "Social Capital and Dropping Out of High School: Benefits to At-Risk Students of Teachers' Support and Guidance." *Teachers College Record* 103 (4): 548–581.
Crowder, K., and S. J. South. 2003. "Neighborhood Distress and School Dropout: The Variable Significance of Community Context." *Social Science Research* 32 (4): 659–698.
Ellenbogen, S., and C. Chamberland. 1997. "The Peer Relations of Dropouts: A Comparative Study of At-Risk and Not-At-Risk Youths." *Journal of Adolescence* 20 (4): 355–367.

Flores-Gonzalez, N. 2002. *School Kids/Street Kids: Identity Development in Latino Students*. New York: Teachers College Press.

Fordham, S., and J. Ogbu. 1986. "Black Students' School Success: Coping With the Burden of 'Acting White.'" *The Urban Review* 18: 176–209.

Furstenberg, F. F. 2000. "The Sociology of Adolescence and Youth in the 1990s: A Critical Commentary." *Journal of Marriage and the Family* 62 (4): 896–910.

Furstenberg, F. F., T. D. Cook, J. Eccles, G. H. Elder Jr., and A. Sameroff. 1999. *Managing to Make It: Urban Families and Adolescent Success*. Chicago: University of Chicago Press.

Goldsmith, P. R. 2009. "Schools or Neighborhoods or Both? Race and Ethnic Segregation and Educational Attainment." *Social Forces* 87 (4): 1913–1941.

Haller, W., A. Portes, and S. M. Lynch. 2011. "Dreams Fulfilled, Dreams Shattered: Determinants of Downward Assimilation in the Second Generation." *Social Forces* 89 (3): 733–762.

Harding, D. J. 2003. "Counterfactual Models of Neighborhood Effects: The Effect of Neighborhood Poverty on Dropping Out and Teenage Pregnancy." *American Journal of Sociology* 109 (3): 676–719.

Harding, D. J. 2010. *Living the Drama: Community, Conflict, and Culture Among Inner-City Boys*. Chicago: University of Chicago Press.

Harris, A. L. 2011. *Kids Don't Want to Fail: Oppositional Culture and the Black-White Achievement Gap*. Cambridge, MA: Harvard University Press.

Hirschfield, P. J. 2008. "Preparing for Prison? The Criminalization of School Discipline in the USA." *Theoretical Criminology* 12 (1): 79–101.

Hirschfield, P. J. 2009. "Another Way Out: The Impact of Juvenile Arrests on High School Dropout." *Sociology of Education* 82 (4): 368–393.

Jones, N. 2009. *Between Good and Ghetto: African American Girls and Inner-City Violence*. New Brunswick, NJ: Rutgers University Press.

Kirk, D. S., and R. J. Sampson. 2012. "Juvenile Arrest and Collateral Educational Damage in the Transition to Adulthood." *Sociology of Education* 86 (1): 36–62.

Lamont, M., and M. L. Small. 2008. "How Culture Matters: Enriching our Understanding of Poverty." In *The Colors of Poverty: Why Racial and Ethnic Disparities Persist*, edited by D. Harris and A. Lin, 76–102. New York: Russell Sage.

Lareau, A. 2003. *Unequal Childhoods: Class, Race and Family Life*. Berkeley: University of California Press.

Massey, D. S., and N. Denton. 1993. *American Apartheid: Segregation and the Making of the Underclass*. Cambridge, MA: Harvard University Press.

Noguera, P. 2003. *City Schools and the American Dream: Reclaiming the Promise of Public Education*. New York: Teachers College Press.

Ogbu, J. U. 1983. "Minority Status and Schooling in Plural Societies." *Comparative and International Educational Society* 27 (2): 168–190.

Orfield, G. 2004. Dropouts in America: Confronting the Graduation Rate Crisis. Cambridge, MA: Harvard Education Press.

Orfield, G., E. D. Frankenberg, and C. Lee. 2003. "The Resurgence of School Segregation." *Educational Leadership* 60: 16–20.

Owens, A. 2010. "Neighborhoods and Schools as Competing and Reinforcing Contexts for Educational Attainment." *Sociology of Education* 83 (4): 287–310.

Papachristos, A. 2009. "Murder by Structure: Dominance Relations and the Social Structure of Gang Homicide." *American Journal of Sociology* 115 (1): 74–128.

Papachristos, A., D. M. Hureau, and A. A. Braga. 2013. "The Corner and the Crew: The Influence of Geography and Social Networks on Gang Violence." *American Sociological Review* 78 (3): 417–447.

Pattillo, M. E. 1998. "Sweet Mothers and Gangbangers: Managing Crime in a Black Middle Class Neighborhood." *Social Forces* 76 (3): 747–774.

Pong, S.-L., and L. Hao. 2007. "Neighborhood and School Factors in the School Performance of Immigrants' Children." *International Migration Review* 41 (1): 206–241.

Portes, A. 1998. "Social Capital: Its Origins and Applications in Modern Sociology." *Annual Review of Sociology* 24: 1–24.

Portes, A., and P. Fernandez-Kelly. 2008. "No Margin for Error: Educational and Occupational Achievement Among Disadvantaged Children of Immigrants." *The Annals of American Academy of Political and Social Science* 620 (1): 12–36.

Ream, R. K., and R. W. Rumberger. 2008. "Student Engagement, Peer Social Capital, and School Dropout among Mexican American and Non-Latino White Students." *Sociology of Education* 81 (2): 109–139.

Reardon, S. F. 2011. "The Widening Academic Achievement Gap Between the Rich and the Poor: New Evidence and Possible Explanations." In *Whither Opportunity: Rising Inequality, Schools and Children's Life Chances,* edited by G. J. Duncan and R. Murnane, 91–116. New York: Russell Sage Foundation.

Reese, C., T. Pederson, S. Avila, K. Joseph, K. Nagy, A. Dennis . . . F. Bokhari. 2012. "Screening for Traumatic Stress Among Survivors of Urban Trauma." *Journal of Trauma-Injury, Infection, and Critical Care* 73 (2): 462–468.

Rendón, M. G. 2014. "Drop Out and 'Disconnected' Young Adults: Examining the Impact of Neighborhood and School Contexts." *The Urban Review* 46 (2): 169–196.

Rendón, M. G. Forthcoming. "The Urban Question and Identity Formation: The Case of Second Generation Mexican Males in Los Angeles." *Ethnicities* 15 (2).

Rumberger, R. W. 1991. "Chicano Dropouts: Research and Policy Issues." In *Chicano School Failure and Success: Research and Policy Agendas for the 1990s,* edited by R. R. Valencia, 64–89. New York: Falmer Press.

Rumberger, R. W. 2004. "Why Students Drop Out of School." In *Dropouts in America: Confronting the Graduation Rate Crisis,* edited by G. Orfied, 131–155. Cambridge, MA: Harvard Education Press.

Rumberger, R. W. 2011. Dropping Out: Why Students Drop Out of High School and What Can Be Done About It. Cambridge, MA: Harvard University Press.

Sampson, R. J., J. D. Morenoff, and T. Gannon-Rowley. 2002. "Assessing 'Neighborhood Effects': Social Processes and New Directions in Research." *Annual Review of Sociology* 28: 443–478.

Sampson, R. J., S. W. Raudenbush, and F. Earls. 1997. "Neighborhoods and Violent Crime: A Multilevel Study of Collective Efficacy." *Science* 277 (5328): 918–924.

Sharkey, P. 2010. "The Acute Effect of Local Homicides on Children's Cognitive Performance." *Proceedings of the National Academy of Sciences* 107: 11733–11738.

Small, M. L., and J. Feldman. 2012. "Ethnographic Evidence, Heterogeneity, and Neigbourhood Effects After Moving to Opportunity." In *Neighborhood Effects Research: New Perspectives,* edited by M. Van Ham, D. Manley, N. Bailey, L. Simpson, and D. Maclennan, 57–77. Dordrecht: Springer.

Stanton-Salazar, R. 2001. *Manufacturing Hope and Despair: The School and Kin Support Networks of U.S.-Mexican Youth.* New York: Teachers College Press.

Swidler, A. 1986. "Culture in Action: Symbols and Strategies." *American Sociological Review* 51 (2): 273–286.

Valencia, R. R., ed. 2002. *Chicano School Failure and Success: Past, Present, and Future.* New York: Falmer Press.

Valenzuela, A. 1999. *Subtractive Schooling: U.S.-Mexican Youth and the Politics of Caring.* New York: State University of New York Press.

Venkatesh, S. A. 1997. "The Social Organization of Street Gang Activity in an Urban Ghetto." *The American Journal of Sociology* 103 (1): 82–111.

Warikoo, N. 2011. *Balancing Acts: Youth Culture in the Global City.* Berkeley: University of California Press.

Wilson, W. J. 1987. *The Truly Disadvantaged: The Inner City, the Underclass, and Public Policy.* Chicago: University of Chicago Press.

Wodtke, G. T., D. J. Harding, and F. Elwert. 2011. "Neighborhood Effects in Temporal Perspective: The Impact of Long-Term Exposure to Concentrated Disadvantage on High School Graduation." *Americal Sociological Review* 76 (5): 713–736.

Appendix

Table 4.1 Racial and Ethnic Composition of Neighborhoods, 2000 Census

	Latino(%)	Mexican Origin(%)	Other Latinos (%)	Non-Latino White(%)	Black (%)	Other (%)
Mexican Neighborhood: Pueblo Viejo	92.3	76.3	16	2	1.5	4.2
Black-Latino Neighborhood: Central City	52.4	32.4	20	1	45.4	1.2
Los Angeles County	44.6	32	13	31.1	9.8	14.5

Table 4.2 Social Characteristics of Residents by Neighborhood, 2000

	Female-Headed Household, No Husband (%)	Males 16+, Not in Labor Force (%)	Males 16+, Unemployment (%)	Median Household ($)	Individuals Below Poverty (%)
Los Angeles County	21	32	8	42,189	18
Latinos	22	32	9	33,820	24
African-Americans	47	40	16	31,905	24
Pueblo Viejo	30	43	12	22,429	37
Latinos	30	41	11	22,942	37
Central City	40	41	14	22,091	37
Latinos	22	32	11	26,031	37
African-Americans	57	53	19	19,065	38

Part III

Gender, Self-Identity, and the Cultivation of Sociopolitical Resistance

5 Beyond "Warming Up" and "Cooling Out"

The Effects of Community College on a Diverse Group of Disadvantaged Young Women

Kelly Nielsen

The schooling environment is often hostile to the success of nondominant students. Collective narratives of appropriate development and beliefs about good and bad student qualities serve to marginalize their experiences and categorize them as incapable, non-intellectual, and generally unsuited for higher education. Many poor and minority students develop learner identities and aspirations while embedded in school contexts where learning is associated with busywork; students are described in deficit terms, and low expectations are widespread (Foley 1990; Oseguera, Conchas, and Mosqueda 2011; Rubin 2007). In these settings, academic success is largely predicated on facility with cultural interactions shaped by race, class, and gender in ways that disadvantage poor and minority students (Bourdieu 1977; Heath 1982; Khan 2011; Lee 1995; Mullen 2011). By comparison, when students are deeply embedded in academic contexts that scaffold and support their experiences and ambitions, schooling can be transformative in a positive sense by expanding students' capabilities, raising their aspirations, and shifting the conceptions they have of themselves and others (Armstrong and Hamilton 2012; Conchas 2001; Mehan 2012). Research on both secondary and four-year college and university students has shown the many similar ways that these institutions impact both positively and negatively the lives of disadvantaged students. To what extent, if at all, do community colleges differ from these two tiers of American education?

Research has shown that community colleges are, in many respects, unlike either secondary or four-year institutions. Community colleges are ambiguously located between them as a consequence of the institution's various roles as "a doorway to educational opportunity, a vendor of vocational training, a protector of university selectivity, and a defender of state higher education budgets" (Dougherty 1994, 8). How do students respond to this ambiguous and contradictory institution? This chapter examines how 23 low-income women attending community college developed educational and occupational trajectories and identities over a three-and-a-half-year period. Scholars have largely focused on the extent to which community college students divert their aspirations from transfer to four-year institutions or unrealistically elevate them beyond vocational programs and degrees. In contrast to the binary framework of student transformation employed in much of the scholarly research on community colleges, the results of this study suggest four possible paradigms of student experience developed in the broader education literature that are well-suited for studying community college students' experiences. I refer to these models as (1) competing pathways, (2) institutional agents, (3) status competition, and (4) figured worlds. At the same time, I go beyond applying preestablished frameworks by focusing on the narratives that students generate to explain their experiences and formulate pathways through college. I argue that how disadvantaged students' experiences in community college align with these models is contingent upon the narratives that they form prior to, and outside of, community college. This is due to the fact that disadvantaged students are more loosely embedded in the community college environment compared to their four-year college and university peers. Rather than providing the strong cultural frameworks for self-making that many four-year institutions provide, community colleges act as key sites for the intersection of narratives developed in other aspects of students' lives, such as work, family, and community.

By drawing on these four paradigms of student experience, scholars can connect more directly to the large body of education literature to understand the effects of community colleges. Moreover, through attention to students' narratives and their lives outside of school, research can sketch out the boundaries of community colleges' influence, given their central role as institutions of social mobility and the high expectations that scholars and policymakers hold for them. The following section first considers the relationship between community colleges and the other tiers of American education before briefly outlining the dominant framework for understanding the experiences of community college students. Next, I propose an alternative framework that draws on concepts employed in the broader field of sociology of education. I then discuss the role of narrative in explaining variation in student experience. After, I present the data and methods, followed by a discussion of four representative cases. The chapter concludes with an emphasis on reevaluating the role that community colleges can be expected to play in the lives of disadvantaged students.

REVIEW OF LITERATURE AND THEORY

Community colleges have grown tremendously over the past half century; whereas four-year college and university enrollments have doubled since the mid-1960s, community college enrollments have expanded at twice that rate (Deil-Amen 2011). At the end of the twentieth century, approximately half of the students in public colleges and universities were enrolled in community colleges (Roksa et al. 2007). This growth has been characterized by the overrepresentation of poor and minority students in community colleges, which tends to reflect the socioeconomic and racial makeup of the communities they serve, creating segregated schools that mirror neighborhood segregation (Goldrick-Rab and Kinsley 2013). As a result, studying community colleges provides a critical entry point into the study of on-going segregation and inequality in American communities.

Since Clark (1960) argued that community colleges "cool out" student ambitions, diverting them away from transfer to four-year institutions, the debate over the role of the community college has swirled around the cooling out function (Brint and Karabel 1989; Dougherty 1994; Deil-Amen and Rosenbaum 2002; Alexander, Bozick, and Entwisle 2008). For the most part, scholars have clung to a narrative that community colleges either divert the dreams of ambitious, working-class young adults motivated by the democratic promise and economic necessity of postsecondary education (Brint and Karabel 1989) or else "students are promised college for very little effort" (Rosenbaum 1998, 56) so that their ambitions warm up, at least temporarily, which only delays recognition of a more suitable pathway (Deil-Amen and Rosenbaum 2002). Focusing on the production of skills and labor market returns to community college attendance, sociologists have largely ignored how college students' experiences move through and ultimately use this large and complex system (Bahr 2011).

If scholars are concerned with the democratic consequences of community college and hope to understand the effects of community colleges on students' lives, they must examine the way that community colleges are incorporated into students' understandings of who they are, as well as where they are headed and how they get there. This means moving beyond the binary framework of warming up and cooling out, which developed as a result of community colleges' ambiguous institutional location between secondary schools and four-year colleges and universities. As this study developed, I saw that students did not conform neatly to either warming up or cooling out. Whereas many students' aspirations changed, the reasons were often more complex than previous community college research would expect. Moreover, warming up and cooling out did not explain the experiences of students whose aspirations remained stable while their self-understandings and worldviews changed during their time in community college. Drawing on research across the secondary and postsecondary literatures, I identified four alternative ways that scholars have understood the experiences of students that can be applied more specifically to community college students. These are the competing pathways, institutional agents, status competition, and figured worlds approaches. Each casts a different light on student experiences, and by incorporating these concepts into the study of community colleges this chapter generates an important link with the much larger secondary and postsecondary research agendas.

First, the *competing pathways* approach argues that schools provide one cultural model of attainment among a range of competing images of success and available opportunities for disadvantaged students, such as professional athletics, gangs, or family businesses (Armstrong and Hamilton 2012; Collins 2009; Harding 2011; Lee 1994; Lew 2010; MacLeod 1995; Mehan 2012; Ogbu 1987; Willis 1977). In contexts where students must navigate multiple, legitimate models of attainment, community colleges may have limited sway over students' ambitions and sense of self. Second, the *institutional agents* approach argues that individuals who occupy high-status positions can transmit, or facilitate the transmission of, resources to students, such as distinct discourses, academic support, advice or guidance, and role modeling (Collins 2009; Stanton-Salazar 2011). In this case, individual actors may have a decisive influence over students' aspirations and the development of an academic and occupational identity, even in contexts where students are generally marginalized. Third, the *status competition* approach argues that students pursue postsecondary credentials in response to power imbalances between social groups and for access to particular occupations (Collins 1979; Khan 2011; Schleef 2000). Students engaged in status seeking through higher education may believe that they do not need to go to college in order to technically do the kind of work they are pursuing, or to become a more capable person. Nevertheless, they recognize the necessity of attaining a degree for access to particular jobs and membership in specific groups. Finally, the *figured worlds* approach argues that colleges are sites where new self-conceptions and ways of acting can emerge and take hold through links between broadly shared discourses and personal experiences (Binder and Wood 2013; Cech, Rubineau, Silbey, and Seron 2011; Kaufman and Feldman 2004; Rose 2012; Urrietta 2007). The particular way in which students are embedded in schooling environments is critical for explaining the transformative effects of schools. Organizational features such as class sizes, housing arrangements, campus traditions, and support programs structure the interaction between widespread cultural forms, shared understandings about particular schools, and personal beliefs about students' present and future lives. For disadvantaged students, academic contexts that incorporate student experiences, community problems, and the collective histories of marginalized groups can affect how students understand themselves and others. These four categories represent ideal-typical pathways through the intersecting terrain of institutional narratives of educational and occupational attainment and individual biographies. In order to make sense of this intersection, however, it is necessary to understand how the community college functions as a meeting point, or hub, for different stories.

NARRATIVES, NARRATIVE FRAMEWORKS, AND NARRATIVE HUBS

An enduring aim of public education has been the provision of a common cultural heritage. In addition to this cultural heritage, schools provide narratives, in part, through their organization and the correlations between the degrees they offer and the occupation and lifestyle degrees holders have. In this way, students with distinct biographies can partake in historical narratives of advancement and democratic citizenship (Brint and Karabel 1989). At the same time, particular pathways promote expectations about the people they are meant to serve, which can be understood in narrative terms as the plots, characters, and key events of a given trajectory (Armstrong and Hamilton 2012; Somers 1994). In particular, sociologists of education have focused on the way that schools have promoted the achievement ideology—the belief that if students work hard they will get ahead, and are to blame for their own failures (MacLeod 1995; Mehan 1992; Turner 1960)—and shown how schools have managed to alter marginalized students' personal narratives to fit within dominant, oppressive ones. In cases where students develop counternarratives to discourses that erase their experiences and the experiences of others like them, gatekeepers such as teachers have the power to silence them through the "terms of their inclusion" in mainstream settings (Collins 2009, 4), or else students may develop alternative frameworks of success and cultural belonging (Carter 2006; Delpit 1988; Lee 1994; Ogbu 1987; Willis 1977). However, schools can also provide the institutionalized pathways for students to imagine alternative futures and identities. Marginalized students can and do hold multiple, often competing, narratives about themselves and their future opportunities, what O'Connor (1999) refers to as co-narratives. Often, particular individuals, classes, or programs support co-narration. As a consequence, disempowered learners "must find a way . . . to synthesize the best of what the school teaches and what they know from their life experiences" within institutions that did not have them in mind when they were formed (Collins 2009, 10).

How do narratives of educational and occupational trajectories interact with narratives that take other institutional realms, such as the family or the community, as their focus? I argue that community colleges operate as hubs for student narrative frameworks.[1] This emphasizes both the narrative material that students bring and the variable ways that this material is linked and understood through the schools and the narratives that they provide. At the same time, it recognizes the priority of schooling in the lives of many students and their families. The expansion of higher education systems and the rising wage premiums to postsecondary credentials since the 1980s have made the belief in the necessity of a college education commonplace (Goldin and Katz 2008; Grubb and Lazerson 2005). For many students, the alternative to community college is the low-wage workforce, which provides few opportunities for imagining a future, or welfare programs that place constraints on recipients' abilities to imagine anything beyond entry into the low-wage workforce.

Narratives are central to identities and trajectories. Personal biographies are linked to collective stories, and their extension in time facilitates sense making about the past and imaging the future. In this way, narratives carry students' lives from outside the school through higher education to the future of work, family, and democratic citizenry. By taking narratives as a key component of how community colleges affect poor and minority students, researchers are better able to account for students' lives both outside and within the community college. The specific form that students' experiences take—competing pathways, institutional agents, status competition, or figured worlds—is determined by the way community colleges function as narrative hubs. To understand how student experiences vary in community college, I ask how community college students narrate their trajectories through school. How do community college students incorporate collective narratives into personal biography? And how does this process of incorporation lead to distinct experiences in community college?

DATA AND METHODS

Data for this study consists of four waves of in-depth, semi-structured interviews with 23 poor and working-class young adult women[2] in a large metropolitan area of Southern California for a total of 92 interviews (Solórzano, Datnow, Park, and Watford 2013).[3] Participation in the study was based on eligibility for income-based support to attend community college in California. Support for low-income students included CalWORKS, a program to support welfare recipients attending school, and a state-sponsored fee waiver from the California Community Colleges Board of Governors, commonly referred to as the BOG waiver. Of the 23 women in the study, 13 had one or more children and three reported being married in September, 2010. The women represented a range of racial and ethnic backgrounds: nine Latinas (39%), seven Black women (30%), three White women (13%), two Asian American women (9%), and two women who identified as multiracial (9%). They averaged 23 years of age at the first interview and 25 years of age at the fourth interview. The ages of the women ranged from 18 to 29 years old at the start of the study and 22 to 31 years old at the last interview. At the outset of the study, 18 of the 23 women (78%) said they planned to transfer to a four-year university, and by the final interview, all but two of the women (91%) reported that they would ideally like to earn a bachelor's degree or more. However, only seven (30%) had transferred to a four-year university by the fourth interview.

The women were initially recruited from three community colleges that were part of the Southeastern Metro Community College (SMCC) district. Together, the three colleges are part of the largest community college system in the nation, which consists of 112 colleges. The student population of the district is approximately 40% Latina/o, 30% White, 11% African American, and 5% Asian American. The completion rate for the 2005–2008 cohort—the percentage of students who attained a certificate or degree or became "transfer prepared" during the three-year period—was 21.93%, and the transfer rate for the 2002–2003 cohort showed that 28% of first-time students showing intent to complete subsequently transferred to a four-year university within six years. Among the SMCC student body, Latino and African American students are underrepresented in the population of transfers to four-year institutions.

The interviews were conducted over a three-and-a-half-year period from September, 2010 to March, 2014. Each interview was conducted in person by one of four researchers, and the author conducted 56 interviews in total. Interviews lasted from one-and-a-half to three-and-a-half hours and took place in a location chosen by the respondent. The researchers inquired about their life history, social networks, and school experiences, along with their perceptions of opportunity, sense of barriers and oppression, and hopes for the future. They were particularly interested in understanding how students had come to enroll at the community college and their educational and occupational trajectories. By asking for specific examples, interviews can access narrative reasoning (i.e., the meanings behind the frameworks they describe and the actions they frame) (Pugh 2013), and the longitudinal nature of the study allowed us to examine how narratives developed and the extent to which action and narrative were linked. Multiple interviews allowed for reflexivity and revision, but also indicated how identities can resist instability and insecurity.

Interviews were digitally recorded and transcribed. I focused on identifying the use of stories to describe particular episodes or critical junctures. These were the personal stories that students used to elaborate their understanding of particular moments within a longer story arc. I also looked for broad narrative patterns in students' trajectories and identity formation over time, such as a deepening attachment to an educational identity. Finally, I identified collective narratives that the women drew upon to make sense of themselves and their trajectories, such as narratives about the role of post-secondary credentials in socioeconomic mobility. In subsequent analysis, I looked for the intersections of personal and collective narratives, as well as the intersection of school and non-school narratives. I considered these intersections in relation to their attachments to community college, or the extent to which they were embedded in the community college environment, educational and occupational trajectories, and aspects of identity that were separate from concerns about occupational attainment. Throughout the discussion of findings I refer to narrative frameworks and narrative hubs to refer to the way students tell life stories within the narrower context of schooling and the way that stories from different areas of students' lives intersect in the context of the college.

FINDINGS

I turn now to the stories that students bring with them, how they intersect with their experience in community college, and their combined effects on the way they talk about their future and their selves. Out of the 23 women I interviewed, I analyze four women's stories in order to examine in greater detail their experiences over time and show how they fit within the expanded framework I have presented. Each case was selected for analysis because it exemplifies the experience of competing pathways, institutional agents, status competition, or figured worlds. At the same time, each of the women discussed below shares experiences with other women in the study. The four women—June, Monica, Rachel, and Nancy—were also similar in several ways. First, each said that they were academically capable of attending a four-year institution at the end of high school. Moreover, each progressed academically throughout the study, with three of the four women eventually transferring to local universities. All four women arrived at the community college with relatively clear academic and occupational goals in mind: two had plans to transfer and two were aiming for associate degrees. Also, each woman initially described weak attachments to SMCC, which meant limited involvement in the life of the school, few peer relationships, and limited interaction with institutional actors. Overall, they held largely instrumental attitudes toward community college. Finally, they were close in age, the youngest being 19 years old at the start and the oldest being 25 years old. One important difference, however, is that two of the women were single parents. Whereas parenthood has been shown to strongly affect the world-views of working-class women (Silva 2013), here it serves to emphasize the importance of non-school aspects of the students' lives.

Competing Pathways

College is often only one cultural model of attainment that students have available to them. For several of the students in this study, already weak ties to SMCC became weaker or were severed entirely over time as narrative frameworks developed. One reason is that these students did not form narratives that linked educational and occupational trajectories, or they developed competing narratives to ones that emphasize degree attainment, which made leaving SMCC a plausible option. One student with multiple, conflicting narrative frameworks was June, a Korean American woman who was 19 years old at the start of the study. She explained her attendance at SMCC as a consequence of several missteps on the way to enrolling at a nearby California State University after high school. In the process, she reflected on the relative status of the community college, saying, "to me, UC is top notch. Cal State is eh, ok. SMCC is like bad, bad, bad . . . So I was like, 'ok, I'm going here but I'm smart . . . I'm not like these people'". Knowing she was qualified to attend a four-year university, June worked hard to craft a coherent narrative about her educational trajectory. Over time, she "met other people that were really educated", but couldn't afford to attend a four-year university. These examples helped her reframe community college as an alternative pathway for smart but disadvantaged students. Eventually, she developed a fragile understanding of her unsuccessful transition to a four-year university and subsequent attendance at SMCC. During the second interview, she explained that by enrolling at the community college she could save both time and money while pursuing a nursing degree. Nevertheless, she often felt like school was "such a waste of time".

June's educational trajectory was made more tenuous by her ambivalence about her career goals and the role of credentials in the labor market. The idea to become a nurse stemmed from the example of her sister, who was pursuing a nursing degree at a local for-profit school, and reinforced by the experience of her father's kidney transplant. Yet, nursing was a recent goal, and prior to choosing it as a possible career she hadn't planned on having a job. She explained, "I think for the longest time when I was younger I wanted to be a house mom because I saw my mom as a house mom, and watching Korean dramas all the wives are house moms. So I'm like, ok, I want to be a house mom".[4] By the third interview, she was still pursuing nursing at the community college, but was learning more about nursing from her sister who had started working as a nursing assistant. Her sister described the patients as "rude" and detailed the hard work of patient care, to which June responded, "I'm not patient like that. I'll slap her [the patient] in the face if she bugs me (laughing) . . . and I don't even like touching my own poop; how would I be able to touch someone else's"? She explained that she was "really scared", then added, "I can do it because I like helping old people. I love my grandparents so if I'm put in the position I'll be able to do it". Although she relied on a repertoire of helping others through the lower rungs of the healthcare industry to explain her motivation, her expressed desire to help others appeared largely as the presentation of an honorable self.

Central to her decision to pursue nursing was her understanding of the broader economy and the specific labor markets for occupations. During the first interview, she said her favorite class was sociology, where she learned about the precariousness of low-status work. This knowledge helped frame popular and personal narratives that suggest the value of a college degree is declining. Popular narratives included teachers being unable to get jobs and Harvard graduates becoming "bums". Personal narratives included a story of a co-worker's daughter who was long-term unemployed after a two-year vocational program. By contrast, nurses were "guaranteed" jobs right out of nursing programs. She concluded, "if I want to do something else, I won't get a job. So I'm just stuck with nursing". The fear of nursing as a difficult job outweighed the fear of doing something else. In addition, June believed that nursing would allow her to "make a lot of money, go travel everywhere", and work part time. By narratively framing nursing as a "good job" that would allow her to work as little as possible and still provide her with the future life she imagines for herself, she was able to persist for over a year despite her general dislike of school and distaste for the perceived hardships of the job. In this way she is like other students who pursued nursing based on expectations about future work opportunities garnered from widely available beliefs about the profession, although she was often ambivalent about her choice and open to alternative narratives of mobility.

June often turned to the example of her immigrant parents, who she described as successful entrepreneurs—her dad in landscaping and real estate, her mom selling Amway cosmetic products. Detailing their rise from poor immigrants to self-employed business people, June drew on their stories to valorize trajectories outside of college. She described her mother's immigration story to the United States from Korea as a young adult who "didn't graduate any college or anything" but who nevertheless succeeded. Moreover, she was "learning biology and chemistry" as she learned about beauty products, suggesting that people who left school did not have to give up learning more academic bodies of knowledge. Through her mother's example and encouragement, June considered the Amway business, saying, "I want a job like that, and a nursing job isn't like that . . . I could become really big and people will be working under me and then I'll just be staying home and just making money, which is what I want to do". As Lew (2010) found in a study of poor Korean American youths, ethnic networks can affect youths in contradictory ways in terms of their schooling and career choices. Whereas June's parents encouraged her to go to college and complete a college degree, her mother also encouraged her explicitly and implicitly to follow a more entrepreneurial path.

June noted that her mom had "been reading a lot of those books and speeches from Obama, people who started low who built their way up top". She added that her mother "always brags about how Oprah started out in the ghettos and then raised up to the top. She tells me, 'oh you could be like that too just if you try'". Using Steve Jobs as an example, June affirmed that it was possible to forego college and still be successful, while also resenting the degree requirements for jobs that were still out of reach. She complained that reliance on social networks in the hiring process meant that qualified applicants without ties are overlooked. She asked, "so why study? Why go through all that money to study and apply for jobs when people who have friends in the corporation already have the upper hand to get hired"? These narratives reinforced her understanding of how education intersects with the labor market to diminish the value of a college education.

These anxieties over the labor market, the value of college degrees, and upper-middle-class status attainment are similar to the anxieties that motivate middle-class students to pursue professional degrees. However, for disadvantaged students heterogeneous and conflicting narrative frameworks mean that professional degree attainment is not necessarily viewed as the most appropriate or inevitable trajectory. By the fourth interview, June had left the community college to work with her mother as an Amway representative. The stories, people, and information that she used to construct a narrative framework came from outside of the community college. Already weak attachments to school and the community college were completely undone by the intersection of popular and personal narratives that offered competing pathways.

Institutional Agents

Student trajectories may be shaped in important ways by institutional actors who share resources with students. For some of the women in this study, tenuous ties to the community college were balanced by the recognition that a college education is an unavoidable piece of their imagined future. However, there was a consistent uncertainty about how much and what kind of education was required or even desirable. In these cases, the presence of institutional agents that provided new frameworks of attainment was central to their transformation as a result of attending community college.

One example is Monica, a single Latina mother in her early 20s pursuing a career in criminal justice. Monica believed that college was an essential step toward a particular career path and quality of life, and over time her ideas about education and career were transformed by the community college. Beginning in high school, she decided she wanted to work in criminal justice. Specifically, she wanted to become a probation officer, after being sent to a military high school for a short time. She explained her early career choice as a consequence of television images of law enforcement, as well as the example set by a woman in a role similar to that of a probation officer at the military academy, saying, "seeing everything she did, how she interacted with the kids . . . once I met her, I decided I wanted to be a probation officer". Her difficulties in high school were compounded when she got pregnant and gave birth at 17.

Together, these challenges did not prevent her from graduating with her class, but they did interrupt her plans to enroll in a four-year university, much as June's trajectory was redirected toward the community college. She said, "I hate going to SMCC. It's so depressing, like ahh! I go to a community college". Upon graduating, Monica's goal was to get an associate degree in a field that would prepare her for some kind of criminal justice-related job. Although she originally wanted to be a probation officer, by the second interview she had begun to consider alternatives. Here, she explains her thought process and the role of an influential professor:

> MONICA: Well before I wanted to do clerical stuff, right. I was okay with something like an associates, just helping out with the probation officer, something clerical but simple, like you didn't need much, and now it is like I still want to do paperwork stuff, but more into that, so maybe like writing the DA's reports . . . well after the police officers turn in their police reports . . . someone else goes through them and corrects them, files them, and gives them to the county, and stuff like that, and so it's still paperwork, but . . . obviously higher education is required.

INTERVIEWER: How do you know that, about correcting police reports?

MONICA: Because in my administration of justice class my professor . . . was the chief of police for like 20-something years . . . and then he was a police officer for Southeastern Metro Police Department for I don't know how many years, and he was like lieutenant I don't know what, was all these whatever crap, and I would ask him random stuff, like what do you do with the guns you find, and the drugs you find, and . . . I'd just be watching Law and Order . . . and I would just e-mail him.

She shows how her personal story intersects with the story of a professor and popular narratives in the media, which open the way for her to raise her aspirations. Later, she described how becoming a probation officer was also less ideal now that she had been in school for over a year, particularly in light of the fact that she didn't have any debt from attending community college. Reflecting on her changing ambitions, she said, "I find this really weird, but the more I study, the more I want. Like before I just wanted, you know, just an associates, just a probation officer, and now I am looking at the job description, at the salary, at what it is, and it's like, why would I settle for this when I can do this"? When Monica later explained how her view of her future had changed since starting college, she referred to her changing ideas about working in the field of criminal justice. This time, however, she described what she imagined her life as a probation officer would look like, including details about the hours and interactions with parolees. Moreover, she combined these details with a story about a local police department that she learned had reduced the number of probation officers to deal with budget cuts, all of which came from her criminal justice teacher.

Key to this transformation is the filling out of an imagined future with details about the job. The narrative of becoming a probation officer becomes less desirable as she imagines being on call, tracking down parolees, managing expanding caseloads, and being exposed to the negative effects of budget cuts. By the third interview, Monica had taken several classes with the same administration of justice teacher, had been accepted to a local state university, and was starting to imagine not just a bachelor's degree but even a doctorate in criminal justice. This imagined future took shape in relation to her experience with this particular teacher who told exciting stories of his own experience as a police chief and combined a display of intelligence with the appearance of understanding students on a personal level. As she explained, "he reads you, he looks at you and he can tell you your whole life story". She further remarked, "he didn't even go to law school but he's just so education smart. I just admired him so much and then I was like, I want to do that".

The importance of this example of educational and occupational success is underscored by the lack of other models in her day-to-day life and the absence of support for her goals. For instance, the trajectory that she imagines through the stories and example of her teacher contrast sharply with the expectations of her family. After looking unsuccessfully for a job, her parents mocked her aspirations. She recalled, "I know that if I go in and apply at McDonalds or Del Taco, or something like that . . . they'd probably hire me when they start hiring 'cause they hire everybody. But I don't want to do it, and . . . my mom and my dad are like, 'oh, well, what do you want to do? You want to work for President Obama'"? She described her parents as "talking so much shit", and their seeming inability or unwillingness to adopt her narrative of future success contrasts sharply with her teacher's perceptive reading of her "like a book". When strong attachments are forged with particular institutional actors, it is largely because students' stories are incorporated into interactions that are otherwise highly routinized, short, and impersonal.

Rather than take a low-wage service job, Monica preferred to do something that would start her toward developing the disposition required to work in criminal justice. Although she was starting to consider extending her education beyond a bachelor's degree and began to express interests that drew more on the liberal arts aspects of college than the occupational, she also pointed to the limits of education in helping her achieve her career goals. After recounting a story about an acquaintance who works as a parole officer, she concluded that "education's not everything . . . I mean, I know it must be something big, but at the same time I know that experience being around, and especially that type of environment, you could have the highest degree possible, but it's not the same as if you've been around something like that". Believing that a college degree, even a doctorate, is "just to get your foot in the door", Monica considered a volunteer opportunity with a rape crisis hotline she learned about at a local coffee shop. In her mind, surrounding herself "with a lot of those pessimistic stories" would help her "later in the future to relate to it". Unlike June, however, Monica did not abandon the college narrative.

The community college and, in particular, her criminal justice courses served as a narrative hub where she brought together aspirations and experiences with family, work, and school. Over time, new people and new episodes transform a narrative that runs from a military high school to an eventual doctorate. The early experience with a probation officer and an interest in crime dramas established a trajectory from which Monica was able to develop an occupational and educational identity. Most importantly, the presence of an institutional agent during her time in community college was a critical resource for Monica that facilitated the narrative framing of her life's course, which included higher levels of education and specific work experiences.

Status Competition

Power imbalances between social groups and stratified access to occupations may lead some students to pursue postsecondary credentials as status signals. The previous two models of student transformation have shown how the community college was an important narrative hub for either deterioration or strengthening attachments to the institution. However, many students experience little change in their trajectories, persisting toward more or less defined ends in spite of the ups and downs of college. For example, Rachel, a Black woman in her early 20s, expressed ambivalence about credentials and skepticism toward the uniqueness of the intellectual environment of colleges and universities. Nevertheless, she earned an associate degree and transferred to a private university where she was near completion of a bachelor's degree in psychology when we last spoke. Her persistence can be explained by her recognition of the status that attaches to postsecondary credentials, particularly in a context of widespread, negative stereotypes about Black women.

Like Monica, Rachel's career goals emerged from an unstable childhood that included periods of homelessness, addiction, and abandonment. And like both Monica and June, community college was "plan b" for Rachel, framed by the negative attitudes toward community college she formed in high school as a result of popular beliefs about the relative status of the institution. Nevertheless, she was committed to enrolling because she initially believed that it would help her achieve the goal she set for herself at 13 to open up a non-profit chain of family outreach centers.

Unlike June, who was pursuing nursing largely for financial reasons and material gain while relying on repertoires about helping others as a way to frame the work as meaningful in itself, Rachel placed helping others at the center of her aspirations: "I don't have to have a huge car . . . I don't have to have the best job in the world. At the same time I'm not going . . . to stop at minimum wage doing something with no progress. I'm helping the people above me? No, I need to be helping the people that were me". She believed education would provide her both the skills and the status to help others.

Through her own story of "surviving" a difficult upbringing, she developed an academic and occupational path that she believed would allow her to help other people arrive at "a better understanding of themselves and why they're in the predicament that they're in". Unlike women whose career goals necessitated degree attainment, however, Rachel's aims were less structured around credentials. As she explained,

> yes the degree looks nice, yes in the real world you have a degree, okay we might be able to work with you. I just want to be able to get the knowledge, learn how do I do this, how do I speak to someone who has been through something different but worse than what I've gone through; how do I deal with a child that's running off of learned behavior that's gonna send them to jail one day if they don't change it; how do I start this nonprofit so that I can help these people and convince them, you know not convince them but give them the resources to help themselves. I just want the education so I can retain it and apply it to my life and help others.

She could, conceivably, do the work she imagined without completing a degree. By the second interview, Rachel was considering leaving the community college because she didn't "feel like you have to go to college to be successful". Moreover, she not only believed she would still be able to pursue her goal but that leaving school might free her up to focus more intently on it. Similar to June, she acknowledged, "not everybody has a degree who opens up anything". She explained the problem with following the college trajectory, saying, "I'm so tied up with school in addition to working full time just because I have to support myself some way". It is possible that, without the added burden of full-time work, Rachel might have felt less willing to leave school to focus on her career goals. But this does not alter her perception, similar to June's, that school was only one possibility in the overall plot guiding her decision making. In other words, it would be a "different route" to the "same goal". She did not deny that there were specific skills involved in the kind of work that she wanted to do, only that she could acquire them outside the structure of the college.

Yet, Rachel persisted and transferred to a four-year university to complete a degree in psychology. She returned to the framework of helping others, saying, "I want to be able to help people who were in my position and were helpless because at one point that was me . . . I'm using that thought process to push me forward to saying ok let me get myself to the point where I can help somebody". Importantly, the point where she could help others was also where she could help herself transcend constraints placed on her and other members of marginalized groups. Specifically, Rachel saw college as a way to combat images of Black women through her own success:

> when I even look at my own people, my own race of people, sometimes I have to put my head down because to see where we started in Africa and all the accomplishments we made that nobody knows about . . . And to see where we are today, not an ounce of that history can be seen, not an ounce. And every day when I get up and I strive it's because I want to be who I know I'm supposed to be, not who society dictates. Because if I am to become who society says that I'm supposed to be, then I'm gonna be that low-income Black mother with a bunch of illegitimate children . . . And so yes, when I wake up in the morning I get up because not only am I gonna be a successful Black woman, I'm gonna be a successful woman, I'm gonna be a successful young woman. So many things going against me, you know what I mean? It's one thing to be a man. It's one thing to be a Black man. It's one thing to be a woman, and then to be a Black woman.

In this reflection on the relationship between her academic trajectory and her accomplishment of a successful, Black female identity, Rachel draws on historical narratives of Black achievement, popular narratives of Black female lives, and her personal biography of growing up in poor, Black neighborhoods.

College acts as a narrative hub through which she is able to challenge status hierarchies.

Despite the turn to a discourse that minimized the role and value of a college education, she not only saw the study of psychology as a way to better help others but also believed that getting an education beyond an associate degree at the community college would allow her "to have a more complex job" that, she says, would put her "in a position to help a little bit more people in a different type of way". Like Monica, she frames education as a source of greater authority and a foot in the door. For Rachel, however, her experience with postsecondary education did not move her from her original dream of opening a community center for disadvantaged families. Instead, community college served as one step toward the status she would need to achieve her goals.

Figured Worlds

Colleges are often sites where new self-conceptions emerge as new links are forged between collective discourses and personal biographies. Like Rachel, many of the women in this study reported seeking and/or learning skills that they believed would get them a job when they graduated. But some of the students at the community college also referred to less tangible critical thinking and analysis skills that allowed them to develop a sense of themselves as knowledgeable and intellectually capable adults. Students also emphasized that they had changed their attitudes toward themselves and others, which in turn affected how they approached their education, their career choices, and other aspects of their lives. Nancy, a Chicana mother of two young boys, had enrolled at the University of California, Riverside upon graduation from high school, but dropped out after a year because, she says, she felt directionless. She soon got married and had two children, but was separated from her husband a few years later. Living alone with her two boys, she entered community college with a clear academic and career trajectory. She developed her goal of becoming a speech and language pathologist in the course of caring for her severely disabled son, who required intensive speech and language services, among others. As her son reached school age, she found herself in regular conflict with her son's school as she agitated for increased attention and support. Through these experiences she says she learned to advocate for herself and others, and saw her career path as one of advocacy on behalf of Spanish speakers in need of speech and language services.

Bringing this narrative of transformation and community uplift with her, she came to see herself differently as a result of being in community college. She said, "I'm a strong person, stronger than I give myself credit. I used to be like, how do people do it, and once you get in the habit of doing things, like I call people's bullshit out all the time, I've changed completely . . . I say it how it is . . . I've learned that from school". As a low-income single mother of two children, Nancy sought out as much support from the community college as possible. This included enrolling in the Puente program—a counseling, mentoring, and writing program aimed at increasing the number of transfer students to four-year institutions. Through Puente, she discovered and enrolled in Chicano literature courses. Additionally, she took a work-study job in the college counseling office where she found herself helping other in-need students. Over time she felt a greater sense of herself as an intellectual and independent actor: "I'll call myself an intellectual . . . I'm a go-getter. I feel like I'm more like a leader than a follower now; before I was more of a follower, just like, ok, go with the flow, and now I'm like, no, I'm doing what I'm gonna do for me, and for my kids, 'cause I want to, not because you're telling me to do it". This attitude is consistent with the highest ideals of democratic societies, which "call for a citizenry that is fully capable of administering its own affairs" and the empowerment of ordinary people (Brint and Karabel 1989, 227). At the level of individual language, performance, and embodiment, Nancy also expressed that she had been transformed by her experience with community college. This transformation in one's mode of interacting with others often overlapped with their understanding of their occupational trajectory. Drawing on the idea of a professional mode, Nancy said,

> I'm not the same old person I used to be. The way I express myself, the way I write, the way I communicate with others is totally different. I still use cuss words . . . it's just that's what you're comfortable with . . . so it's like, whatever. That's never gonna go away, so . . . bummer . . . but, I feel like having the education that I have definitely does help put me in a better position because not only am I expressing myself better, but if I were to get hired on to a place, I'm representing that company or whoever I'm working for, so if I didn't have the education I wouldn't know how to deal with problems that come up, and having the education, it makes you really flexible in the way you think.

Here, she draws together learned language patterns, new modes of thinking, and the relationship between learned patterns and one's sense of comfort.

At the same time, Nancy experienced weakening ties to many of the people in her life. She described how she had learned to manage relationships:

> so, I'm a whole lot more demanding too, I'm demanding on what type of people I surround myself with. I've cut a whole lot of people out of my life, and people don't understand . . . I explained it to my sister and my mom, people who I feel are bringing me down have no place in my life because I need people who are gonna motivate me.

Through college, the networks that made up past figured worlds began to change. Moreover, Nancy developed an increased awareness of others outside of her personal network and greater tolerance toward difference, what Kaufman and Feldman (2004) refer to as growing cosmopolitanism, as well as changes to within-group beliefs. This meant reflecting on oppression within Mexican American families and communities, as well as developing a historical knowledge of Mexican Americans that she could connect with her personal history. She had to generate a narrative framework outside of traditional role expectations. When talking about the education of Latina students, she explained,

> it's like, you're staying home, you're having children, taking care of them; that's it. Like, my dad . . . to this day he still fights me, he tells me, 'why you going to school? Your job is to stay at home and wipe your kids' asses and feed them; that's your job'. He's like, 'stop spreading your legs'. He thinks I'm a slut or something and I'm like, that's not what I'm doing when I go to school, I'm educating myself.

More than just resisting role expectations, attending and completing a degree at community college became an important aspect of managing the expectations of others. Nancy believed that completing an associate degree at the community college would "feel good" because she would be "proving everybody wrong" and "just shut up all the people who are negative" in her life. At the same time, community college provided her with the intellectual tools to make sense of her own identity as a Chicana and an "advocate" for herself and her community. She said she first learned the meaning of the term Chicano when she enrolled in Puente, and her Chicano studies class taught her "how America subordinated Mexico". This knowledge helped her to make sense of the stories she had about her grandmother in Mexico during the 1930s by connecting world history to her own family history. Through personal and collective history, the symbols of Chicano identity, and experiences of gendered and classed forms of oppression, Nancy entered into the figured world of Chicana/o activism, "identifiable cultural, political, social, and historical landscapes" that provided "access to a more enduring identity, and other persons similar to them that they could relate to" (Urrietta 2007, 124).

By the fourth interview, Nancy had transferred to a local, public, four-year university and was still committed to her goal of becoming a speech and language pathologist. Although she had not changed her academic and career trajectories, she experienced widespread changes in attitude, language, behavior, and social networks. These changes began prior to community college and were amplified as her personal biography intersected with narratives of empowerment, attainment, and struggle encountered in programs, classrooms, and on-campus jobs. Over the three-and-a-half years of the study, Nancy entered into a new figured world.

CONCLUSION

Drawing on popular frameworks of typical community college students, many students in this study worked to construct narratives that explained their enrollment in community college as opposed to a four-year institution. On the one hand, some students developed weakened attachments to the college and left. In contrast to the organizationally focused community college literature, these women were not cooled out (Clark 1960), but rather were narrating alternative pathways due to a multiplicity of competing pathways, or cultural models of success. On the other hand, some of the 23 women in this study experienced a transformation in their trajectories, expanding their educational and occupational aspirations. This was a consequence of interactions with particular institutional agents who provided narrative frameworks for them to imagine futures other than what they entered with. Other students maintained weak attachments to the college while persisting. Though their trajectories through school did not change, they either questioned the value of a college education and postsecondary credentials or else they did not draw on the college as a source of identity and direction. Nevertheless, concerns about status motivated them toward completion. Finally, some students entered entirely new figured worlds that allowed them to reconstruct personal biographies in light of collective narratives of achievement encountered in support programs and classes. These students relied on personal and collective narratives that stemmed from outside of the community college, but over time the community college became more central to their identities. The four women highlighted above exemplify these experiences shared by other women interviewed for this study.

There are, of course, many overlaps and alternative experiences that these categories do not easily account for. Some of the women in this study reported that they had developed new skills, ways of thinking and communicating, and different conceptions of themselves as competent adults. For the most part, they did not attribute these changes to particular organizational arrangements or individual encounters with institutional agents. Instead, these changes appeared to happen as a result of attending college and being challenged in classes. Often, just their personal narratives of going to college served as counternarratives to collective narratives about social groups to which they belonged or the expectations of other people in their lives, such as family or friends. However, this only reinforces the main argument of this chapter that sociologists studying community colleges can benefit from adopting and developing alternative frameworks to warming up and cooling out, which have dominated the field. By drawing on four approaches that are widely used in secondary and postsecondary research, and employing the concept of narrative to navigate these approaches, this chapter will hopefully provide a model for moving community college research from its ambiguous location between the secondary and four-year institution literatures. It will also help us recognize the limits to what community colleges are able to do. The concepts of warming up and cooling out assume a great deal of responsibility for an institution that serves approximately half of American college students, most of who plan to transfer and earn a bachelor's degree. Yet, as this chapter has shown, students are often loosely attached to community colleges to begin with, and their trajectories and identities are drawn from many sources. Moreover, the effects on students should be understood outside of simple income metrics.

As this chapter shows, for each of the students the college functioned as a narrative hub. Due to the centrality of higher education to the lives of so many American students and their families, future trajectories and individual identities were narrated in relation to higher education and the community college. The community college served as an institutional site to weave together narrative frameworks related to family, friends, work, education, and community. Unlike four-year colleges and universities, community college did not present the women with dominant repertoires that they felt they needed to adopt, nor did it marginalize women whose narratives included aspects of their lives outside of school.

Given the importance of non-school factors in identity and trajectory transformations, the community college should move more visibly into the communities that they serve. This is in addition to the efforts to channel graduates into the local labor force or encourage high school students to continue their education. Community colleges should expand their presence in religious settings, workplaces, drug and alcohol recovery centers, shopping malls, and anywhere else that community colleges can foster attachments with students. As state support for public higher education has declined, community college leaders and policymakers have shifted attention from expanding access to increasing timely completion (Moore and Shulock 2011). Research will need a more complex picture of community college experiences if it is to contribute to this effort.

NOTES

1. Available cultural forms within college and university settings are partly a consequence of the intersection of a range of social institutions, such as the family, the broader economy, labor markets, and so on. Stevens, Armstrong, and Arum (2008) refer to this as the "hub" function of postsecondary institutions, because they have historically brought together elite interests in the organization of resources. Here, I shift the focus to the students and the cultural material they bring. Additionally, Small (2002) suggests that narratives—the on-going and complex plots that individuals use to interpret their lives and take action—are shaped by narrower frames that provide cultural categories that filter particular contexts.
2. All names used throughout this chapter are pseudonyms.
3. This research is an outgrowth of a larger study on community colleges and the sense and decision making of poor and minority youth. The project, *Pathways to Postsecondary Success*, was a Bill and Melinda Gates Foundation-funded project conducted by a research team under the direction of University of California/All Campus Consortium on Research for Diversity (UC/ACCORD). It consisted of quantitative analyses of various nationally representative data sets, a statewide survey of California youth between the ages of 18 and 26 years old, and three case studies of poor and minority youth in three Southern California cities. For more, see http://pathways.gseis.ucla.edu/.

4. In her work on the mobility stories of Korean women, Abelmann (2003) draws on the concept of melodrama to explain how the women made sense of their lives. This use of melodrama as an explanatory device emerged from the women's constant reference to Korean television dramas. By drawing on this narrative form, June's experience points to the intersection of narrative forms across and within social systems.

REFERENCES

Abelmann, N. 2003. *The Melodrama of Mobility: Women, Talk, and Class in Contemporary South Korea.* Honolulu: University of Hawaii Press.

Alexander, K., R. Bozick, and D. Entwisle. 2008. "Warming Up, Cooling Out, or Holding Steady? Persistence and Change in Educational Expectations After High School." *Sociology of Education* 81: 371–396.

Armstrong, E. A., and L. T. Hamilton. 2012. *Paying for the Party: How College Maintains Inequality.* Cambridge, MA: Harvard University Press.

Bahr, P. R. 2011. "A Case for Deconstructive Research on Community College Students and Their Outcomes." Paper presented at the Mapping Broad-Access Higher Education conference, Stanford, CA, December 1–2.

Binder, A. J., and K. Wood. 2013. *Becoming Right: How Campuses Shape Young Conservatives.* Princeton, NJ: Princeton University Press.

Bourdieu, P. 1977. *Outline of a Theory of Practice.* Cambridge: Cambridge University Press.

Brint, S., and J. Karabel. 1989. *The Diverted Dream: Community Colleges and the Promise of Educational Opportunity in America, 1900–1985.* New York: Oxford University Press.

Carter, P. L. 2006. "Straddling Boundaries: Identity, Culture, and School." *Sociology of Education* 79: 304–328.

Cech, E., B. Rubineau, S. Silbey, and C. Seron. 2011. "Professional Role Confidence and Gendered Persistence in Engineering." *American Sociological Review* 76: 641–666.

Clark, B. 1960. "The 'Cooling-Out' Function in Higher Education." *The American Journal of Sociology* 65: 569–576.

Collins, P. H. 2009. *Another Kind of Public Education: Race, Schools, the Media, and Democratic Possibilities.* Boston: Beacon Press.

Collins, R. 1979. *The Credential Society: An Historical Sociology of Education and Stratification.* New York: Academic Press.

Conchas, G. Q. 2001. "Structuring Failure and Success: Understanding the Variability in Latino School Engagement." *Harvard Education Review* 71: 475–504.

Deil-Amen, R. 2011. "The 'Traditional' College Student: A Smaller and Smaller Minority and Its Implications for Diversity and Access Institutions." Paper presented at the Mapping Broad-Access Higher Education conference, Stanford, CA, November.

Deil-Amen, R., and J. E. Rosenbaum. 2002. "The Unintended Consequences of Stigma-Free Remediation." *Sociology of Education* 75: 249–268.

Delpit, L. 1988. "The Silenced Dialogue: Power and Pedagogy in Educating Other People's Children." *Harvard Educational Review* 58: 280–298.

Dougherty, K. J. 1994. *The Contradictory College: The Conflicting Origins, Impacts, and Futures of the Community College.* Albany, NY: SUNY Press.

Foley, D. E. 1990. *Learning Capitalist Culture: Deep in the Heart of Tejas.* Philadelphia: University of Pennsylvania Press.

Goldin, C., and L. F. Katz. 2008. *The Race between Education and Technology.* Cambridge, MA: Harvard University Press.

Goldrick-Rab, S., and P. Kinsley. 2013. "School Integration and the Open Door Philosophy: Rethinking the Economic and Racial Composition of Community Colleges." In *Bridging the Higher Education Divide: Strengthening Community Colleges and Restoring the American Dream*, edited by The Century Foundation, 109–136. Washington, DC: Brookings Institution Press.

Grubb, W. N., and M. Lazerson. 2005. *The Education Gospel: The Economic Power of Schooling*. Cambridge, MA: Harvard University Press.

Harding, D. J. 2011. "Rethinking the Cultural Context of Schooling Decisions in Disadvantaged Neighborhoods: From Deviant Subculture to Cultural Heterogeneity." *Sociology of Education* 84: 322–339.

Heath, S. B. 1982. "What No Bedtime Story Means: Narrative Skills at Home and School." *Language in Society* 11: 49–76.

Kaufman, P., and K. A. Feldman. 2004. "Forming Identities in College: A Sociological Approach." *Research in Higher Education* 45: 463–496.

Khan, S. R. 2011. *Privilege: The Making of an Adolescent Elite at St. Paul's School*. Princeton, NJ: Princeton University Press.

Lee, C. D. 1995. "A Culturally Based Cognitive Apprenticeship: Teaching African American High School Students Skills in Literary Interpretation." *Reading Research Quarterly* 30: 608–630.

Lee, S. J. 1994. "Behind the Model-Minority Stereotype: Voices of High- and Low-Achieving Asian American Students." *Anthropology and Education Quarterly* 25: 413–429.

Lew, J. 2010. "Asian American Youth in Poverty: Benefits and Limitations of Ethnic Networks in Postsecondary and Labor Force Options." *Journal of Education for Students Placed at Risk* 15: 127–143.

MacLeod, J. 1995. *Ain't No Makin' It: Aspirations and Attainment in a Low-Income Neighborhood*. Boulder, CO: Westview Press.

Mehan, H. 1992. "Understanding Inequality in Schools: The Contribution of Interpretive Studies." *Sociology of Education* 65: 1–20.

Mehan, H. 2012. *In the Front Door: Creating a College-Going Culture of Learning*. Boulder, CO: Paradigm Publishers.

Moore, C., and N. Shulock. 2011. *Sense of Direction: The Importance of Helping Community College Students Select and Enter a Program of Study*. Sacramento, CA: Institute for Higher Education Leadership and Policy.

Mullen, A. 2011. *Degrees of Inequality: Culture, Class, and Gender in American Higher Education*. Baltimore: Johns Hopkins University.

O'Connor, C. 1999. "Race, Class, and Gender in America: Narratives of Opportunity among Low-Income African American Youths." *Sociology of Education* 72: 137–157.

Ogbu, J. U. 1987. "Variability in Minority School Performance: A Problem in Search of an Explanation." *Anthropology & Education Quarterly* 18: 312–334.

Oseguera, L., G. Conchas, and E. Mosqueda. 2011. "Beyond Family and Ethnic Culture: Understanding the Preconditions for the Potential Realization of Social Capital." *Youth and Society* 43: 1136–1166.

Pugh, A. 2013. "What Good are Interviews for Thinking about Culture? Demystifying Interpretive Analysis." *American Journal of Cultural Sociology* 1: 42–68.

Roksa, J., E. Grodsky, R. Arum, and A. Gamoran. 2007. "United States: Changes in Higher Education and Social Stratification." In *Stratification in Higher Education: A Comparative Study*, edited by Y. Shavit, R. Arum, and A. Gamoran, 165–194. Stanford, CA: Stanford University Press.

Rose, M. 2012. *Back to School: Why Everyone Deserves a Second Chance at Education*. New York: The New Press.

Rosenbaum, J. E. 1998. "College-For-All: Do Students Understand What College Demands?" *Social Psychology of Education* 2: 55–80.

Rubin, B. C. 2007. "Learner Identity Amid Figured Worlds: Constructing (In)competence at an Urban High School." *The Urban Review* 39: 217–249.

Schleef, D. 2000. "'That's a Good Question!' Exploring Motivations for Law and Business School Choice." *Sociology of Education* 73: 155–174.

Silva, J. 2013. *Coming Up Short: Working-Class Adulthood in an Age of Uncertainty*. New York: Oxford University Press.

Small, M. L. 2002. "Culture, Cohorts, and Social Organization Theory: Understanding Local Participation in a Latino Housing Project." *American Journal of Sociology* 108: 1–54.

Solórzano, D., A. Datnow, V. Park, and T. Watford. 2013. *Pathways to Postsecondary Success: Maximizing Opportunities for Youth in Poverty*. Los Angeles: UC/ACCORD.

Somers, M. R. 1994. "The Narrative Constitution of Identity: A Relational and Network Approach." *Theory and Society* 23: 605–649.

Stanton-Salazar, R. D. 2011. "A Social Capital Framework for the Study of Institutional Agents and Their Role in the Empowerment of Low-Status Students and Youth." *Youth and Society* 43: 1066–1109.

Stevens, M. L., E. A. Armstrong, and R. Arum. 2008. "Sieve, Incubator, Temple, Hub: Empirical and Theoretical Advances in the Sociology of Higher Education." *Annual Review of Sociology* 34: 127–151.

Turner, R. H. 1960. "Sponsored and Contest Mobility and the School System." *American Sociological Review* 25: 855–867.

Urrietta, L., Jr. 2007. "Identity Production in Figured Worlds: How Some Mexican Americans Become Chicana/o Activist Educators." *The Urban Review* 39: 117–144.

Willis, P. E. 1977. *Learning to Labor: How Working Class Kids Get Working Class Jobs*. New York: Columbia University Press.

6 Bicultural Myths, Rifts, and Scripts
A Case Study of Hidden Chicana/ Latina Teacher's Cultural Pedagogy in Multiracial Schools

Glenda M. Flores

Scholarship has noted that Latino culture is unwelcome in the teaching jobs. Up until the middle of the twentieth century, Mexican-origin children in the U.S. were forced to undergo "Americanization" programs that urged them to shed their ethnic culture and assimilate into a White mainstream (González 1990b; Urrieta 2009). In many instances, Latino culture and foreign language capabilities were perceived as obstacles to schooling success and as pathological deficiencies (Ochoa 2007). It was not until the Civil Rights Movement and the Chicano Blowouts of the 1960s when celebratory multiculturalism and multicultural education formally entered schools after pressure from teachers, students, and parents challenged institutionalized discriminatory practices in public educational institutions (Garcia 2011). Celebratory multiculturalism became institutionalized in the U.S educational system (Banks 1989) and was used to promote ethnic diversity in school settings, but these aspects of Latino culture in schools have largely remained symbolic, limited to foods and festivities.

Today, multicultural education practices (Washburn 1996; Delpit 2006) are encouraged in schools, but there is a paucity of research showing how Latina teachers implement their Latina cultural resources in the teaching jobs. Previous scholarship has noted that when Latina teachers display Latino culture in schools where the majority of students are of Latino background, they are met with resistance and hostility from White co-workers (Flores 2011b). Other studies have noted that Latina teachers feel that they must hide their cultural and ethnic heritage in White spaces when working amongst a majority of White colleagues (Ochoa 2007; Urrieta 2009). Yet other studies argue that schools "subtract" the cultural and social resources of Latino students in schools (Valenzuela 1999).

In this chapter, I focus on Latina teachers because, in the late 1990s and early 2000s, Latina women entered the teaching profession in droves in California and Los Angeles schools (U.S. Department of Labor 2010; see Flores and Hondagneu-Sotelo 2014) and found work in school districts that serve predominantly immigrant and racial/ethnic minority families. Today, more than eight million Mexican-origin children and youth, the largest Latino subgroup, have Mexican-born parents (Passel 2011). One out of every four students in K–12 schools is of Latina/o origin nationwide (Fry and Lopez 2012), and in California alone, Latino children comprise over 50% of the school-age population (Fry and Lopez 2012; Ed-Data 2012), and many are increasingly attending multiracial schools (Orfield et al. 2011). These demographic shifts are especially pronounced in Los Angeles, where Latino students now make up nearly two-thirds of the K–12 population, and Latina/o teachers constitute nearly 30% of the teacher force (Ed-Data 2012). Drawing from interview and extensive ethnographic data in two Southern California "majority-minority" schools, I examine how Latina teachers are implementing Latino cultural resources in schools and how they are quietly reshaping the way that schools are run and classrooms are taught. I contend that they are transforming the ways that Latino students and their immigrant parents are received, engaged with, and incorporated into American ways of life. Their efforts, however, are met in contrasting ways in two scholastically underperforming, multiracial schools in Los Angeles.

Research has identified a myriad of factors that contribute to the low academic achievement of Latinos in school (see Flores 2011a; Simón 1997; Valenzuela 1999; Feliciano 2006). Multicultural educational practices have been formally instituted in schools to aid the academic outcomes of Latino children, but Latino youth continue to falter in U.S. schools (Romo and Falbo 1996; Velez 2000), and their cumulative disadvantages have been hailed a "crisis" (Gándara and Contreras 2009). Telles and Ortiz (2008) find notable educational progress between the first and second immigrant generation, but this socially mobile trend stagnates beyond the second generation. Educational policymakers have directed their attention towards developing effective multicultural education practices to prepare teachers for a racially and linguistically diverse classroom and nation (Ochoa 2007; Ladson-Billings 2005). However, most school curricula still stress Anglo conformity, and, whereas multicultural education practices are growing, they are not well integrated, with lessons limited to a few days of the year, falling under the food, fun, faces, and festivities rubric (Washburn 1996). Sociologist and educational scholar Angela Valenzuela (1999) adds that for U.S.-Mexican youth schools are a "subtractive process" where Mexican-origin students feel there is a lack of caring by teachers and a lack of respect for Mexican culture and migration experiences. Yet, other scholars detail urban school success stories that explain the ways racial/ethnic minority youth navigate unequal schooling conditions that place them at a disadvantage (Conchas 2006).

As we will see, the Latina teachers included in this chapter encourage one another to actively incorporate symbolic aspects of Latino culture, as well as the "hidden Chicana/Latina cultural pedagogy"—thus, amplifying our conceptualization of Latino culture in schools. By serving as cultural liaisons Latina teachers may facilitate the incorporation patterns of Latino youth.

LATINO EDUCATION IN THE UNITED STATES

The Era of *De Jure* School Segregation

Historically, cultural deficit models were prominent in the literature when it came to understanding the role of Latino culture in schools (Valenzuela 1999; Ochoa 2007; González 1990). So much so that Mexican-origin children experienced mandatory segregation in U.S. schools until the middle of the twentieth century (Sanchez 1997), with court cases and schools battling over whether it was justifiable to segregate Mexican children based on racial markers or ethnic ones.[1] Ethnic markers such as language fueled segregationist policies against Mexican-origin children in schools (Ochoa 2007; Sanchez 1995). One of the earliest court cases dealing with Mexican desegregation was *Roberto Álvarez v. the Board of Trustees of the Lemon Grove School District* (1931), the first successful desegregation court decision in the history of the United States, preceding *Brown v. The Board of Education* (1954) by over two decades. The ruling in the "Lemon Grove incident" established the rights of Mexican-origin children to equal education, despite local, regional, and national sentiment that favored segregation and deportation of the Mexican-origin population. Mexican children were perceived to be lazy and backwards, and Spanish language abilities were perceived as hindrances to schooling success that resulted in children being labeled as mentally disabled (González 1990). School officials urged that Mexican children needed to go through Americanization programs before full integration with White children could take place. As the education historian Gilbert González (1990, 45) states, "through the program of Americanization, the Mexican child was taught that his/[her] family, community and culture were obstacles to schooling success". However, because the Mexican-origin population was deemed to be racially White during this era, the judge assigned to the case rendered in his ruling that "this separation denie[d] the Mexican children the presence of American children, which is so necessary to learn the English language" (Alvarez 1986, 47).

Although no state in the American Southwest upheld legally the segregation of U.S.-Mexican youth, the practice continued. Teachers and school administrators argued that their presence in integrated, multiracial schools "would hinder the progress of white American children" (Moore 1970, 77). This perception was not just held by Whites. In fact, many middle-class Latinos favored Catholic school education for their children rather than schools for the Mexican laboring class, whose children were relegated to public educational facilities that prepared them for vocational jobs (Garcia 1991). The Latino elite believed that Catholic schools groomed their children to be *"gente decente"* [more civilized], and wanted their children to attend schools that promoted limited Spanish use. Shedding their native language, they believed, would ensure the elimination of racial prejudice (Sanchez 1997). In effect, Latinos themselves were fragmented on the inculcation of culture in schools.

Post-1965: *De Facto* Segregation and Latino Culture in Schools

In the twenty-first century, Latino-origin children are still segregated in U.S. schools, but the form has shifted to *de facto* school segregation, giving the impression that the segregation of Latino students and families is incidental. In the 1960s, Mexican Americans took part in a national quest for civil rights, and staged a series of protests and the Chicano Blowouts against unequal schooling conditions in Los Angeles Unified School District high schools (Gonzalez 1990a). Mexican-origin students were suffering from massive drop-out rates and were tracked into vocational courses and jobs. Protestors requested more Latina/o-origin teachers, bilingual education, equitable schooling facilities, and culturally relevant curriculum. The 1970s witnessed the emergence of multicultural and pedagogical approaches that addressed ethnic and racial diversity. Much of the efforts in multicultural education were aimed towards preparing White teachers to work with and teach students of color (Delpit 2006; Sleeter 2001), but schools still stressed culturally oppressive teaching approaches (Sleeter and Grant 2009; Ladson-Billings 2005, 1995). The 1980s and 1990s saw the resegregation of Latino children in schools mainly due to residential and linguistic segregation, the latter of which was propelled by the English-only movement and Proposition 227, billed as the "English for the Children" initiative in 1998. These studies contextualize schools as key sites of assimilation in the past.

Today, teachers are encouraged to promote diversity in the classroom and to expose students to various cultural customs and traditions. These, however, are often celebrated and implemented occasionally where teachers develop a lesson plan to teach a subject during a particular day (Washburn 1996; Nieto 1999). For instance, González et al. (2005) propose a cultural funds of knowledge frame and suggest that teachers should attempt to learn and understand the political, historical, and personal life contexts of their students, because their households contain rich cultural and cognitive resources—for example, they might use Mexican candy to help children learn to count (Moll et al. 1992). Yosso (2005) coins the concept of "community cultural wealth" to challenge the notion that Latino students come to the classroom with cultural deficiencies, and focuses on the underutilized assets that they bring with them from their homes and communities. Additionally, Prudence Carter (2007) suggests that Black and Latino youth are multicultural navigators, culturally savvy youth who draw from multiple social locations to navigate schools. Although these studies promote Latino culture in schools, there is a gap in the research on how Latina teachers serve as "institutional agents" (Stanton-Salazar 2010) between the educational institution and Latino communities and families.

Drawing on ethnographic data, I argue that Latina teachers are quietly implementing another form of Latino ethnic culture in their daily practices in schools—the hidden Chicana/Latina cultural pedagogy. The pedagogy that Latina teachers are enacting in schools is not what is found in teacher instructional materials or daily curricular lessons. It is also not what is popularly taught or celebrated during popular festivals such as Cinco de Mayo[2] or Cesar Chávez Day. Rather, the hidden Chicana/Latina cultural pedagogy in schools refers to the subtle and nuanced cultural cues that Latina teachers are able to pick up, discern, and communicate with Latino families because of their own connections to immigrant origins and familiarity with, for instance, Latino communication styles. These are fluid cultural practices that Latina/o parents and children bring with them to schools daily, and Latina teachers have the prior situated knowledge that allows them to discern slight indications about how they should alter their teaching and interactions in particular circumstances in order to effectively reach and communicate well with Latino families. Their efforts, however, are met in different ways in two racial/ethnic minority and multiracial elementary schools.

DESCRIPTION OF RESEARCH SITES AND METHODOLOGY

This case study draws from 20 interviews with Latina teachers[3] and extensive ethnographic research in two predominantly immigrant and multiracial school districts and communities in Southern California. The Latina teachers included in this study worked as full-time teachers for the Compton Unified School District (n = 10) and Garvey Unified School District (n = 10). These school districts were selected because they experienced considerable growth in their Latina teacher workforce. Although the city of Compton is racialized as an African American city in popular culture, today 80% of students in Compton schools are of working-class Latino origin, whereas African American students comprise only 20% of the student population and are decreasing yearly (California Department of Education 2012). The teacher force in Compton schools is predominantly African American and Latino (66%), with African American teachers outnumbering Latinos/as 41% and 25%, respectively (CDE 2013). The Garvey district, however, is comprised of Asian (56%), Latino (41%), and White (1%) students (CDE 2013). The teacher distribution mirrored the student breakdown with Asian teachers (40%) outnumbering Latinas (26%) in the district. In both of these school districts, Latinas comprised a significant percentage of teachers, were growing in size, and served primarily working-class Latino and racial/ethnic minority populations.

Semi-structured interviews were conducted with several generations of Latina-origin school teachers—one-and-a-half, second, third, and later generations. At both schools, snowball sampling was used to recruit participants. The interview guide included open-ended questions on three broad central domains: pathways into the occupation, the implementation of Latino culture in minority schools, and interracial relationships and interactions. Each interview lasted between one and three hours. All face-to-face interviews took place after school, before school, during lunchtime, or in interviewees' homes. Interviews were transcribed verbatim for the analysis and Strauss's (1987) coding scheme was used to evaluate the data.

Prior to beginning the interview, each teacher was asked to fill out a demographic face sheet, which queried them about their marital status, their parents' place of birth and occupation, their own place of birth, city of residence, and the highest level of schooling obtained, as well as their credentialing institution and whether or not they had a CLAD or a BCLAD.[4] At the time of the interview, with the exception of one teacher in Compton, all teachers were fully credentialed.

Latino-origin families living in the U.S. are a heterogeneous group. Table 6.1 gives an overview of the Latina teachers included in this study. Over half are the daughters of Mexican immigrants. Of the Latina teachers interviewed for this study, two-thirds of them (13 out of 20) had at least one parent born in Mexico, two had parents born in Central America, one the Caribbean, and two were multiracial. The asterisk next to each teacher's last name indicates his/her generation level in the U.S., and we see that two-thirds were either one-and-a-half or second generation. Seven teachers were a part of the third and fourth generation, but still from working-class origins, and all worked in Rosemead. Table 6.1 also provides a brief snapshot of the Latina teachers' parental backgrounds, including information about their place of birth and the occupations their parents held, both at the time of our interview and while these Latina teachers were growing up. These Latina teachers had immigrant origins and came from working class homes, with parents that worked in low-skilled, manual jobs. All teachers were asked to approximate their own annual income, excluding sources of income such as second jobs. Two declined to state income information. The average annual income was $64,000.

To assess how Latina teachers implemented Latino culture as strategic tools to bridge the cultural gaps between a White mainstream institution and Latino children, I immersed myself in the professional and home lives of Latina teachers for two academic school years to capture daily interactions between teachers, students, and parents during school hours and at off-campus activities. I began participant observation in August of 2009, when the academic school year officially began for these schools. I spent four days a week documenting the interactions at both of the research

Table 6.1 Demographic Characteristics of Teachers

Pseudonym	Age	Teacher (POB)	Parent (POB)	Father Occupation	Mother Occupation	Undergrad Inst.	Credential Inst.	Years Teaching	Annual Income
Compton									
Mrs. Kingston*	40	Mexico	Mexico	Retired Teacher in MX	Retired Teacher in MX	Cal Poly Pomona (Finance)	Compton District Program* (CLAD)	9	$60,000
Ms. Gutierrez**	35	Mexico	Mexico	N/A	Retired	Cal State LA (Liberal Studies)	Cal State LA* (CLAD)	4	$54,000
Mrs. Crescent**	33	Orange County	Cuba/El Salvador	Bank Executive	Nurse	Cal Poly Pomona (Liberal Studies)	Compton District Program* (CLAD)	6	$56,000
Mrs. Madrigal*	33	Mexico	Mexico	Welder	Homemaker	Cal State LA (Multicultural Education)	Cal State LA* (CLAD)	5	$45,000
Mrs. Estrada**	34	Santa Ana, CA	Mexico	Welder	Independent Distributing Company Owner	Cal State Fullerton (Liberal Studies)	Compton District Program* (CLAD)	5	$36,000
Ms. Tiscareno**	27	Long Beach, CA	Mexico	Shipper/Custodian	Homemaker	Cal State Long Beach (Liberal Studies)	Cal State Long Beach (CLAD)	4	$52,000
Mrs. Godinez**	39	East LA	Mexico	Clerk	Seamstress	Cal State Dominguez (Spanish/Mex-Am Studies)	Cal State Dominguez Hills (BCLAD/MA in Multicultural Education)	14	$76,000

Mrs. Velásquez**	34	Chicago	Mexico/Texas	Car Wash/Electronic Tech	Teacher aid	Cal State Long Beach (Chicano/Latino Studies)	National University (CLAD)	5	N/A
Mrs. Rivas**	39	Sacramento, CA	Mexico	N/A	Operator	Cal State Dominguez (Psychology/Chicano/Latino) Studies	San Jose University* (CLAD)	15	$78,000
Mrs. Ybarra**	39	East LA	Mexico	Clerk	Seamstress	Cal State Dominguez Spanish/Mex-Am Studies	Cal State Dominguez Hills (BCLAD)	14	N/A
Rosemead									
Ms. Davila***	34	Bellflower, CA	Kansas/Iowa	Warehouse	Cashier	UCLA (Theater)	Cal State LA* (CLAD)	9	$51,000
Mrs. Robles****	36	Rosemead, CA	Los Angeles, CA	Mail Carrier	Pharmaceutical Clerk	Cal State LA (Health Sciences)	Cal State LA* (CLAD/MA in Arts in Education & Reading Specialist)	14	$80,000
Ms. Maciel**	40	Rosemead, CA	Mexico	Warehouse	Homemaker	Cal State LA (Child Dev.)	Cal State LA* (BCLAD/MA in Reading)	14	$80,000

(Continued)

Table 6.1 (Continued)

Pseudonym	Age	Teacher (POB)	Parent (POB)	Father Occupation	Mother Occupation	Undergrad Inst.	Undergrad Inst.	Years Teaching	Annual Income
Mrs. Arenas***	61	San Gabriel, CA	CA	Agriculture	Agriculture/ Pre-school Teacher	Cal State LA (Liberal Studies)	Cal State LA (CLAD/MA in Education & Reading Specialist)	21	$86,000
Mrs. Franco**	30	Montebello CA	Mexico/CA	Plumber	Teacher Aid	UCLA (Sociology)	University of Phoenix (CLAD/MA in Education)	9	$70,000
Mrs. Larry***	36	San Dimas, CA	OK/Mexico	Painter in Aeronautics	Homemaker	Cal State LA (Social Science)	Cal State LA (CLAD/MA in Education)	11	$68,000
Mrs. Cadena***	41	Orange, CA	Santa Ana, CA	Welding Supervisor	Factory	Cal State LA (Child Dev.)	Cal State LA (CLAD/MA in Admin.)	11	$67,000
Ms. Sanchez***	39	East LA	East LA	Core Maker	Teacher Aid	Cal State LA (Computer Information Systems)	University of Phoenix (CLAD/MA in Education)	5	$50,000
Mrs. Quiroz**	29	San Gabriel, CA	Guatemala	Mechanic	Homemaker	Cal State LA (Child Dev.)	Cal State LA (CLAD/MA in Reading)	5	$44,000

Mrs. Perez***	57	Texas	Texas	Warehouse Man- ager	Homemaker	Cal State LA (Languages)	Cal State LA (CLAD)	29	$85,000
Avg.	37							11	$64,026
N = 20									

* Teacher generation level noted by asterisk next to last name (i.e., *1.5 generation, **2nd generation, ***3rd generation, ****4th generation)
Asterisk in credential institution cell denotes if hired with emergency credential/only marked those that explicitly mentioned it.

sites. I conducted ethnographic participant observations in a number of contexts, including faculty meetings, classrooms, the teachers' lounge, the front office, PTA meetings, and all-campus events. Sociologist Erving Goffman (2001) explains the process of "getting into place" when conducting field work at any site. Therefore, I actively volunteered for any social events on and off school grounds and served as a translator for teachers during parent-teacher conferences and other events. I also shadowed four Latina teachers, two in Compton and two in Rosemead. Observations on campus allowed me to examine the topics teachers discussed, how they interacted with co-teachers, parents, and students of various racial/ethnic backgrounds, and how and under what circumstances Latina teachers expressed their culture with members of multiple racial/ethnic categories. In all, I logged over 400 hours of ethnographic participant observation. All "jottings" (Emerson, Fretz, and Shaw 1995) were converted into sets of field notes that were placed into conceptual categories.

To obtain a complete view of the social worlds of Latina teachers, I also conducted four focus groups with Latino parents in both schools.[5] I conducted two focus groups solely for Spanish-speaking, Latino immigrant parents, one at each site. Although there is a tendency to homogenize the Latino experience and subsume them under one umbrella, pan-ethnic label (Oboler 1995), the Latina teachers in the study made reference to the daily lived distinctions between newly arrived immigrant Latino parents and those who were second or third generation.

The Sites: Compton and Rosemead Schools

Site selection for this study was key. I purposefully and strategically selected two school districts that had a sizeable Latina teacher population and served multiracial populations. Orfield and his colleagues (2011) find that today, around 40% of Latino and Black students in the U.S. are concentrated in schools that are over 90% Black and Latino, and just 5% of Southern California's Asian students attend intensely segregated racial/ethnic minority schools. This led me to the Compton and Garvey districts in metropolitan Los Angeles. In popular culture, the city of Compton is rarely recognized for its once White and Black middle-class inhabitants. Its dramatic racial/ethnic transformation into a predominantly Latino immigrant city within the last two decades is relatively unknown by those who do not actually live in the city. In the 1950s, fewer that 50 African Americans lived among Compton's 45,000 residents (Sides 2003). Today, 65% of Compton's 96,455 residents are of Latino origin. They are primarily Mexican immigrants and their children (U.S. Bureau of the Census 2005). The African American population has steadily declined to 27.2%, reaching parity with Whites, who also comprise 27.2% of Comptonites (U.S. Bureau of the Census 2010). As recently as 1985, African American pupils constituted 60% of the students in the district, whereas Latinos formed only 37% of the student body (Camarillo 2004). In 2011, the percentages reversed, with an astounding 78% of students being Latino, whereas only 17% are African American (CDE 2013).

Rosemead, a much smaller city in the larger west San Gabriel Valley, goes virtually unnoticed by popular media. Rosemead is a region where two racial/ethnic minority groups, Asian and Latinos, live side by side. It is described as an "ethnoburb" (Li 1997), a suburb with a large racial/ethnic minority population. It is much smaller than Compton, with a population of approximately 55,500. The Latino population is 34% of the population, whereas Whites comprise 19.3%. The Asian-origin population is 58% and growing. Until the 1950s, when urban renewal programs and freeway construction helped lure in Asian, immigrant, middle-class residents to the region, most residents in the San Gabriel Valley were working-class Whites, with pockets of large Latino sectors. Today, the San Gabriel Valley region of Los Angeles County has one of the most prominent collections of U.S. suburbs, with large, foreign-born, Chinese-speaking populations, ranging from working-class residents living in Rosemead and El Monte, to wealthier immigrants living in Arcadia and Diamond Bar (American Community Survey 2009). Whereas the Asian-origin population is very class heterogeneous, many Mexican-origin families have remained working class.

The Elementary Schools

Table 6.2 shows the demographic breakdown of teachers and students at both the district level and within the schools that are the focus of this study. Compton Elementary school is a K–5 school that serves approximately 850 students. It is a big school. In the 2010–2011 academic school year 78% of students at Compton Elementary were of Latino origin, and 19.3% were African American (Ed-Data 2012). Whereas some Latina teachers referred to the student population as "biracial", others negated the idea that it was diverse, because most students were of Latino origin. They served only one Samoan family. Over 80% of the student body receives free and reduced lunch, and 85% are considered socioeconomically disadvantaged. Their Academic Performance Index (API) score was 736, and at the time I was in the field they were considered a program improvement (PI) school in year five. Goodwill Elementary, however, is comprised of roughly 600 students and serves children ranging from preschool to the sixth grade. Whereas at times the Asian- and Latino-origin population were evenly split, when I began my field work 52.5% of the student population was Asian, whereas 45% were Latino (Ed-Data 2012). African American students numbered between two and four. 85% of children in the school were considered to be socioeconomically disadvantaged. The API score was 783, and they were in their second year as a PI school, losing their title as Title 1 Academic Achievement school.

Table 6.2   Racial/Ethnic Demographics of Teachers and Students

	Latinas/os	Blacks	Asians	Whites
Compton District				
Teachers	24%	41%	1%	21.2%
Students	77%	19.3%	>1%	>1%
Compton Elementary				
Teachers*	30%	35%	4%	26%
Students	78%	17%	>1%	0%
Garvey District				
Teachers	28%	3%	44%	23%
Students	41%	>1%	56%	1%
Goodwill Elementary				
Teachers**	45%	0%	41%	14%
Students	45%	>1%	52.5%	>1%

*Total: 48 teachers
**Total: 29 teachers

In this chapter, I illuminate how Latina teachers incorporate Latino cultural resources in schools mainly through the hidden Chicana/Latina cultural pedagogy to facilitate the incorporation patterns of the children of Latino immigrants. As we will see, some elements of the pedagogy are values (immigrant narratives), some are a means of conveying information (*amabilidad*), and some are truly an alternative curriculum (mathematics).

HEROIC FOLKLORIC LATINO CULTURE VS. THE HIDDEN CHICANA/LATINA CULTURAL PEDAGOGY

A Diego Rivera painting with white calla lilies hung neatly above Mrs. Cadena's cluttered desk. Surrounding the painting were an ensemble of various Mexican crafts, such as *Día de los Muertos calacas* (Day of the Dead skeletons), red, white, and green paper maché flowers, Mexican *lucha libre* (free wrestling) masks, and a poster of César Chávez with "¡*Como Siempre!*" emblazoned across the middle. Sections of her room were partitioned off and engulfed with several of these items. A display of biographical books about famous Latino icons were propped along the entrance of her room, right below her windows scratched up with graffiti. This was the setting during the interview with Mrs. Cadena, a self-identified, fourth-generation Latina teacher, who had blond hair and green eyes.

If we look in many classrooms, we may come across many of these items for various reasons. Whereas these items may hold important ties to Latino culture and history, these are perceived as non-threatening and decorative. These are what I categorize as heroic, folkloric, Latino culture, because within the educational context, Latino culture has been "canned" and is reproduced in schools across the United States in very contained ways (Washburn 1996). In the era after the Civil Rights Movement, socially sanctioned multiculturalism was instituted in schools, and teachers were encouraged to expose children to the symbolic forms of ethnic culture such as cuisines, Latino icons, dances, and popular festivals. These aspects of culture help students learn important historical events, and they validate Latino children's traditions; but these aspects of Latino culture are largely symbolic (Gans 1979; Waters 2001). This is the version of ethnic culture that is expected, reproduced, symbolic, and lived.

Immigrant Narratives' Scripts

One of the ways that Latina teachers described connecting with their Latino students was by sharing their own immigrant origins and histories to develop a homologous link with them the very first day of school. The Latina teachers revealed that they would discuss being the children of immigrants adapting to a new American culture, and the intergenerational and bicultural dynamics that emerged within their families in their classrooms. For example, Mrs. Kingston, a Latina teacher in Compton who moved to the United States at 15 years of age and had schooling in Mexico, expressed that she would "share stories about when [she was] little and how [school was] different in Mexico" to show the transition into a new American schooling system. Similarly, Mrs. Estrada, a U.S.-born Latina teacher that learned to speak English at eight years of age, explained to her students that she always felt "lost" in school because she could not understand her teacher's instructions in the English language. She would tell her students, "in kindergarten the teacher only spoke English and I was kind of like to the side . . . I was always lost. I think the teacher was like 'she is not going to succeed, amount to anything. She's Latina'".

Latina teachers used these education-related immigrant narratives to convey that they were once "in their shoes" and to motivate Latino students to succeed in school. Latina teachers who had roots from other regions in Latin America also shared their immigrant narratives to spur educational success. Mrs. Crescent, a Latina teacher of Salvadoran and Cuban descent and whose parents were fleeing political turmoil in their countries of origin, explained the anecdote she shared with her students to accentuate the parallels within their experiences:

> [I talk to them about] how my mom was boarded on a plane with a note stapled to her shirt from El Salvador [at] four years old . . . We talk a lot

about why your parents came, about struggle, about sacrifice—because some were born there [Latin America], but probably right after they were born they came over. Once in a while you will get a kid who lived there for a little bit, but for the most part they have lived most of their lives in the U.S. We talk about why they immigrated and of course I get on my college soapbox and why [their parents] want a better life for their kids.

(Mrs. Crescent, Compton)

Mrs. Crescent's quote reflects how, as the daughter of Central American and Caribbean immigrants, she is cognizant of the internal heterogeneity within the migration histories of the Latino population, intragenerational divides, and varying contexts of reception (Menjívar 2000; Suarez-Orozco and Suarez-Orozco 2001).[6] Mrs. Crescent also invokes stories of Latino migration to the U.S. and struggle in order to promote educational success, but she also does it to push her students to "give back" to their parents through a college education because of the sacrifices their parents made for them. This finding mirrors the "immigrant bargain" (Smith 2005)—a process that stresses educational and occupational success, and suggests that second-generation, young, Latino adults measure their moral worth or failure based on upward mobility. Much like immigrant Latino parents who use this strategy in Smith's study, here we see Latina teachers working as intermediaries in the incorporation process for the children of Latino immigrants, instilling the immigrant bargain and parental sacrifice in their teaching to spur college-going behavior among their Latino students.

The Latina teachers credited their parents' immigrant backgrounds for giving them an inner drive to succeed in school. They attempted to develop this immigrant narrative in their classrooms to give Latino students a purpose behind "making it" in schools, and would highlight the backbreaking jobs that their own parents held. As Agius Vallejo and Lee (2009) show, many Latinas/os from working-class backgrounds, who experience upward social mobility and are one generation removed from the immigrant experience, wish to "give back" socially to their families and poorer co-ethnic communities. The immigrant narrative is borne out of parental sacrifice and struggle, and the expectation is that the children should reciprocate with their parents. Here we see how college-educated Latinas are verbally communicating and transmitting the immigrant narrative on behalf of immigrant Latino parents, naturalizing migration status in the classroom and making it a part of their curriculum.

Although Latina teachers saw their immigrant narratives as offering important insights in schools, they were also acutely aware that U.S. immigration issues were disproportionately framed around the Latino experience, resulting in a negative racialization process of Latinos.

For instance, Mrs. Crescent said that, during volatile political climates like HR4437, an anti-immigrant bill that emerged in 2005, she was more cautious about exchanging her immigrant experience with other teachers, but would do so with her students in the classroom. She said,

> a Caucasian woman made a comment . . . It was very misguided and so I pounced on her. I regretted it . . . She ha[d] this view that "they should be deported, they have no rights here". Then she walks into her classroom with the faces of the very kids whose parents are at jeopardy of being deported and to me I'm like, "you don't have that sensitivity". So I talk about that [immigration] in class.
>
> (Mrs. Crescent, Compton)

Whereas prior research has observed that second-generation Latina teachers often feel uncomfortable discussing their immigrant roots in the teaching jobs and, in many cases, prefer to self-segregate when working among a majority of White co-workers (Flores 2011b), within their classrooms, with Latino children, we see a different pattern emerge where Latina teachers verbally convey immigrant narratives as a way to promote educational attainment in an ethnic group whose parents suffer from lower levels of human capital.

Latina teachers also felt that Latino immigrant parents carried with them a *"rancho* mentality". This did not mean that Latina teachers indicated that Latino immigrant parents did not care about their children's education, but that they experienced obstacles related to the working-class Latino immigrant experience. Mrs. Madrigal, a one-and-a-half-generation Latina teacher whose family settled in Compton, explained,

> you want someone who is illiterate to be literate [the parents]. It's that wave that gets out of the ranches and gets out of Mexico and just comes here for the first time trying to make the best of their life . . . [They think] let me get out of poverty, let me start all over again . . . My mom and dad were part of that wave. They never volunteered because they were always working . . .
>
> (Mrs. Madrigal, Compton)

Mrs. Velásquez also added, "[Latino parents] are coming straight from a little *pueblito* and they are struggling . . . They come here and they don't even know that they are supposed to be involved in their kids' school. They are just trying to put bread on the table and it is a different mentality".

Mrs. Madrigal and Mrs. Velásquez's quotes demonstrate that immigrant narratives contrasted for Latino families who had lower levels of human capital. Latina teachers adamantly challenged the notion that Mexican culture and families did not value education or that they possessed an inferior culture. In fact, the teachers highlighted that Latino parents would provide verbal encouragement (Gándara 1995) to their children and helped them with schooling in the ways that they could. The teachers perceived that Latino families' socioeconomic constraints and low levels of human capital in the home country traveled with them to the U.S., influencing Latino immigrant parents' ability to participate in their children's schooling in the ways that American schools expect. As Mrs. Madrigal's quote illustrates, working-class Mexican immigrant families who settle in the U.S. are initially unaware of the differences between the characteristics of Mexican educational institutions and the American schooling system. In Mexico, many teachers serve as surrogate parents who ensure that Mexican children are *bien educado* [well mannered] and also explain the consequences of migration to their students (Rosas 2011).

Even Latina teachers who were one or two generations removed from the immigrant experience and did not directly possess immigrant narratives recognized them as important. This was the case in Rosemead. Mrs. Arenas, a third-generation Latina teacher whose parents had less than a middle school education, would tell her students about her experiences working in the fields alongside her U.S.-born, Mexican parents to stress the importance of education. She said, "my parents did not graduate from high school . . . [I tell them that] I worked in the fields. I was a farm worker and we used to work in the summer. We would miss school . . . I knew I didn't want to do that for the rest of my life and I knew how important education was". Despite being third generation, her U.S.-born parents worked in agriculture. Although a part of the fourth generation, Mrs. Cadena, a Mexican/Irish teacher who had limited Spanish speaking skills and was born to two working-class, teenaged parents, explained that she told her students of the words reverberating in her head from her grandfather, who was of Mexican origin and had less than a third grade education: "finish school, [he would say]. I would have loved to stay in school, but I didn't have the choice". Although removed from the immigrant experience, Mrs. Cadena would also purposefully include lessons that would get students to ponder the immigrant experience. Many Latina teachers attempted to expose their students to the immigrant narrative to resonate with their Latino students' experiences and to promote future collegiate aspirations.

Communication Codes: Personalismo, Simpatía, *and* Amabilidad *(Personable, Sympathy, and Kindness)*

"[I] know how to talk to them" was a quote that Mrs. Rivas, a second-generation Latina teacher in Compton, imparted to me during our interview when probed about how she communicated with Latino immigrant parents. Whereas prior studies have shown that Latina teachers and children are often admonished for speaking Spanish in schools (Ochoa 2007;

Valdes 1996; Valenzuela 1999), here I show that Latina teachers were aware of the stigma associated with the Spanish language in schools, but were also highly cognizant of communicative forms of speech in the Spanish language exhibited by Latino immigrant parents. Mrs. Rivas, a bilingual teacher who was raised by a single mother in East Los Angeles, said that she learned how to speak to Latino immigrant parents: "you just need to learn to speak to parents . . . to be able to adjust to speak to different parents . . . It helps being bilingual that they actually come up to you".

Like Mrs. Rivas, many Latina teachers noted that Latino immigrant parents would approach them and seek them out to translate or interpret for other teachers who had difficulties fully communicating in the Spanish language. Even when non-Latino, monolingual, English teachers spoke some Spanish, Latina teachers described that Latino immigrant parents felt more at ease and comfortable with a native Spanish speaker to discuss their child's academic progress. This was the case when a White teacher asked a Latina immigrant mother, "*¿se siente comfortable con mi Español?*" [do you feel comfortable with my Spanish?] for a parent-teacher conference. The Latina immigrant mother looked at her and opted to have a second-generation Latina teacher translate for her because "comfortable" (correct word is *comoda*) was the incorrect word to signal feeling at ease. Latina teachers also explained that they were sought out because Latino immigrant parents felt a number of negative emotions such as nervousness, embarrassment, or intimidation when trying to interact with monolingual, English-speaking teachers. Valdes (1996) explains that the Latino immigrant parents in her study purposefully missed parent-teacher conferences with monolingual, English-speaking teachers because they were fearful of being judged, but the Latina teachers in this study explained that parents actively sought them out to help themselves and their children. Mrs. Estrada explained, "a lot of parents would come to me to go and translate to the teacher they had now. They were embarrassed or something. Like intimidated that they couldn't speak the language, so I think they kind of like don't defend their kid like they would if they could". I found that it was not solely speaking Spanish that would draw Latino immigrant parents to Latina teachers; rather, it was also understanding their forms of speech and experiences as immigrants adapting to the host society. Mrs. Kingston said, "I'm able to communicate to most of the parents . . . Not only because of the language but because of where I come from, Mexico. I relate to their struggling to come across. They have issues like 'oh well my husband was taken in [deported]'".

The Latina teachers included in this study communicated in Spanish with Latino immigrant parents invoking language codes that Carter (2003) would characterize as "nondominant" forms of expression in marginalized conversational etiquette in institutions that privilege English and Anglo ways of "talking the talk". Bernstein (1971, 1973) refers to these sociolinguistic patterns among working-class groups as the "restricted code" which is common knowledge shared among families, children, and extended kinship and friendship networks. Many Latina teachers noted that they did not know speaking Spanish was an asset for them in their jobs until they experienced it firsthand in their interactions with parents, noting that it was a "big deal to be Latina and to be able to communicate to the kids and with the parents". For instance, Mrs. Franco, a second-generation Latina teacher in Rosemead, who sometimes felt nervous using Spanish with Latino immigrant parents, still evinced these communication codes in her classroom when she received a phone call from the grandmother of one of her Latino students that was put on the speakerphone. This is how it was captured in my field notes:

> Mrs. FRANCO: *Mijo* [Son], can you answer the phone?
> CALLER: *Si, es la abuelita de Mayito. Namas queria saber si se iba a quedar despues de escuela.* [Yes, it's Mayito's grandmother. I just wanted to know if he will stay after school.]
> STUDENT: It's Mayito's grandma.
> Mrs. FRANCO: (grabs phone) *Mayito se va a quedar en la clase* [will stay in class].

Research shows that bilingual Latina teachers often code-switch between Spanish and English during informal conversations with one another (Flores 2011); however, in this case, the field notes were saturated with examples illustrating the nuances in Spanish conversational language codes among working-class Latino immigrant parents and Latina teachers who were one generation removed from the immigrant experience. Latina teachers used *mi-ja* and *mi-jo* (shortened version of *mi hija*, meaning "my daughter") to refer to their students, even though they were not related by blood. Spanish phoneticists, such as Schwegler (2009), would also call this "*encadenamiento*", the process of blending letters together depending on the combination of consonants and vowels by native Spanish speakers. Mrs. Franco also invoked the ending "*ito*" (indicating size) to signify an endearing way of saying a name in Spanish.

Mrs. Madrigal also invoked these language codes when she spoke to Mrs. Martinez, a Latina immigrant mother in Compton, during a parent-teacher conference that lasted more than 25 minutes to discuss her son's academic performance.

> Doña Martinez stood at Mrs. Madrigal's door, hesitating to come in. "*Hola maestra*"! [Hi teacher] "*Pasele, señora Martinez. Con confianza. ¿Gusta de un cafecito*"? [Come in Mrs. Martinez. With confidence. Would you like coffee] "*No Gracias*". [No, thank you] "*¿Cómo ha estado*"? [How have you been] "*Muy bién, gracias. ¿Y usted*"? [Very well, thank you. And you] . . . She turned to Mrs. Martinez's baby and asked, "*¿Cuántos meses tiene*"? [How many months is she] "*Ocho*"

[Eight], she responded. "You're going to college". The mother chuckled. Then the conference began. "*Cristian es un niño agradable. ¿Así se dice verdad? ¿Agradable*"? [Cristian is a pleasure to have in class. That's how you say it right? A pleasure] "*Si*"! [Yes].

There are a couple of items that stand out about this interaction. First, Mrs. Madrigal refers to the mother as *señora* Martínez, not Cristian's mom, which several non-Latino teachers used when speaking with Latino parents. Second, she uses the diminutive when she says "*cafecito*", a common form of expression in the Spanish language. She also encourages Mrs. Martinez to enter her classroom by using the word "*confianza*" (a form of confidence). Lastly, many Latina teachers began these meetings with initial "small talk" conversations, which deviated from the child's academic achievement, before the scholastic portion of the conference began. These conversational elements and cultural codes and signals, which Latina teachers exercise daily, are imperative to build positive social relations with working-class, Latino immigrant parents.

In contrast, the following field note excerpts show how language codes were lost in translation between the Latina immigrant mother and a Caucasian male colleague of Mrs. Madrigal's in Compton. Mrs. Madrigal was holding a parent-teacher conference with a Latino immigrant father when Mr. Allen came into her room to see if she could translate for him, but noticed she was busy. He made a "come here" motion with his right arm and mouthed in a very low voice, "can you translate for me"? We walked into his room and Mrs. Martinez, Cristian's mother, was waiting by the door. Mr. Allen walked in and motioned her to sit down at a semi-round table in the back of his room. Mr. Allen asked me to ask Mrs. Martinez if she had any questions. She looked at me and said, "*a si, vine a preguntar por qué Cristian esta tan bajo en el lenguaje. Si me puede explicar por que se saco un dos*". I turned to Mr. Allen and translated, "Mrs. Martinez says she wants to know why Cristian was doing so poorly in language. If you could explain to her why he has a two as his language score". Mr. Allen kept his eyes on me or the children, the English speakers in the room. It was rare that he directed his glance at Mrs. Martinez. At one point Mr. Allen turned around in his chair and picked up a chapter book that was on a shelf. "This is Judy Blume's *Tales of a Fourth Grade Nothing*", he said. He opened the book to the first chapter, slammed the book on the table and demanded that Cristian "read the first paragraph out loud"! Panicked, Cristian started sounding out the words and breaking them into meaningful syllables. "Chaaap-ter . . . one . . . Th-e . . . Big . . . Win-ner". Before he could finish the paragraph Mr. Allen grabbed the book from his tiny hands and fluently, but haughtily, read, "Chapter One, The Big Winner". He began to wave his arm in a figure eight motion to insinuate the pace of his reading style: "as a fourth grader you need to be reading like that. Not Ch-Ch-Chap-ter One. No stuttering. It should be fluid"! He continued in an abrasive tone and pointed his index finger at Mrs. Martinez, "*MÁS LÉA, LÉA, LÉA*"! [MORE READING, READING, READING] . . . She stared at the index finger pointed at her . . . "you've got to be stern and direct with these parents", he said.

Whereas this may seem like an extreme example, versions of these abuses in language codes were not uncommon. Mrs. Ybarra said, "*hay maneras de comunicarse*" [there are ways to communicate], but monolingual English teachers and personnel "*no se prestan para comunicar*" [don't lend themselves to communication]. This was a linguistic pattern that Latina teachers observed between some monolingual English speakers and Latino immigrant parents. Chong (2002) argues that Latino immigrants and their children respond positively to politeness of demeanor, comportment, and address, and favor the pleasing forms vs. the direct, businesslike messages conveyed by the English language. An intense emotive style and person-centered approach is more appealing than a businesslike, structured approach. Having proper demeanor and *simpatía*, the ability to create smooth, friendly, and pleasant relationships that avoid conflict (Chong 2002; Falicov 2002) with authority figures, are preferred.

Latina teachers often served as translators for teachers that could not speak Spanish, and were attuned to the differences in interactional forms between teachers of different racial/ethnic backgrounds and Latino parents. Mrs. Quiroz, a Guatemalan and Salvadoran teacher in Rosemead, said, "*les trato de suavizar el mensaje*" [I try to smooth out the message] whenever she would serve as a translator. Mrs. Quiroz emphasized that she would make the effort to direct her focus at the parents' eyes, because non-Spanish-speaking teachers would avert their glance from the parent and direct it to the child or the translator. Many teachers like Mrs. Quiroz sympathized with monolingual, English-speaking teachers who had difficulty communicating in Spanish during parent-teacher conferences, but added that this could potentially affect rapport between teachers and parents. She said, "I can see the frustration that a lot of English teachers have during parent teacher conferences . . . if they don't have a translator, they can't communicate . . . I've always seen the distance. The fact that they don't speak the [Spanish] language creates . . . the barrier".

This rift was also the case for third- and fourth-generation Latina teachers who could not articulate themselves very well in the language and felt they were disappointing Latino families. As Mrs. Cadenas explained, "a lot of the Latino families think that I speak Spanish, and I feel like I let 'em down. I can't speak it. I understand for the most part what they're telling me, but [it] makes me feel like I'm somehow letting them down". To compensate for their limited bilingual skills, many third-plus-generation Latina teachers would invite former bilingual Latino students who had graduated from high school to facilitate these meetings, or relied on translators provided by the school.

Mathematical Rifts

Unlike the transmission of values to Latino children and implementation of a different means of communication, Latina teachers described another cultural rift in regards to math algorithms. Many said they resonated with their students' experiences because they too grew up in homes with parents that had low levels of education and only received *"primaria"* [primary] education in the home country. This was the case especially in regards to long division and multiplication equations that were daily sources of contestation between Latina teachers and their students.

Latina teachers explained that Latino immigrant parents would schedule meetings with them because their children cried or grew "frustrated" when doing math homework. This cultural mismatch was evident during a "Swun family night",[7] an event held for parents in Compton who wanted to aid their children with their homework. When the question and answer portion began after a Latina teacher finished a presentation on addition and subtraction, a Latina mother exclaimed, *"mi niña se frustra y se pone a llorar porque como yo le enseño no es como le enseña la maestra"* [my daughter gets frustrated and starts to cry because how I teach her is not how her teacher shows her]. Another Latina immigrant mother chimed in, *"a la mía ya la pusieron en clases especiales"* [mine has already been placed in special education classes]. The presenter, in her broken Spanish, said, *"nosotros queremos enseñarle la manera mas fácil para el niño"* [we want to teach the child the easiest way possible]. A second-generation Latina mother said, *"me enseñaron a mi diferente. Yo le decia a mi mamá, 'le tengo que hacer como le hizo el maestro'"* [they taught me differently. I would tell my mother, "I have to do it how the teacher taught me"]. *"Allí es donde existe la confusion"* [this is where the confusion begins], said another mother.

There is a long history in the education literature of Latino children labeled as special needs (Gonzalez 1990a) due to a perceived language impairment, but here we see how a Latino child was placed in a special education classroom for her mathematical abilities, even when she showed advanced forms of solving them. Mosqueda (2010) suggests that English language proficiency is necessary to handle the linguistic complexity of math content. Similarly, Civil (2008, 2009) argues that cultural misunderstandings arise between Latino immigrant families and school officials because mathematical word problems do not use examples that relate to a Latino student's home life. In this study we see that not all teachers validated the mathematical, nondominant forms of capital that Latino parents brought with them from the home country when they attempted to help their children in the ways that they were able. This study finds that it is not only language proficiency that matters, but also that acknowledging and allowing alternative mathematical problem-solving strategies is crucial in the classroom for the children of Latino immigrant parents to succeed. When probed about this rift, some

Latina teachers, like Mrs. Rivas, said that if it "made sense to the child and they could explain it to the teacher, then it was fine." Other Latina teachers such as Mrs. Madrigal said that she was unaware of this method because her parents did not have much schooling in their country of origin, but informed me that once Latino parents met with her and "discussed the steps" she was more receptive to allowing the strategy. Latina teachers such as Mrs. Godínez also informed me that some non-Latino teachers in Compton were less receptive to this method and urged Latino parents to learn the "U.S. way" of solving long division and multiplication. Mrs. Godínez elaborated that the perception was that if immigrants were in the U.S., they needed to assimilate and learn the mainstream "American way" of solving problems to keep the learning process "standardized". This led to disagreements between Latino immigrant parents, who indicated that their child's teacher would claim the child "cheated" on homework assignments. These findings reso- nate with Delpit's (2012) work on how teachers can connect math concepts to community issues relevant to African American students; but here we see something different, where Latina teachers allow a completely alternative problem-solving strategy among Latino students in schools.

Teachers such as Mrs. Franco, Mrs. Cadena, and Ms. Sánchez—all upper- grade Latina teachers at Rosemead—acknowledged that their Latino stu- dents were instructed to solve math problems at home in a different way by their Latino immigrant parents. They allowed the practice for both their Latino and Asian students. Mrs. Cadena, in particular, said, "oh yeah! The Latinos solve them differently . . . I let them do it. I always tell them, I have to teach you this way, but if you are more comfortable doing it the way your parents showed you, then that's fine".

Similarly, Mrs. Cadena explained,

> Latinos will tell me, "my dad taught me like this". I tell them, "whatever way you're comfortable with, continue it". I teach it a certain way in class. It's gonna confuse 'em when they go home and their dad says, "no, you do it like this. This is how I learned". I can't tell them, "your dad's been teaching you all this time, but because I'm your teacher this year you have to change it to this". It's harder for them. I do run into that.
>
> (Mrs. Cadena, Rosemead)

Figures 6.1 and 6.2 show how Latina teachers instructed their students in their daily curricular lessons, and also show how some Mexican immigrant parents learned to solve math problems in the home country. The focus group data compiled for this study, based on both Latino immigrant and English-speaking Latino parents, asked Latino parents to solve both a mul- tiplication and long division math problem. The prompt read: please solve the following math problem/*por favor hágame esta operación*: $1238 \div 84$ or 29×34, written vertically. As we can see from Figure 6.1, the long divi- sion math problem, Latino immigrant parents arrived at the same quotient, but did not detail all of their steps. One parent was enthused that they were able to showcase their expertise and showed the method they were taught to assess if they came to the correct answer. The multiplication math prompt in Figure 6.2, in particular, posed problems for some Latino immigrant parents during the focus group because I wrote the problem vertically. During the focus group with Spanish-speaking, Latino immigrant parents, one Latina mother asked me, "*¿me la puedes escribir hací? Es más fácil. De este modo no le entiendo*" [can you write it for me this way (arm horizontal, across her chest)? It's easier. I don't understand the problem written that way]. Not all Latino parents knew how to solve problems using Mexican math methodologies. In fact, I filled out the demographic face sheet for one immigrant Latina mother in the Spanish language focus group because she was not Spanish literate.

I asked Latina teachers if they could show me how Latino parents were instructing their children, but many of them had trouble explaining the procedure. Mrs. Arenas said, "Mexican parents solve part of the problem in their head. They don't write everything down". Mrs. Franco made sure to validate Latino immigrant parents' ways of solving math problems during parent-teacher conferences so Latino students would not undermine their parents' authority and intelligence. She expressed that Latino children worried about this and needed to hear that what their parents were teaching them was accepted and validated in schools. She explained,

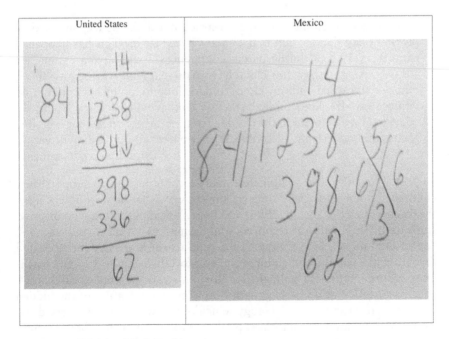

Figure 6.1 Division Math Problem

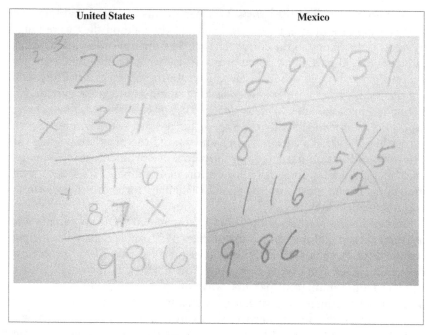

United States	Mexico

Figure 6.2   Multiplication Math Problem

[my students] tell me, "my mom learned it a different way in Mexico. Is that okay that she did that" [in a worried tone]? This has happened almost every year during parent conferences. I will have a parent say, "I was trying to show [my child] how to do math this way because this is the way I learned and [my child] told me 'no, no, no'! They couldn't do it because Mrs. Franco taught them". So they will ask me if I can validate . . . I will explain to the child in front of the parent so that everyone hears the same thing, "it is okay if your parents have a different way".

(Mrs. Franco, Rosemead)

As Mrs. Franco's quote illuminates, many Latino parents do support their children at home with their homework in the ways that they are able. Unlike the teachers in Valenzuela's (1999) and Lopez's studies (2002), who divested students of their cultural resources and seemed to reflect a "subtractive" educational model, here we see how Latina teachers actively incorporated them to make parents and children feel comfortable, and how Latina teachers were attempting to validate Latino immigrant parents' local knowledge base in U.S. schools. The math examples, a key feature of the hidden Chicana/Latina cultural pedagogy, elucidate how Latina teachers draw from the nondominant cultural capital of poorer Latino families to generate parental involvement, which is crucial to social advancement in schools

(Valdes 1996). This example illustrates that Latina teachers are not just "cultural brokers", a unilateral form of translating and communicating from the institution to the Latino immigrant parent; rather, this is a reciprocal process where they take from the knowledge that Latino parents bring with them from their home countries and incorporate such in schools to aid the learning process. Latino students who were not validated for this were at risk of being downwardly and negatively tracked in school.

CONCLUSIONS

This chapter illuminates how Latina teachers play a pivotal role in mitigating the incorporation trajectories of Latino students and their families—teachers are the success stories in Latino communities and are intermediaries in the adaptation process. Based on the ethnographic evidence presented in this paper, I argue that there is a quiet transformation in California's public schools in Latino and mixed neighborhoods through an institutionalizing of "giving back" socially in schools by Latina teachers. There are limits to the ways education scholars have been conceptualizing cultural funds of knowledge in schools, and formal, institutionalized, celebratory multiculturalism is not enough, because it is mostly symbolic. I distinguish between two different kinds of culture: heroic folkloric Latino culture—symbolic forms that take place only certain times of the year—and the hidden Chicana/Latina cultural pedagogy that occurs daily. I found that Latina teachers are already implementing Latino cultural resources in schools, albeit unknowingly even to them at times.

Latino culture is an asset in schools for Latina teachers, and I show this through communication styles, the immigrant narrative, and mathematics. Latina teachers used immigrant narratives, communication, and alternative math-solving strategies as a teaching tool in their workplaces. I contend that because of their working-class roots and immigrant backgrounds, Latina teachers are able to more successfully tap into the subtle Latino cultural cues that immigrant Latino families bring with them from their countries of origin, even those Latina teachers that are further removed from the immigrant experience recognize these cultural signals as important. The hidden Chicana/Latina cultural pedagogy in schools provides us with resources that can be tapped into, and practical measures that can be implemented, to make Latino families feel welcome in schools. This is important because Latino culture has previously not been accepted in schools, and Latino families have been greeted with hostility and acute nativism. Latina teachers are aware of this anti-Latino and anti-Mexican sentiment and are trying to address hostile contexts of reception that Mexican families are exposed to in schools (Portes and Rumbaut 2001). However, their efforts to include Latino cultural elements are met in contrasting ways in multiracial schools, experiencing more resistance in Compton than in Rosemead.

This research contributes to sociological and educational scholarship by expanding our idea of Latino culture in education. This chapter argues that Latina teachers, the mostly college-educated daughters of working-class, Mexican immigrants, draw from the "hidden Chicana/Latina cultural pedagogy" to facilitate the incorporation of their Latino students. Because Latino culture has historically been prohibited in American public schools and the children of Latino immigrants have been greeted with one of the most hostile contexts of reception of all immigrant groups (Portes and Rumbaut 2001; Lopez 2002), I suggest that Latina teachers use culture to curtail and buffer the downwardly mobile pathways of Latino youth in schools. I argue that the mostly second-generation and bilingual Latina teachers in this study are intermediaries, because these practices are not unidirectional, and simply come from Latina teachers that filter the information down to the children of Latino immigrants. Rather, there is a reciprocal process—one that is a cooperative effort that facilitates on-going relationships between Latino families and the teacher. These are, indeed, important counterhegemonic spaces that lead to empowerment and success.

NOTES

1. Unlike African American children that suffered *de jure* segregation because they were deemed racially inferior, Mexican-origin children held a racially ambiguous status because they were granted citizenship under the Treaty of Guadalupe Hidalgo in 1848. Mexican families who opted to stay in the newly acquired territories were guaranteed the right to maintain the Spanish language and their culture (Ochoa 2007; Sanchez 1995).
2. Often confused as Mexican Independence Day (September 16, 1810), Cinco de Mayo [May 5] marks the Mexican army's defeat of the French at the Battle of Puebla.
3. The names used for the Latina teachers throughout this chapter are pseudonyms.
4. Cross-cultural, Language, and Academic Development and Bilingual, Cross-cultural, Language, and Academic Development.
5. Focus group breakdown: Rosemead: five Latina immigrant mothers, four Mexican American parents (one man), six Asian immigrant mothers (one was one-and-a-half immigrant). Compton: five Latina immigrant mothers, four Mexican American mothers, four Black parent figures.
6. The first wave of Cuban migrants, the Golden Exiles, is the Latino subgroup that was warmly received by the U.S. government.
7. SWUN Math is a mathematical model developed by Si Swun, an English Language Learner who struggled with math as a student. His model is based on math methodologies found in Asia, namely Singapore. SWUN Math has spread throughout Southern California and is used in school districts with low socioeconomic, English Language Learner, and minority student populations.

REFERENCES

Agius Vallejo, J., and J. Lee. 2009. "Brown Picket Fences: The Immigrant Narrative and Patterns of Giving Back Among the Mexican Origin Middle-Class in Los Angeles." *Ethnicities* 9: 5–23.

Alvarez, R. R. 1986. "The Lemon Grove Incident: The Nation's First Successful Desegregation Court Case." *San Diego Historical Society Quarterly* 32: 116–135.

American Community Survey. 2014. "State & County Quick Facts." Retrieved January 8, 2015 from http://quickfacts.census.gov/qfd/states/06/0662896.html.

Banks, J. 1989. "Multicultural Education: Characteristics and Goals." In *Multicultural Education: Issues and Perspectives*, edited by J. Banks and C. Banks, 3–26. Boston: Allyn and Bacon.

Bernstein, B. 1971. *Class, Codes and Control: Theoretical Studies Towards a Sociology of Language*. New York: Routledge.

California Department of Education. 2013. *Certificated Staff by Ethnicity for 2009–2010: State Summary, Number of Staff by Ethnicity*. Retrieved September 22, 2010, from http://dq.cde.ca.gov/dataquest/Staff/StaffByEth.aspx.

Camarillo, A. 2004. "Black and Brown in Compton: Demographic Change, Suburban Decline, and Intergroup Relations in a South Central Los Angeles Community, 1950 to 2000." In *Not Just Black and White: Historical and Contemporary Perspectives on Immigration, Race, and Ethnicity in the United States*, edited by N. Foner and G. M. Fredrickson, 358–376. New York: Russell Sage Foundation.

Carter, P. 2003. "Black Cultural Capital, Status Positioning, and Schooling Conflicts for Low-Income African American Youth." *Social Problems* 50: 136–155.

Carter, P. 2007. *Keepin' It Real: School Success Beyond Black and White*. New York: Oxford University Press.

Chong, N. 2002. *The Latino Patient: A Cultural Guide for Health Care Providers*. Yarmouth, ME: Intercultural Press.

Civil, M. 2008. "Language and Mathematics: Immigrant Parents' Participation in School." *Center for the Mathematics Education of Latinos/as* 32: 329–336.

Civil, M. 2009. "Mathematics Education, Language, and Culture: Ponderings From a Different Geographic Context." *Center for the Mathematics Education of Latinos/as* 1: 131–136.

Conchas, G. 2006. *The Color of Success: Race and High-Achieving Urban Youth*. New York: Teachers College Press.

Delpit, L. 2006. *Other People's Children: Cultural Conflict in the Classroom*. New York: The New Press.

Delpit, L. 2012. *"Multiplication Is for White People": Raising Expectations for Other People's Children*. New York: New Press.

Ed-Data. 2012. *Fiscal, Demographic and Performance Data on K-12 Schools*. Retrieved March 18, 2013, from http://www.ed-data.k12.ca.us/Pages/Home.aspx.

Emerson, R. M., R. I. Fretz, and L. L. Shaw. 1995. *Writing Ethnographic Fieldnotes*. Chicago: University of Chicago Press.

Falicov, C. J. 2002. *Latino Families in Therapy: A Guide to Multicultural Practice*. New York: The Guilford Press.

Feliciano, C. 2006. *Unequal Origins: Immigrant Selection and the Education of the Second Generation*. El Paso, TX: LFB Scholarly Publishing.

Flores, G. M. 2011a. "Latino/as in the Hard Sciences: Increasing Latina/o Participation in Science, Technology, Engineering and Math (STEM) Related Fields." *Latino Studies* 9: 327–335.

Flores, G. M. 2011b. "Racialized Tokens: Latina Teachers Negotiating, Surviving and Thriving in a White Woman's Profession." *Qualitative Sociology* 34: 313–335.

Flores, G. M., and P. Hondagneu-Sotelo. 2014. "The Social Dynamics Channeling Latina College Graduates into the Teaching Profession." *Gender, Work and Organization*. doi:10.1111/gwao.12051.

Fry, R., and M. H. Lopez. 2012. *Hispanic Student Enrollments Reach New Highs in 2011*. Washington, DC: Pew Research Hispanic Center.

Gándara, P. 1995. *Over the Ivy Walls: The Education Mobility of Low-Income Chicanos*. Albany, NY: State University of New York Press.

Gándara, P., and F. Contreras. 2009. *The Latino Education Crisis: The Consequences of Failed Social Policies.* Cambridge, MA: Harvard University Press.

Gans, H. J. 1979. "Symbolic Ethnicity: The Future of Ethnic Groups and Cultures in America." *Ethnic and Racial Studies* 2: 1–20.

Garcia, R. 1991. *Rise of the Mexican American Middle-Class: San Antonio, 1929–1941.* College Station, TX: A&M Press.

Goffman, E. 2001. "On Fieldwork." In *Contemporary Field Research: Perspectives and Formulations,* edited by Robert M. Emerson, pp. 153–158. Prospect Heights, IL: Waveland Press.

Gonzalez, G. 1990a. *Chicano Education in the Era of Segregation.* London: Balch Institute Press.

Gonzalez, G. 1990b. "Culture, Language and the Americanization of Mexican Children." In *Chicano Education in the Era of Segregation,* 30–45. Philadelphia: The Balch Institute Press.

González, N., L. C. Moll, and C. Amanti. 2005. *Funds of Knowledge Theorizing Practices in Households, Communities, and Classrooms.* Philadelphia: Routledge.

Ladson-Billings, G. J. 2005. "Is the Team All Right? Diversity and Teacher Education." *Journal of Teacher Education* 56: 229–234.

Li, W. 1997. "Ethnoburb versus Chinatown: Two Types of Urban Ethnic Communities in Los Angeles." *Cybergeo.*

Lopez, N. 2002. *Hopeful Girls, Troubled Boys: Race and Gender Disparity in Urban Education.* New York: Routledge.

Menjívar, C. 2000. *Fragmented Ties: Salvadoran Immigrant Networks in America.* Berkeley: University of California Press.

Moll, L. C., C. Amanti, D. Neff, and N. Gonzalez. 1992. "Funds of Knowledge for Teaching: Using a Qualitative Approach to Connect Homes and Classrooms." *Qualitative Issues in Educational Research* 31: 132–141.

Moore, J. 1970. *Mexican Americans.* Englewood Cliffs, NJ: Prentice Hall.

Mosqueda, E. 2010. "Compounding Inequalities: English Proficiency and Tracking and Their Relation to Mathematics Performance among Latina/o Secondary School Youth." *Journal of Urban Mathematics Education* 3: 57–81.

Nieto, S. 1999. *The Light in Their Eyes: Creating Multicultural Learning Communities.* New York: Teachers College Press.

Oboler, S. 1995. *Ethnic Labels, Latino Lives: Identity and the Politics of (Re)presentation in the United States.* Minneapolis: University of Minnesota Press.

Ochoa, G. 2007. *Learning from Latino Teachers.* San Francisco: Jossey-Bass.

Orfield, G., G. Siegel-Hawley, and J. Kucsera. 2011. *Divided We Fail: Segregated and Unequal Schools in the Southland.* Los Angeles, CA: The Civil Rights Project at UCLA.

Passel, J.S. 2011. "Demography of Immigrant Youth: Past, Present, and Future." *The Future of Children* 21: 19–41.

Portes, A., and R. Ruben. 2001. *Legacies: The Story of the Immigrant Second Generation.* Berkeley: University of California Press.

Romo, H. and Falbo, T. 1996. *Latino High School Graduation: Defying the Odds.* Austin: University of Texas Press.

Rosas, A. 2011. "Breaking the Silence: Mexican Children and Women's Confrontation of Bracero Family Separation, 1942–1964." *Gender & History* 23: 382–400.

Sanchez, G. 1995. *Becoming Mexican American: Ethnicity, Culture and Identity in Chicano Los Angeles, 1900–1945.* Oxford: Oxford University Press.

Sanchez, G. I. 1997. "History, Culture and Education." In *Latinos and Education: A Critical Reader,* edited by A. Darder, R. D. Torres, and H. Gutierrez, 117–134. New York: Routledge.

Schwegler, A., J. Kempff, and A. Ameal-Guerra. 2009. *Fonética y Fonología Españolas: Teoría y Práctica,* 4th ed. New York: John Wiley & Sons.

Sides, J. 2003. *L.A. City Limits: African American Los Angeles from the Great Depression to the Present*. Berkeley/Los Angeles: University of California Press.

Simón, L. 1997. *Fear and Learning at Hoover Elementary*. Hohokus, NJ: Transit Media.

Sleeter, C. E., and C. A. Grant. 2009. *Making Choices for Multicultural Education: Five Approaches to Race, Class and Gender*, 6th ed. New York: Wiley.

Smith, R. C. 2005. *Mexican New York: Transnational Live of New Immigrants*. Berkeley: University of California Press.

Strauss, A. L. 1987. *Qualitative Analysis for Social Scientists*. Cambridge: Cambridge University Press.

Suarez-Orozco, C., and M. Suarez-Orozco. 2001. *Children of Immigration*. Cambridge, MA: Harvard University Press.

Telles, E. E., and V. Ortiz. 2008. *Generations of Exclusions: Racial Assimilation and Mexican Americans*. Berkeley: University of California Press.

Urrieta, L. 2005. *Working from Within: Chicana and Chicano Activist Educators in Whitestream Schools*. University of Arizona Press.

Valdes, G. 1996. *Con Respeto: Bridging the Distances between Culturally Diverse Families and Schools: An Ethnographic Portrait*. New York and London: Teachers College Press.

Valenzuela, A. 1999. *Subtractive Schooling: U.S. Mexican Youth and the Politics of Caring*. Albany, NY: State University of New York.

Velez, W. Y. 2000. "The Invisible Minorities in Mathematics." *Mathematics and Education Reform Forum* 12: 3–7.

Washburn, D. E. 1996. *Multicultural Education in the United States*. Philadelphia: Inquiry International.

Waters, M. 2001. *Black Identities: West Indian Dreams and American Realities*. Harvard University Press.

Yosso, T. 2005. "Whose Culture Has Capital? A Critical Discussion of Community Cultural Wealth." *Race, Ethnicity and Education* 8: 69–91.

7 Gendered Expectations and Sexualized Policing

Latinas' Experiences in a Public High School

Gilda L. Ochoa

Everything is fenced up, and I feel like everybody is watching us. You can't do this; you can't do that.

(Angelica Vega, high school senior)

As a Hispanic there's discrimination, and I think gender-wise there's discrimination too.

(Summer Reyes, high school junior)

As with many of her schoolmates, senior Angelica Vega feels her Southern California High School (SCHS) is "like a prison". Wrought iron gates enclose it, several security guards patrol it, and occasionally drug-sniffing dogs scour it. Such security and punishment are part of what has been called a discipline regime in public schools (Morris 2006; Kupchik 2010). These forms of social control are part of the movement from a welfare state to a penal state, characterizing the neoliberal agenda of privatization and defunding of social programs (Fleury-Steiner 2008). Emerging in the context of "tough on crime" policies and fueled by a culture of fear and the demonizing of youth of color, schools are increasingly using prisonlike tactics, including zero tolerance policies where students caught violating school rules face stricter penalties, including suspensions, expulsions, and maybe even police interventions (Beres and Griffith 2001; Noguera 2008; Nolan 2011).

However, as high school junior Summer Reyes clarifies, these constraints are not meted out equally. Some students are given the benefit of the doubt and multiple chances; others are presumed guilty and receive no chances at all. They are heavily surveilled and punished. These are among the forms of discrimination Summer believes Hispanics or Latinas, such as herself, encounter at her high school.[1]

Recently, there has been significant public and academic focus on the experiences of young boys and men of color, including the extensive policing they encounter in U.S. schools (Noguera 2008; Rios 2011; Conchas and Vigil 2012). President Obama's initiative, *My Brother's Keeper*, is a contemporary, high-profile example centering boys of color. Launched in January 2014, this initiative focuses on providing mentors, support networks, and skills to enhance opportunities for all boys and young men of color.

Conversely, less attention has been placed on the experiences of girls and women of color and the types of constraints, surveillance, and punishment they endure in schools. With larger percentages of young women graduating from high school and matriculating at colleges and universities, some may divert attention away from girls and women with the false pretense that schooling is working for them and that it is just young boys of color who are struggling or who are maybe even the problem. This approach may inadvertently pit groups against one another in a zero-sum game where attention is directed at young men and away from women of color. It also ignores how groups are defined in relationship to one another and the ways race, gender, sexuality, and class intersect to differentially influence experiences and life chances. To more thoroughly understand the multifaceted components and implications of today's system of social control in U.S. schools, it is important to consider varied students' experiences. A wider range of narratives enables a fuller story about the belief systems, practices, and everyday dynamics structuring U.S. schools and students' opportunities.

LISTENING TO LATINA VOICES AS A CASE STUDY APPROACH

Drawing on in-depth interviews with educators and students from a Southern California public high school, this chapter considers dominant constructions, school practices, and everyday relationships on Latinas' schooling. Because elsewhere I detail academic barriers at the school (see Ochoa 2013), this chapter focuses specifically on raced-gendered expectations, including sexualized policing, where Latinas at the high school encounter constant monitoring of their bodies, beliefs, and actions. These are among the disciplining mechanisms occurring in our schools. By limiting students' ways of being, such expectations and policing are assimilationist. Justified by individualistic ideologies, these processes deflect attention away from societal and school conditions and instead blame Latinas/os and their families for educational inequalities. Together, they reinforce gender, racial/ethnic, and class hierarchies.

Although politicians, pundits, and the public talk at length about educational reform, students' perspectives are largely absent from contemporary discussions. New programs are instituted and marketed with the pretense that they are best for students, schools, and society. However, few speak with those impacted on a daily basis by what happens in our schools. Instead, students are increasingly evaluated *quantitatively* as though performances on standardized tests are meaningful measurements of all that needs to be known. Going inside our schools and listening to students is more telling. Students' narratives unmask the hidden curriculum—the many unspoken lessons transmitted in schools.

Eager to learn from students, I spent over 18 months at the school I refer to as Southern California High School (SCHS). Located in Los Angeles County, SCHS has a population of nearly 2,000 students with relatively equal percentages of Asian Americans (46%) and Latinas/os (43%); the remaining student body is about 7% White, 2% African American, and 1% Native American. Over 30% of students are eligible for free and reduced lunch, and about 10% are English Language Learners. As is the case nationally, the school personnel at SCHS do not represent the racial/ethnic backgrounds of the student body. About half of the teachers and administrators are White, one-fourth are Latina/o, one-fifth are Asian American, and less than 3% are African American or Native American (California Department of Education 2008).

SCHS is a relatively well-funded public high school. In addition to honors and Advanced Placement courses, it boasts an International Baccalaureate (IB) program that provides a special counselor and courses including Theory of Knowledge, Art History, and Twentieth-Century History for the 30–40 juniors and seniors in the program. SCHS is known for having high standardized test scores and rates of college attendance. As a result, it has appeared in *Newsweek Magazine*'s list of the top 1,000 public schools in the nation. However, as students' testimonials reveal, not all have access to the same quality and quantity of school resources.

In May and June 2001, and again from May 2007 to December 2008, I sat in on classes and attended campus assemblies, graduations, and meetings. Working with several students from the Claremont Colleges, I interviewed over 50 teachers, counselors, and parents; but most of my time was spent listening to students. Across from tables, gathered around benches, and sitting in circles, in 50- to 75-minute interviews, we asked 139 students about their schooling, friendships, and future plans. The interview questions were broad and open-ended, allowing students to share their experiences in ways that were meaningful for them. As a result, students provided a range of testimonials about peer groups and high school life, some highlighting the institutional and daily constraints in school connected to gender and sexuality. For this chapter, I focus on these aspects of the interviews, specifically centering on the 46 interviews with Latina students. With the exception of a few of the interviews, most were audiotaped, transcribed, and then analyzed for recurring themes and patterns. The quotations appearing throughout this chapter are verbatim from the transcripts, but as is the custom in qualitative research the names of the participants and their school have been changed.

On average, the 46 Latinas were nearing the end of their sophomore years in high school. With parents in sales, construction, and trucking, most will be the first generation in their family to attend college. They are the children or grandchildren of immigrants, and many identify as Mexican or Mexican American. Some identify pan-ethnically as Hispanic or Latina, and a few are Central American or identify with multiple ethnic groups.[2]

GENDERED EXPECTATIONS AND SEXUALIZED POLICING

At SCHS, school personnel and students reveal disturbing experiences that highlight how females' bodies and actions—especially Latinas'—are sexualized, hyperscrutinized, and patrolled. Together, dominant myths, school practices, and everyday exchanges perpetuate strict dress codes, objectifying gazes, and labeling that are bolstered by an assimilationist imperative endorsing White, middle-class, and upper-class modes of comportment; narrow gendered and racialized constructions of femininity; and heteronormativity. Underlying these practices and imperatives are prevailing ideologies that blame young women for their experiences and cast Latinas as hypersexual and potentially pregnant teenagers. Together, these dynamics foster a discriminatory environment of sexualized policing that reinforces hierarchies and limits a sense of belonging in school. However, as their narratives suggest, students do not always acquiesce to such school climates; they construct counterspaces, and critique and contest exclusionary dynamics in multifaceted ways.

Dominant Myths about Latinas

Latinas' schooling experiences must be understood in the context of a legacy of exclusionary ideologies that justify power, privilege, and inequality. Ranging from biological and cultural deficiency perspectives that assume Latinas/os lack intellectual and cultural capabilities for academic success to constructions of Latinas as sex objects, these myths are part of larger belief systems maintaining and reproducing social, economic, and political inequality. It is because of the magnitude of these constructions that Patricia Hill Collins (2001) refers to them as "controlling images".

These myths or controlling images manifest themselves in multiple arenas, and they may become self-fulfilling. They are historically rooted and permeate all aspects of our society, including attitudes and dynamics at schools. At SCHS, there are several recurring myths categorizing Latina/o students as uncaring about education, hypersexual, and potentially pregnant teenagers. These beliefs impact experiences and material conditions.

Uncaring About Education

The Asians seem to be motivated and driven. The Latinos don't seem to value education in the same way.

(Anthony Castro, SCHS teacher)

Such sweeping generalizations about Latinas/os not valuing education relative to Asian Americans permeate the campus of SCHS. These generalizations exist despite multiple studies indicating that Latinas/os tend to have *higher* aspirations to go to college than do students from the general population and that 94% of Latina/o parents expect their children to go to college (Delgado-Gaitan 1992; Kao 2000; Pew Hispanic Foundation/Kaiser Family Foundation 2004). Nevertheless, stereotypical views proliferate. They are rooted in deficiency perspectives, and they pit Latinas/os against Asian Americans.

In schools through the 1950s, White middle- and upper-class researchers and educators often used both biological and cultural deficiency arguments to explain differences in educational outcomes (Gonzalez 1990). For example, proponents of biological arguments believed that Mexican American students were predisposed physically to perform agricultural labor and lacked the mental capabilities to excel in academically rigorous courses (Gonzalez 1990). By the 1920s, as cultural deficiency perspectives became more popular, educators aimed to Americanize Mexicans and Mexican Americans who they believed came from homes and cultures that did not value education, were too present-time oriented, or were disorganized (Gonzalez 1990; Ochoa 2007). These racist theories justified unequal schools, punished those who spoke languages other than English, and prepared students for low-wage and gender-specific occupations. For Latinas, this meant preparation to fulfill domestic labor (Gonzalez 1990). Meanwhile, Euro-American students were largely schooled for higher paying occupations in accordance with their gender and class positions. Thus, these biological and cultural arguments reproduced a race-based capitalist and gendered labor system.

Today, in places such as SCHS, racist cultural deficiency explanations prevail in the dominant representations of Asian Americans as a so-called model minority in comparison to Latinas/os. Emerging in the midst of the 1960s social justice struggles and gaining prominence in the 1980s, this construction praises Asian Americans as a model group which has supposedly advanced in the U.S. because of their believed cultural emphasis on hard work and determination. At a time when Latinas/os and Blacks were demanding access into dominant institutions and engaging in mass demonstrations that critiqued U.S. society, the mainstream media depicted Asian Americans as good citizens who were advancing on their own (Lee 1996). Since the 1960s, popular magazine and newspaper articles have promulgated the false image that if Asian Americans can succeed without assistance, something must be wrong with Latinas/os and Blacks who are lagging behind educationally and economically (Lee 1996). Recently, high-profile academics have also promulgated such cultural beliefs, ignoring the significance of class resources and institutional disparities (see Chua and Rubenfeld 2014). The model minority myth lumps together heterogeneous groups with diverse histories and class backgrounds and assumes that all Asian Americans are advancing, that we live in a meritocracy, and that African

Americans and Latinas/os are to blame for their positions in society. The ramifications of such assumptions are felt widely. They work in tandem with myths about Latinas/os and permeate the SCHS campus climate.

Hypersexual and Potentially Pregnant Teenagers

A second prevailing assumption apparent at SCHS is that Latinas are hypersexual and potentially pregnant. This myth is also historically rooted, specifically in images deeming Latinas as "hyper-fertile baby machines", "teenage mothers", and barriers to children's educational success (Gutiérrez 2008). For example, early theorists, such as a 1928 Los Angeles assistant supervisor of education, alleged that Mexican teenagers were naturally inclined toward sex over education: "authorities on the Mexican mind agree that after the age of 12–14 educational and higher ambitions turn to inclinations of sex impulse . . . The average [Mexican] boy and girl revert to the native instinct" (quoted in Gonzalez 1990, 37). These racist representations have been used to camouflage systemic inequality and justify discriminatory practices (Gonzalez 1990).

A common narrative in society, and repeated at SCHS, is that the sexuality of Latinas, relative to Whites, Asian Americans, and their male counterparts, is a problem needing control (Garcia 2012). Underlying this concern is a fear of teen pregnancy and acceptance of a cultural deficiency framework positing that Latinas, as a group, are promiscuous and favor young motherhood. An established teacher at SCHS, Margaret Albert most explicitly articulates these myths:

> I've felt that there was a marked difference between the Hispanic female, and I remember reading a very interesting article on how it was a status symbol practically, you know, you're proud that you're pregnant at an early age . . . If you're in one part of the subculture, it's kind of cute for the girl to walk around pregnant. And she's young and then he's young and then there's the limit to how much education you can get.

Adopting the belief that culture is to blame, teacher Margaret Albert characterizes teen pregnancy as a so-called Hispanic value. Despite false convictions such as these, there is not one Latina/o culture or value, and research indicates that having a child as a teenager is linked to *class* resources, not culture (Blum et al. 2000, as referenced in Denner and Guzmán 2006, 4).

Teacher Margaret Albert expounds on her essentializing of Latina hypersexuality and young parenthood by contrasting Latinas with Asian Americans at SCHS: "among the Asian population, generally dating and really getting involved in boyfriend-girlfriend relationships is something that is delayed a great deal. And therefore they have more time to do other things". This disparate typecasting of Latinas and Asian Americans is reinforced in the mainstream media and influences public perceptions (Espiritu 1997; Rodríguez 1997). It is a gendered component of the problematic conceptualization of Asian Americans as so-called model minorities relative to Latinas (see Ochoa 2013).

When Latinas are not invisible in the media or "symbolically annihilated", they have been depicted as sex objects and teen mothers (Rodriguez 1997). During various historical periods, Latinas have been cast as sexually promiscuous and flaunting their sexuality, or as asexual and virgins until marriage. As hegemonic constructions, such representations are as oppressive as the myth of not caring about education: (1) they divide entire groups of women into whore/virgin dichotomies and pit women against each other in bad/good categories, (2) they blame Latinas, rather than consider larger factors influencing life changes, (3) they do not allow for the individual agency of women to determine their own sexualities, (4) they reinforce heteronormativity by presuming all sexual relationships are female-male partnerships, and (5) they assume that education is necessarily sidelined by relationships and pregnancy. The few studies centering the perspectives of Latina teens actually suggest that motherhood increases educational aspirations for some (Russell and Lee 1994), and that, as a whole, Latina adolescents are *less likely* to be sexually active than most other racial/ethnic groups (Blum et al. 2000, as referenced in Denner and Guzmán 2006, 4).

With so many racist and sexist assumptions about the supposed biological impulses and cultural values of Latinas and their families, young Latinas are derogatorily defined as "at risk". They are blamed for their position in society and seen as the source of the believed problem of teen pregnancy (Garcia 2012). Meanwhile, unequal access to resources persist, and sex education remains absent in schools such as SCHS, thereby limiting students' opportunities to learn more about their bodies, relationships, health, and sexual identities. Such absence persists in part because "lessons about sexual pleasure upset the balance of gendered power in our society by introducing women's capacity for self-determination" (Fields 2008, 160).

THE DISCIPLINING MECHANISMS OF SCHOOL PRACTICES AND EVERYDAY EXCHANGES

Students' testimonials reveal how exclusionary beliefs interact with school practices such as dress codes, curriculum tracking, and narrow course curriculum to maintain raced-gendered inequality and sexualized policing that typecasts, limits, and recreates hierarchies. These school practices are often unchallenged, accepted as normal, *and* educators and students internalize and reproduce them through their everyday exchanges. In the context of exclusionary constructions and school practices, interactions such as objectifying gazes, surveillance, labeling, rumors, and low expectations are everyday forms of social control that run the gamut of making select students feel hypervisible or invisible. Such experiences may leave students feeling hurt, angry, apathetic, and disconnected from school. Similar to school practices, these individual actions also foster a chilly or downright hostile campus climate, and they illustrate the multiple forms of policing encountered by Latinas as a result of race/ethnicity, gender, class, and sexuality.

Dress Codes and the Institutionalization of Female Bodies as "Distractions"

Premised on the assumption that students' styles need to be regulated for safety and learning, school dress codes repress and control students (Brunsma 2004; Ochoa 2008). At SCHS, the dress code intersects with hegemonic assumptions that female bodies—in particular female breasts—need to be covered because of a belief that they are distracting. The school's dress code stipulates that clothes should "not distract or interfere with the educational environment . . . Dresses, skirts, and shorts shall be within bounds of decency and good taste".

During a class discussion, Latinas critiqued the school's attempts to contain their bodies. As several Latinos argued, "women can wear clothes that guys can't" and pointed to a Latina classmate wearing a t-shirt with a woman and gun on it. One Latina student quickly corrected, "there are dress codes for prom. We can't wear low-cut dresses or ones that are cut down the back". Her response was met with a chorus of affirming "yea's" from her Latina classmates. A student later shared how, before she could enter the school's prom, school officials required her to cover her chest with a shawl because they believed her dress was "too revealing". Thus, whereas the young men in the class critiqued a double standard where women are perceived to be granted more liberty, some women feel limited by the school's requirement that they cover parts of their bodies. The school's emphasis on "distraction free" dress codes assumes that if girls' tops are low and shorts high, young men are unable to control their sexual desires, placing blame on female bodies for arousing excitement and interfering with schooling.

Given sexualized media representations where girls and women are evaluated by their bodies and clothes, some may support dress codes as a way to combat sexist and consumerist media pressures.[3] Unfortunately, schools such as SCHS do not make this case for such restrictions or provide students with opportunities to deconstruct media representations. Instead, SCHS emphasizes "decency and good taste"—subjective constructs that are influenced by multiple factors, including age, generation, culture, religion, and socioeconomic status. It is assimilationist to assume that all at SCHS share or should share the same conceptions as the school's primarily White, middle-class educators who regulate dress. The assumption too is that those who do not accept the school's conception are somehow indecent and have poor taste. For female adolescents with larger breasts, they may be considered "indecent" simply because they have more to show than their slighter schoolmates (Hyams 2006, 100).

As part of schooling students on mainstream norms and socially preferred body types, students who break the dress code are sent home to change, or they are forced to wear loaner clothes. Whereas female bodies are seen as distractions, being removed from the classroom is an unspoken interference from learning for the students involved.

Taken together, such dress codes simultaneously sexualize and control female bodies and discipline their sexualities (Hyams 2006, 101). These rules imply that female breasts are objects of desire needing to be covered, contained, and controlled. An assumption of heterosexual desire permeates these dress codes, and such rules may also foster shame among young girls who internalize negative messages about their bodies. Furthermore, adolescent females are policed to constrain their perceived sexualities and to enforce what sociologist Julie Bettie (2003) has described as school-sanctioned and middle-class norms of femininity. Thus, the objectification of female bodies and the implementation of school dress codes are not neutral. Not all adolescent girls are equally impacted by, or punished for, their styles of dress, and the subjective interpretations of the primarily middle-class and White school officials determine modes of comportment.

Objectifying Comments and Gazes

Objectifying comments and gazes also police students' styles of dress and bodies. Rooted in patriarchy and bolstered by dominant media representations, objectifying comments and gazes are so common that they often become naturalized. They may pass unnoticed by educators and students, or they may be justified as part of school cultures and hormonal changes. Nonetheless, their impacts are strong. They are microaggressions that keep those at the margins in their place (Solorzano 1998). At SCHS, such objectifying comments and gazes are part of the school culture. They occur among students and educators, and the school is implicated when such practices persist as part of a culture of silence.

At a 2008 SCHS awards assembly organized by students, four groups of young women from ninth through 12th grade each took turns dancing and entertaining their schoolmates and teachers through choreographed performances. Their matching outfits and synchronized moves revealed the time they invested in perfecting their dances to the latest hip-hop songs. However, schoolmates' catcalls and judgments about the performers' bodies, such as "the girl in the middle is going to make an earthquake", clouded the camaraderie, skill, and work displayed by the students. In schools where dance and cheer is given less status than football and basketball and young women's bodies are perceived as fair game for commentary, some schoolmates treated the performers' bodies as objects to be evaluated. In this case, students not fitting prevailing constructions of beauty based on body size were ridiculed.

The scrutinizing that some young women receive on campus because of dominant constructions of beauty is not only apparent among students. Teacher Marilyn Garcia, for example, is very concerned that "prettier girls with bigger breasts seem to get [certain male teachers'] attention more".

Garcia reveals that this pattern has detrimental impacts, including unequal practices by a couple of male teachers known for granting select female students desired classes and a severe case of negligence by a teacher who overlooked a student accident because the teacher was believed to be "checking out the girls". Such disparate treatment and objectifying gazes create a dangerous and even hostile environment. They send powerful messages about women's worth and pit students against one another by reinforcing a pattern of favoritism steeped in systems of race/ethnicity, gender, class, and sexuality.

As illustrated in school dress code policies, part of the objectification of females is the assumption that their bodies—in particular their breasts—are distractions academically. This was also evident when a veteran, White, male teacher, Tom O'Brien, joked before a faculty meeting, "ninth grade girls do well until they get the two Bs—boobs and boyfriends". Although his comments were loud enough for most of his colleagues to hear, no one challenged them, suggesting that other teachers tacitly agree. Tom O'Brien's specific reference to breasts implies that he believes anatomical development disrupts the academic performance of ninth grade girls, a group he assumes are attracted to and attract boys. In this example, females are reduced to their body parts, and their bodies are considered the source of their problems—removing any role of the school in hindering students' academic achievement.

Surveilling and Labeling

Politically active Latinas and those who use their bodies in ways that disrupt hegemonic constructions of femininity encounter equally confining assumptions and forms of surveillance. For example, junior Summer Reyes, a leader in MEChA (Movimiento Estuduantil Chicano de Aztlán), a student organization established in the 1960s, believes that school administrators suspiciously watch her and her group's activities, whereas other students and groups are granted more liberty.

Summer explains how, as a self-identified Hispanic woman, she is subjected to racial and gender monitoring in ways not experienced by MEChA's male president:

> as a Hispanic, there's discrimination, and I think gender-wise there's discrimination too. I noticed that for the president of MEChA, they've never given *him* dirty looks, or they're never watching what he does, and for me, they are . . . I guess because they always notice me. They kind of know who I am. They don't know my name, but after all that was going on with MEChA and they weren't letting us do a thing, I started noticing that they were watching where I was going . . .

Along with gender and race, Summer attributes this differential treatment to her unwillingness to concede to the administrators' attempts to cancel

MEChA's campus events. Because SCHS's administrators are predominately White males, Summer may encounter more surveillance than her male counterpart; not only is she involved with an antiracist and social justice organization, but by calling attention to racism and working to "empower Hispanics", she is also transgressing normative raced and gendered expectations of acquiescence and passivity.

Typically, students who are involved with the production of school-sanctioned dances, assemblies, newspapers, and yearbooks receive special status from school officials, and they are granted *greater* freedom of movement on campus (Eckert 1989). However, Summer's experiences illustrate how not all student leaders are granted such privileges. As a Mexican woman involved with an overtly political organization, Summer recounts more surveillance in the form of sexualized policing as well:

> ok, there's a lot of couples around school and they are constantly making out, and no one ever tells them anything, and me and my boyfriend are just talking and I can see the administration. They're just standing right next to us. And I'm like, "we're not even doing anything". It kind of gets me angry that they don't do it to anybody else. They just do it to me.

Summer's experience must be seen in the context of the overall campus climate where other members of MEChA, including Latina/o faculty advisors, report constant questions and snide comments from administrators about their club's activities. Participating teachers and students compare what they observe as lack of trust and low expectations of MEChA with praise and celebration for other organizations. Likewise, relative to their Asian American counterparts, Latinas were far more likely to talk about feeling monitored based on their political participation, clothing, and romantic relationships (Ochoa 2013). In particular, the sexualized profiling Summer perceives may also be influenced by dominant myths of Latinas as hypersexual. Overall, when student leaders such as Summer and her MEChA schoolmates contest the status quo by raising awareness about racism, anti-immigrant sentiment, and class inequality, their activities are stifled in a form of political repression.

Sophomore Angelica Vega also describes constant surveillance by school administrators and security guards. In particular, racialized and normative gendered expectations of "being ladylike" influence this monitoring, which for two years has haunted her schooling. During her sophomore year, Angelica befriended a group of girls who she later found out were doing drugs. After about a month of using drugs with them, she successfully quit and helped her friends stop as well. When her mother found out about Angelica's past drug usage, she reached out to the school. In return, the school punished Angelica and her friends, instigating ostracism and fistfights between these former friends who blamed Angelica for the school's actions.

Instead of being praised for no longer using drugs or receiving assistance during a difficult period, for the remainder of high school, school officials branded Angelica with a negative reputation:

> because of all that with those friends that got involved with drugs and I got into a fight with them, [administrator] Johnson still thinks I'm the same type of person. Yet, I don't hang out with them. I don't have any interactions with them, and yet he still judges me from back in the day. It's like, "c'mon. I'm focused on school".

Despite her attempts to establish a new identity and friendship group, Angelica is forced to contend with low expectations and enhanced surveillance:

> just the way security is, they'll sit there [in front of the campus]. They look at the same people to see what they're doing, to see where they're going but not new faces . . . Like me, they'll just watch and watch.

At times, this constant watching is combined with public ridicule by security guards:

> they always give me problems. Like [saying], "here she comes. Be careful". I remember the security guards saying, "watch out! Here comes Tyson", 'cause they know me as fighting. So they call me, "oh, here comes Mike Tyson. She's gonna hit you".

These school officials' comments are humiliating, especially for a student trying to alter a negative image. However, the labeling of Angelica as "Tyson" has other implications as well. It is a form of masculinizing name-calling that reinforces assumptions that women do not engage in fistfights. Such labeling also fuels racist constructions of Black men as aggressive, violent, and ready to strike at any moment (see Feagin 2001).

Each time she is berated, Angelica does all she can to cope with such harassment. However, she is unable to remove the stigmas that have been assigned to her. Thus, when we met her in March of her senior year, she could not "wait to leave this school".

Shaming and Steering

Just as the constant surveillance experienced by Summer and Angelica marginalizes students by making them feel that they are suspect, the spreading of rumors and shaming are also disciplining mechanisms that ostracize and impact belonging. In particular, during a two-hour group discussion with three Latina/o friends, the stigmatizing and shaming of pregnant students were pervasive.

After stopping our discussion to scrutinize a student walking across campus, junior Monique Martinez explained how her schoolmate was the eighth pregnant student at SCHS. When asked how students have reacted to news of these pregnancies, the three friends reveal the gendered judgment and gossip surrounding the young mothers that typically eludes the fathers:

> MONIQUE: Well, people are just talking like, "oh my god! She is pregnant. Did you hear"? That's about it.
> GILDA: Like in a judgmental way or—[students start nodding]? Yeah, it is?
> MONIQUE: Yeah.
> ART: They are judging her.
> GILDA: The guys, what are they saying about the guys?
> MONIQUE: I don't know what they say about the guys. They always talk about the girls. They don't say anything about the guys.
> LAURA: They don't say anything about the guys. They only say things about the girls.

This gendered double standard places blame entirely on young women, who must then navigate a campus climate filled with rumors and sneers, including by these three friends who also belittle their female schoolmates.

The shaming escalates when these friends believe that pregnant teenagers not only embarrass themselves but also defame the entire school. Here, they vilify schoolmates by drawing on racist and classist images of a neighboring school where most of the students are working-class Latinas/os, and the school has an on-campus childcare facility:

> LAURA: . . . [Teen pregnancy] makes our school look bad.
> MONIQUE: We're like the next Northern High School.

Part of their criticism of pregnant teenagers, in addition, comes from their parents' judgmental messages:

> MONIQUE: "They're animals", that's what my mom tells me.
> ART: Yeah.
> MONIQUE: The way I was taught was purity. You do it when you're married. It's like love, and now everyone's doing it. My mom's like, "they're all out there being little bunnies".

Whereas the comments Monique hears at home are harsh, the disparaging lessons she and her schoolmates are subjected to from at least one of their teachers is downright hostile. In opposition, students do what they can to contest such sentiment:

> my English teacher, Ms. Saldana, this year, we were talking about having sex in class or pregnant girls, and she's like, "I think it's

disrespectful if you get pregnant in high school . . . You shouldn't come to school if you're pregnant". All of us are like, "what are you talking about?! . . . Shouldn't you be supporting that the girl comes to school to finish her education"?

By stigmatizing students and associating pregnancy with immorality and disrespect, sentiment by teachers such as Saldana pits students against one another, limits pregnant students' sources of support, and pushes them away from certain classes and maybe even out of school. Whereas in this case, students in Saldana's class critiqued her argument, perspectives such as Saldana's are prevailing, and they seep into worldviews and negatively impinge on young women's lives.

Shaming at SCHS is especially pernicious when educators withdraw support for pregnant students and young mothers. This was the case for junior Ashley Cordero, who initially praised several teachers for providing advice during her pregnancy and while raising her baby. However, an analysis of the larger messages conveyed by her school counselor and school district policies belies what appears to be a seemingly positive reception. Ashley's experiences illustrate the detrimental impacts of institutional practices that stem from a history of exclusion and foster unequal outcomes.

Before her pregnancy, Ashley was one of the only Latinas/os enrolled in the school's top academic program—the International Baccalaureate (IB) program.[4] In the program, she was often tokenized, singled out as a "credit to her race". A difficult position to be in, Ashley was committed to "breaking that mindset" that some educators and schoolmates have about the academic abilities of Latinas/os. However, when Ashley became a mother, her additional workload impeded her ability to stay in this select program. After leaving the program, her treatment by the school changed. Just as Ms. Saldana, the aforementioned English teacher, advocated, Ashley was literally pushed out of the school. First, easy access to the IB counselor, who provides stress release sessions, letters of recommendation, and an open door policy for students in the program, was rescinded:

. . . [T]his last time I had made an appointment with her and I had cleared the time, and she had said yes just to tell her secretary, and I did. And then I ended up going in, and she wasn't there at the time. I was getting ready to leave and then I ended up seeing her, and I had went into her office . . . [a]nd she's like, "oh, my secretary wasn't here to shoo you away".

No longer in the IB Program, Ashley is physically shooed away by a once supportive counselor. This same counselor also eschews Ashley's initial college plans:

I've spoken to [my counselor] about my daughter, with school as far as [the academic program], like how should I go about doing this, which way would be best for me to go. She suggested, that I should just probably go to [a local community college] for now so that way, because money's tight, and then I could transfer out after.

Her counselor's once high expectations receded from attending a competitive university to a community college. Such steering of Latinas/os into often overcrowded and underfunded community colleges is common, and given the low transfer rates from community college to universities, it is a pattern that negatively impacts the percentage of Latinas/os earning advanced degrees (Pérez Huber et al. 2006).

Just as her counselor sends messages that discredit Ashley's abilities, the school district's policies are equally unforgiving. With only one year remaining before graduation, Ashley can no longer remain at SCHS. As a student outside of the school's neighborhood lines, her enrollment as a transfer student was contingent on her participation in the IB Program. Whereas this district policy may appear fair, it is ostracizing. It literally banishes Ashley by not allowing her to complete her senior year at a familiar place. During a period of many transitions, Ashley is forced to change schools and establish new systems of support. This is a significant disruption to her education. Such district policies are inflexible and unaccommodating—they ignore students' differing experiences and unequal struggles.

Silencing and Invisibility

Finally, silencing discussions about sexuality is also a mechanism of social control at SCHS. Despite the apparent concern over teen sexuality and pregnancy, course curriculum on parenting, birth control, and sexual identities is absent in most classrooms. It is what the American Association of University Women refers to as "evaded curriculum"—"matters central to the lives of students and teachers but touched upon only briefly, if at all, in most schools" (AAUW 1992, 131, as referenced in Fields 2008, 72). Given the raced-gendered assumptions at the school about Latinas, these silences are conspicuous. They bolster individualizing discourses that blame and shame young women and remove any responsibility from men, society, or schools to provide education and support. The invisibility also stifles opportunities for enhancing understanding and creating a more inclusive campus climate.

The absence of these discussions is not lost on the three friends introduced earlier. Here, they reflect on how such topics should be part of students' learning, especially given the percentage of students believed to be sexually active:

MONIQUE: I would say about 60% of [SCHS] is sexually active. 60%.
LAURA: Probably.
GILDA: Including ninth [graders] through seniors?
MONIQUE: Yeah, I even found out little middle schoolers do the dirty.

ART: Yeah.
GILDA: And is this being talked about, besides amongst students?
MONIQUE: No, they never talk about it.
GILDA: The teachers? Administrators? Should they be?
MONIQUE: I think they should.
LAURA: Yeah.
ART: I think so.

By denying educational opportunities to students and fueling a climate of shame for pregnant teenagers, adolescent girls are forced to bear much of the weight of learning about sexual heath and birth control.

Another form of stigmatization and silence surrounds sexual identities and desires. These silences perpetuate heterosexuality as the expected social norm because these are the unnamed and idealized relationships (González-López 2010). Heterosexual relationships are assumed to be natural. In contrast, relationships and gendered ways of being perceived to fall outside of these normative expectations are ridiculed or hushed. Whereas the intents of the following exchanges differ, both of these dynamics maintain heteronormativity and stifle nonnormative sexual practices and gender identifications.

Just as sociologist C. J. Pascoe (2012) found at the California high school she studied, "fag discourse", including the ridiculing of others by using derogatory labels, is part of the campus climate at SCHS. Primarily male students use this discourse to ridicule other males. It is a technique that debases gender, nonconforming students, femininity when performed by males, and activities perceived to fall outside of narrowly constructed heterosexual relationships. Such ridiculing polices students' ways of being and enforces assimilationist imperatives—in particular, it maintains what researcher Lorena Garcia (2012) refers to as "heteronormative imperatives".

Whereas "fag discourse" is overt and a form of public shaming that draws attention to students to squelch dissent, silencing any reference to "gayness" also privileges and reinforces heterosexuality. As sophomore Monica Ruiz shares, heteronormativity and homophobia are so pervasive that even speculating that a schoolmate is gay can foster a hostile climate:

the kid that sits next to me was like, "oh did you know that guy was gay"? I was like, "how do you know if he's gay"? and he's like, "oh, he's just gay". I was like, "no, he's not. Don't say that if you don't know if it's true. Now you can't just go around saying stuff 'cause that's how rumors start" and then he was asking some kid in the back [of the class].

Although the tone and intent of this exchange is unclear, that Monica believes her classmate is spreading rumors by calling another student gay reveals the negative connotations and even potentially violent ramifications associated with this identity. Monica's teacher, John Alvarez, has a similar interpretation and reaction to the students' conversation:

> Mr. Alvarez overheard, and he got really mad. He's like, "what do you think you're God? It's not right; you shouldn't say that especially in my class. I won't tolerate that". He got really mad. Then again, you can't just be saying, "oh this guy is gay", like if you don't know if it's true.

Rather that encouraging dialogue, this immediate silencing has the same, and perhaps unintended, effect of Monica Ruiz's response—fueling a perception that being gay is shameful, something to hide, and an insult. As such, it regulates sexual identities by maintaining heterosexual supremacy and perpetuating homophobia.

The one space where students at some schools have found dialogue, visibility, and inclusion about sexuality and nonconforming sexual and gender identities is in organizations such as the Gay-Straight Alliance (GSA) (Clay 2012). GSA chapters are located in schools throughout the nation, including in over 900 active clubs and organizations in California (Marquez and Brickenbrough 2013). However, as one Chicana at SCHS bemoans, the school's GSA is floundering:

> . . . [I]t's not going to last, even though I signed up, it is not going to last because high schoolers are not mature enough to deal with it. It's something you have to do more in college, and it is sad because the person was trying to recruit for the club, and people were just laughing. And then I signed up because I mean that's interesting and that's something that I want to support. But then I know it is probably not going to last it; it's probably going to end.

GSA chapters are crucial student spaces, but they alone cannot change a campus and societal culture filled with silence and stigma surrounding sexuality and identities. To change campus cultures, schools and students need course curriculum and affirming spaces that include materials on the sociopolitical constructions of gender and sexuality.

IMPLICATIONS AND CONCLUSIONS

Going into our schools and listening to students reveal how more than school gates are barring students. Behind fences, students encounter multiple constraints—academically, socially, politically, and sexually. Because much has been written about the academic barriers, and there is growing scholarship on how schools limit student relationships, this chapter focused on the less examined ways that schools also regulate students politically and sexually. In particular, Latinas' testimonials uncover how school practices, educators' messages, and students' interactions police their bodies, monitor radical political activism, and dismiss nonconforming students and identities. The various institutional and interpersonal constraints detailed in this chapter are forms of control conveying what is deemed acceptable and who belongs in our schools and society.

During a period of growth and identity development, such disciplinary measures impinge on students' abilities to form positive self-concepts unencumbered by others' assumptions and limitations. By mandating narrow ways of being and thinking, they also reinforce assimilationist imperatives and exclusionary campus climates. In their most extreme cases, some forms of control foster violence and death based on race, gender, and sexuality (see Fragoso 2003; Marquez and Brickenbrough 2013).

Dominant ideologies about so-called Latina/o values and Latina sexuality bolster these disciplinary measures. In a self-perpetuating cycle, they justify school practices and everyday exchanges. They also blame Latinas/os for their positions in society. Thereby, larger societal and school-level injustices are kept intact, and the cycle of racial inequality and blame continues.

Despite the pervasiveness of these constraints and the prevailing myths about Latinas, there are glaring silences surrounding them. Thus, Latinas are simultaneously positioned as hypervisible and invisible—alternatively spotlighted as problems relative to other girls or dismissed as succeeding compared to boys of color. Meanwhile, Latinas' perspectives and experiences are often ignored in discussions about education, as are the varied constraints they encounter.

A more complete understanding of schooling requires a holistic perspective that names and tackles raced-gendered exclusionary expectations and sexualized policing. This must be part of public debate and educational policy, and it is incumbent upon our schools to alter their campus climates by providing the necessary curriculum and educator training to enhance critical awareness and inclusive spaces. Academically, more research is needed to consider the linkages between multiple disciplinary mechanisms and their implications. We must continue unmasking the many forms of social control occurring in our schools. To do otherwise is to ensure the maintenance of exclusionary belief systems, school practices, and everyday dynamics that have damaging implications for students, communities, and our society.

NOTES

1. Whereas the pan-ethnic categories Latina and Hispanic are broad and refer to over 50 million people in the U.S. from diverse regions, generations, class position, etc., for inclusivity, I use the category Latina throughout this chapter,

except when referring to students' specific racial/ethnic identifications. In addition, all names in this chapter are pseudonyms to protect the identity of the information.

2. Whereas Latinas are the focus of this chapter, it is important to understand the backgrounds of their Asian American schoolmates, because these are the students Latinas are often compared to and evaluated against at this school. Reflecting systemic inequalities and differing immigration histories, most of the Asian Americans interviewed are immigrants and children of immigrants from middle- and upper-middle-class backgrounds and with college-educated parents who are primarily from Hong Kong and Taiwan. Most of the students identify as Chinese or Asian, but some are Korean, Japanese, and Taiwanese American. Although largely ignored at the school, the general class differences between the Latina/o and Asian America students at SCHS are significant and result in unequal economic, social, and cultural capital.

3. Thanks to Laureen Adams for pointing this out.

4. This is a pattern observed across the nation. As a result of historical and contemporary exclusionary practices and unequal forms of support, Latinas/os as a whole are underrepresented in top academic tracks (Oakes 1985). For a detailed discussion of this at SCHS, see Ochoa 2013.

REFERENCES

Beres, L. S., and T. D. Griffith. 2001. "Demonizing Youth." *Loyola of Los Angeles Law Review* 34: 747–766.

Bettie, J. 2003. *Women Without Class: Girls, Race, and Identity.* Berkeley: University of California Press.

Blum, R. W., T. Beuhring, M. L. Shew, L. H. Bearinger, R. E. Sieving, and M. D. Resnick. 2000. "The Effects of Race/Ethnicity, Income, and Family Structure on Adolescent Risk Behaviors. *American Journal of Public Health* 90 (12): 1879–1884.

Brunsma, D. 2004. *The School Uniform Movement and What it Tells Us About American Education: A Symbolic Crusade.* Lanham, MD: ScarecrowEducation.

California Department of Education. 2008. *Students by Ethnicity, 2006–2007* and *Teachers by Ethnicity, 2006–2007.* Sacramento, CA: Education Data Partnership. Retrieved January 15, 2011, from www.ed-data.k12.ca.us.

Chua, A., and J. Rubenfeld. 2014. "What Drives Success?" *The New York Times,* 25 January.

Clay, A. 2012. *The Hip-Hop Generation Fights Back: Youth, Activism, and Post-Civil Rights Politics.* New York: New York University Press.

Collins, P. H. 2001. *Black Feminist Thought: Knowledge, Consciousness, and the Politics of Empowerment.* New York: Routledge.

Conchas, G. Q., and J. D. Vigil. 2012. *Streetsmart Schoolsmart: Urban Poverty and the Education of Adolescent Boys.* New York: Teachers College Press.

Delgado-Gaitan, C. 1992. "School Matters in the Mexican-American Home: Socializing Children to Education." *American Educational Research Journal* 29 (3): 495–513.

Denner, J., and B. L. Guzmán. 2006. *Latina Girls: Voices of Adolescent Strength in the United States.* New York: New York University Press.

Eckert, P. 1989. *Jocks and Burnouts: Social Categories and Identity in High School.* New York: Teachers College.

Espiritu, Y. L. 1997. "Race, Gender, Class in the Lives of Asian Americans." *Race, Gender, and Class* 4 (3): 12–19.

Feagin, J. R. 2001. *Racist America: Roots, Current Realities, and Future Reparations.* New York: Routledge.

Fields, J. 2008. *Risky Lessons: Sex Education and Social Inequality.* New Brunswick, NJ: Rutgers University Press.

Fleury-Steiner, B. 2008. *Dying Inside: The HIV/AIDS Ward of Limestone Prison.* Ann Arbor: University of Michigan Press.

Fragoso, J. M. 2003. "Serial Sexual Femicide in Ciudad Juárez, 1993–2001." *Aztlán* 28 (2): 153–178.

Garcia, L. 2012. *Respect Yourself: Protect Yourself: Latina Girls and Sexual Identity.* New York: New York University Press.

Gonzalez, G. G. 1990. *Chicano Education in the Era of Segregation.* Philadelphia, PA: Balch Institute Press.

González-López, G. 2010. "Heterosexuality Exposed: Some Feminist Sociological Reflections on Heterosexual Sex and Romance in U.S. Latina/o Communities." In *Latina/o Sexualities: Probing Powers, Passions, Practices, and Politics,* edited by M. Asencio, 103–116. New Brunswick, NJ: Rutgers University Press.

Gutiérrez, E. R. 2008. *Fertile Matters: The Politics of Mexican-Origin Women's Reproduction.* Austin: University of Texas Press.

Hyams, M. 2006. "La Escuela: Young Latina Women Negotiating Identities in School." In *Latina Girls: Voices of Adolescent Strength in the United States,* 93–108. New York: New York University Press.

Kao, G. 2000. "Group Images and Possible Selves Among Adolescents: Linking Stereotypes to Expectations by Race and Ethnicity." *Sociological Forum* 15 (3): 407–430.

Kupchik, A. 2010. *Homeroom Security: School Discipline in an Age of Fear.* New York: New York University Press.

Lee, S. J. 1996. *Unraveling the "Model Minority" Stereotype: Listening to Asian American Youth.* New York: Teachers College.

Marquez, R., and E. Brockenbrough. 2013. "Queer Youth v. the State of California." *Curriculum Inquiry* 43 (4): 461–482.

Morris, E. 2006. *An Unexpected Minority: White Kids in an Urban School.* New Brunswick, NJ: Rutgers University Press.

Noguera, P. A. 2008. *The Trouble with Black Boys: And Other Reflections on Race, Equity, and the Future of Public Education.* San Francisco, CA: Jossey-Bass.

Nolan, K. 2011. *Police in the Hallways: Discipline in an Urban High School.* Minneapolis: University of Minnesota Press.

Oakes, J. 1985. *Keeping Track: How Schools Structure Inequality.* New Haven, CT: Yale University Press.

Ochoa, E. C. 2008. "Dress Codes, School Repression, and Misplaced Priorities." *Hispanic Outlook on Higher Education,* 21 April.

Ochoa, G. L. 2007. *Learning from Latino Teachers.* San Francisco, CA: Jossey-Bass.

Ochoa, G. L. 2013. *Academic Profiling: Latinos, Asian Americans and the Achievement Gap.* Minneapolis: Minnesota Press.

Pascoe, C. J. 2012. *"Dude, You're a Fag!" Masculinity and Sexuality in High School.* Berkeley: University of California Press.

Pérez Huber, L., O. Huidor, M. C. Malagón, G. Sánchez, and D. G. Solórzano. 2006. *Falling Through the Cracks: Critical Transitions in the Latina/o Educational Pipeline.* UCLA Chicano Studies Research Report.

Pew Hispanic Foundation/Kaiser Family Foundation. 2004. *National Survey of Latinos: Education.* Washington, DC.

Rios, V. M. 2011. *Punished: Policing the Lives of Black and Latino Boys.* New York: New York University Press.

Rodríguez, C. E. 1997. "Latinos on Television and in the News: Absent or Misrepresented." In *Latin Looks: Images of Latinas and Latinos in the U.S. Media,* edited by C. E. Rodríguez, 13–20. Boulder, CO: Westview Press.

Russell, S. T., and F.C.H. Lee. 1994. "Latina Adolescent Motherhood: A Turning Point?" In *Latina Girls: Voices of Adolescent Strength in the United States,* 212–225. New York: New York University Press.

Solorzano, D. G. 1998. "Critical Race Theory, Race and Gender Microagressions, and the Experiences of Chicana and Chicano Scholars. *Qualitative Studies in Education* 11 (1): 121–136.

Part IV

Immigrant Global Communities, Disparity, and the Struggle for Legitimacy

8 Difficult Transitions
Undocumented Immigrant Students Navigating Vulnerability and School Structures

*Roberto G. Gonzales and
Cynthia N. Carvajal*

FLOR

For many Americans education is viewed as the key to the American dream. But this ideal is lost on Flor Garcia, one of the young people we have been following through the course of our research. Horace Mann's proclamation that education is a great equalizer simply does not match Flor's experiences. Flor is an undocumented immigrant. Together with six siblings and her two parents, she came to the U.S. when she was just nine years old. Flor's formative years were difficult and shaped in her a sense of ambivalence about the future. She realized from an early age that her lack of *papers—papeles—*would keep her from the good jobs she dreamed of as a child. She also felt like an outsider at school, internalizing a belief that no one was looking out for her—that she was on her own.

With so many mouths to feed, Flor's family struggled to make ends meet. She entered the labor force at the age of 14. A family cleaning business allowed her to bypass the typical hurdles involved in seeking work. However, a grueling work schedule forced her to miss too many days of school. She felt frustrated and scared, wondering if her future held anything more than backbreaking work. She left high school during her junior year after being suspended for excessive—work-related—truancies. She felt sad that not a single person at her school "tried to pull me back in".

Flor eventually returned to school. Along the way she married and had children. Due to financial and family issues, Flor took seven years to earn her GED. She later tried to take community college courses, but without the proper guidance and with an unrelenting work schedule she never got very far. Beyond the logistical issues of financing and making time for school, she was deeply ambivalent about the value education held for turning her life around. During a conversation in 2009 she articulated her frustration with school:

> [I thought] if I go to college I'm not gonna have much time to spend with my kids you know, but since my son was already attending kindergarten and he [was] there for four hours, I would just have to leave my

daughter alone for those four hours . . . I ended up not going because I didn't want to leave my kids and I didn't really see the point of making those sacrifices. For what? I don't think it would have changed anything.

Now in her early 30s, Flor has been working for almost 20 years. She is isolated and under constant stress. Her undocumented status is a constant reminder of her limitations. Flor recalls,

I'm obviously an older person now. I mean, I see things different today. Back then I wasn't so much interested in being there, you know, in school. But when I think about it, there was no one there saying, "hey, I care about you and I want to help you stay in school". I was needed by my family and I get that. I'd do anything for them, you know. Being in my situation I really didn't see much of a future for myself. I wonder what would have happened to me if I had someone like that looking after me.

Each year, tens of thousands of undocumented immigrant students like Flor leave American high schools for uncertain futures. Whereas most students face some difficulty transitioning to college, undocumented young people face multiple barriers. Over the last few years, as growing numbers of undocumented students have matriculated to colleges and universities across the U.S., their plight has gained increasing attention. Stories of valedictorians and class presidents whose talents are wasted because current laws do not allow them to pursue their dream careers strike a chord with the American public.

Undoubtedly, there are a great number of high achievers who have faced challenges due to their undocumented status (Gonzales 2010; Contreras 2009; Abrego 2006, 2008). Very little, however, is known about lesser academically achieving young adults like Flor, who, because of legal, financial, and educational barriers, make up a larger share of this population. Young men and women who exit the public school system at or before high school graduation encounter increasing legal risks (Gonzales 2011). These years represent a crucial transition in their lives when the limitations of their immigration status begin to make themselves known (Gonzales 2011; Suarez-Orozco et al. 2008; Abrego 2006). Further, their untenable circumstances force them to deal with additional sources of stress, such as fear of deportation and societal rejection (Perez et al. 2009). As they reach working age, they face the dilemmas of finding full- or part-time work. Such decisions are complicated by the need to make further choices about driving and working illegally. Especially when working and driving are necessities, the need to make such decisions forces these young people to confront their legal limitations and the constricted range of available choices (Gonzales and Chavez 2012). Exclusion from financial aid eligibility and low family socioeconomic status severely limit their ability to matriculate to institutions of higher learning (Salsbury 2003). But little is known about the ways in which school experiences influence postsecondary transitions. Moreover, these achievement narratives tell us very little about the ways in which undocumented immigration status frames the everyday lives of young people, particularly at the onset of exclusions (Gonzales 2011).

This chapter focuses on the high school experiences of a sample of undocumented young adults from the first author's West Coast Undocumented Research Project, a multi-sited longitudinal research project aimed at better understanding what happens to undocumented immigrant youth as they make critical transitions to adulthood. In doing so, we examine the ways in which school structures shape access to resources needed for healthy development and successful postsecondary transitions. Current research suggests that school-based networks are critical for success. However, we argue that these networks are fundamentally shaped by the school structure. For undocumented immigrant youth, school represents the opportunity of inclusion. Whereas their parents are absorbed into the world of low-skilled work, they begin their American lives legally absorbed into a defining institution, the public school system. It is there where they not only meet American-born peers, but are also taught to internalize ideals of meritocracy. But schools do not treat all of their pupils equally. Resources are concentrated on a small number of students who, because of a perceived set of abilities, strong work ethic, and obedience to authority, reap the benefits of small learning environments and access to supportive adults. Meanwhile, a larger majority of the student body must contend with larger classes, outdated materials, and barriers to receiving help.

Our aim in this chapter is to explore the ways in which undocumented immigration status constrains interactions with school structures, cultures, and practices.[1] Whereas most studies focus on academic achievers, we turn our attention to a broader portion of this population that is not tracked for school success and examine the ways in which immigration policies and educational practices conspire to narrowly circumscribe their options. Undocumented immigrant students are particularly vulnerable and have arguably greater needs than their citizen peers. Legal and financial constraints not only erect numerous barriers but also create added layers of need in navigating the successful completion of high school and the transition to college. However, many of these students face challenges forging relationships with teachers and counselors who can provide access to important resources.

Our findings, furthermore, suggest that students' ability to access these relationships is shaped by their position within the school curriculum hierarchy. There are many reasons why undocumented immigrant students do not make successful transitions to college: exclusion from financial aid, resource-challenged families, frustration, and disillusionment, to name a few. But we find that many students are also disadvantaged by school structures that fail to illuminate pathways to resources critical to successful postsecondary transitions. Instead, many schools compound barriers, limiting access to information and support. We situate these students in their relevant school contexts and ask: How do school relationships mediate the various constraints of undocumented status? And how are these relationships structured institutionally?

CONTEMPORARY EDUCATIONAL POLICY AND EDUCATIONAL ACCESS

Until only a few decades ago, undocumented immigrants were mostly seasonal labor migrants who left their children and families back home in their countries of origin (Massey, Durand, and Molone 2002; Chavez 1998; Heyman 1999). However, compositional shifts in settlement involving increasing numbers of women and children started taking effect on communities across the country. By the mid-1970s, these changes were already becoming apparent in states like California, where the political implications of these trends were most felt in debates about the place of immigrants in society and in the schools.

In 1982, the U.S. Supreme Court ruled in *Plyler v. Doe* that states could not discriminate against undocumented immigrant students on the basis of their immigration status in the provision of public elementary and secondary education (see Olivas 1986, 2005, 2012). This decision provided undocumented children the legal means through which to receive both a formal education and an important socialization towards becoming American. By affirming the pursuit of a public education as legally permissible, the Court provided opportunities for undocumented children to be woven into the fabric of American society, just as generations of immigrant students had before them. However, *Plyler's* reach did not extend beyond school. So, although undocumented immigrant youth could receive a public K–12 education, they could not legally work, vote, travel out of the country, or drive in most states. They also faced restrictions from federal and state financial aid.[2] As a result, tens of thousands of undocumented young people leave school each year with uncertain and untenable futures.

Individual states have attempted to rectify the financial hurdles by passing tuition equity bills. As of June 2014, 18 states allow undocumented immigrant students to pay tuition at in-state rates. Sixteen of these states—California, Colorado, Connecticut, Florida, Illinois, Kansas, Maryland, Minnesota, Nebraska, New Mexico, New Jersey, New York, Oregon, Texas, Utah, and Washington—provide provisions through legislation. The remaining two—Oklahoma and Rhode Island—provide similar in-state rates through a Board of Regents decision. Hawaii and Michigan's Board of Regents have also passed similar policy to allow certain undocumented students to be eligible for in-state tuition. In addition, four states—Texas, New Mexico, California, and Washington—have passed legislation that makes undocumented immigrant students eligible for certain state aid.

However, a handful of states have taken a more exclusionary stance. Arizona, Georgia, and Indiana prohibit undocumented students from receiving in-state tuition rates. Furthermore, South Carolina and Alabama bar undocumented students from enrolling in public postsecondary institutions, and Georgia bans undocumented students from its most competitive universities. And although North Carolina attempted to ban undocumented students from enrolling in community colleges, they are permitted to enroll if they have graduated from a North Carolina high school and are able to pay out-of-state tuition.

In addition to the limited access to financial aid opportunities, undocumented students are barred from participating in federally funded programs, such as TRIO and work-study.[3] Both of these programs are designed to assist low-income, first-generation, and ethnic minority students. Because these programs receive federal funds, undocumented students are not entitled to participate. Despite the fact that an overwhelming majority of undocumented students fit this description, they are ineligible for these critical services (Gonzales 2010). Additionally, exclusion from work-study limits students' support systems on campus. Taken together, the inability to receive financial aid and the exclusion from federally funded sources of support place undocumented students on a difficult path towards higher education.

RESOURCE DISTRIBUTION IN THE *PLYLER* ERA

Immigration laws mark individuals either inside or outside of the legal system; similarly, schools also draw boundaries. By tracking students into different curricular pathways and labeling them based on perceived abilities, schools make determinations of worthiness. Scholarly research on the consequences of educational stratification—tracking, labeling, and other forms of ability grouping—has received considerable attention in sociological studies of education. Whereas the long-held assumption of such practices is that students need specialized educational programs to prepare them for different careers and that those homogeneous groupings promote efficient teaching and learning, research has consistently demonstrated that school stratification disadvantages students in the lower tracks (Hallinan 1994; Kilgore 1991; Oaks 1985; Schafer and Olexa 1971).

Most undocumented children from working-class backgrounds outpace their parents in educational attainment. As they reach high school, they are confronted with a range of decisions they must make without parental guidance. College attendance certainly helps them to extend a period of legal participation while it gives them the opportunity to gain knowledge, obtain advance degrees, and prepare themselves to be competitive in the labor market. However, most of these students are at a distinct disadvantage with respect to basic knowledge about what it takes to move from high school to college.

The concept of social capital—how individuals and groups invest in social relationships and share resources—resonates with current concerns about immigration and education. Accordingly, social capital exists in the structure of relationships between and among people (Bourdieu 1986). Its key characteristic is convertibility. That is, it can be translated into other social and economic benefits. People can access social capital through membership in interpersonal networks and social institutions. By converting these relationships into other forms of capital they can pursue their goals and improve their position in society.

Recent scholarship has suggested that a diversity of student outcomes exists within schools, and that relationships with peers and school officials can enable some poor and ethnic minority students to access important social capital in order to mobilize resources necessary for school success (Conchas 2001). In particular, access to resources and improved information are two important benefits that arise from school-based social capital (Faist 2000). In large, urban schools with large classes and high student to counselor and teacher ratios, access to teachers, counselors, and high-achieving peers can provide important advantages. And, improved information about their options and rights can help them make informed choices.

It is important to note that school success or failure often hinges upon whether school officials create a culture that facilitates positive interactions among students, teachers, and staff (Conchas 2006; Pizarro 2005). When teachers take time and effort to assist students, they can be an important source of social capital (Croninger and Lee 2001). Such teacher-based forms of social capital reduce the probability of students dropping out and help students who come from socially disadvantaged backgrounds or who have had academic difficulties in the past. Schools can also structure peer environments to promote academic achievement (Gibson, Gándara, and Peterson-Koyama 2004). This is particularly important for students who have less information about how schools and the broader society allocate resources and opportunity. However, when schools treat their students as outsiders they diminish their chances for success and close off avenues for counseling and assistance.

School officials' decisions are often influenced by a scarcity of resources, differential access to information, and their own personal prejudices and beliefs. Particularly in large, urban schools is a lack of adequate time and resources to be distributed among the entire student body. Consequently, teachers and counselors often expend these resources on those who have been designated as worthy, while the vast majority faces the difficulty of navigating the system on their own. As the following discussion suggests, problems that plague large, urban school systems are doubly felt by undocumented immigrant students who require additional support in order to make successful postsecondary transitions.

STUDYING THE SCHOOL EXPERIENCES OF UNDOCUMENTED YOUNG ADULTS

In this chapter we provide data from several studies on the West Coast. Since 2003 the first author has been engaged in what is arguably the most comprehensive study of undocumented, immigrant young adults in the United States to date. This research has taken place in two strategic sites on the West Coast.[4] Between 2003 and 2012 he carried out longitudinal research in Los Angeles, involving extensive field work and 150 individual life history interviews with Mexicans and Central Americans (El Salvador- and Guatemala-origin young adults, 20–34 years of age) who migrated before the age of 12. The second study began in 2009 in the state of Washington, involving young adults of the same age, immigrant generation, and immigrant status. Whereas respondents in the Los Angeles study are overwhelmingly urban, its Washington counterpart also draws from rural settings. To date, 40 life history interviews have been conducted. In both studies, samples were drawn to include equal numbers of college-going young adults and lesser-achieving young adults who stopped their schooling at or before high school graduation. In addition to these studies, we draw from the work of the second author, who, in 2013, carried out a yearlong study in Los Angeles, involving field work, semi-structured individual inter- views, and group interviews with 15 undocumented youth between the ages of 14 and 18.

Our research sites are ideal for studying contemporary immigration and educational processes. With close to 2.5 million undocumented immigrants, California is home to almost one-fourth of the nation's undocumented pop- ulation. California also educates about 40% of the undocumented student population at all grade levels. In addition, Washington state consists of a large agricultural industry and is one of the top 10 destinations for undocu- mented immigrants (Hoefer, Rytina, and Baker 2012).

Although many of our respondents are now adults, we draw on the aspects of the interview that capture their high school experiences. We asked respondents to describe their high school years (the school setting, their classes, and programs of study) and tell us about their relationships with teachers, counselors, and peers. We were particularly interested in the con- nections they made with adults during these years and how these adults may have shaped their sense of belonging and access to resources. The advantages of this approach are worth noting: interviewing young adults provides the opportunity to examine important events and turning points in childhood, adolescence, and young adulthood. Additionally, comparing the diverse experiences of modestly achieving respondents with their higher-tracked counterparts allows us to identify mechanisms that promoted upward and downward trajectories. The following discussion draws from these studies.

STRUCTURED VULNERABILITY

What happens in the formative years can have a major impact over the course of one's lifetime. For many of our respondents, childhood was wrought with hardship and struggle. Parental work life often entailed long hours away from home and children. Restricted access to decent wages also impacted parents' ability to find affordable housing. These problems not only concentrated families in crowded neighborhoods and in cramped living arrangements, but also funneled children into low-performing, overcrowded, *de facto* segregated school districts. Most of our California respondents attended large public schools with counselor to student ratios as high as 1,000:1.[5]

By the beginning of high school nearly all of our respondents had outpaced their parents in educational attainment. Due to parental work schedules, limited knowledge of the school system, and language barriers, they were at a distinct disadvantage to provide academic assistance to their children. Nevertheless, the vast majority of respondents felt as though their parents supported their educational goals and encouraged them to do well in school. Many even cited their parents' support and sacrifice as their inspiration to continue school even when they did not think they could do much more. Angeles, from western Washington, exemplifies this sentiment:

> I remember talking to my mom and saying that maybe I cannot do it. I have been spending my whole school career trying to do something that I am really not going to end up doing. My parents are very positive and they always say "there is always a way, there is always a solution. You have to look for it and you have to work hard. Don't let it get you down, keep working". It is always this that keeps me going, going strong.

But as we listened to the narratives of our respondents, the common experience shared by those at both ends of school sorting practices was quickly noticeable. Whereas parents were generally supportive of their children's educational pursuits, they were at a distinct disadvantage to provide the kind of guidance needed to navigate school.

Small Learning Communities and the Construction of Engagement

The narratives of our college-going respondents bolstered claims about the benefits of smaller classes and specialized programs in high school. Respondents described positive experiences in programs such as International Baccalaureate, Gifted and Talented Educational (GATE) program, and other small learning academies, as well as Advanced Placement (AP) and honors classes. These learning environments were generally smaller and helped them to foster relationships with key school personnel who could leverage important and scarce resources. High-achieving respondents benefited from positive schooling while being shielded from the broader problems that plagued their large and overcrowded schools. Many of these respondents were placed in specialized programs as early as seventh grade. By the time they reached high school they were capable of competing for seats in gifted and talented programs, specialized academies, and honors and AP classes. As Jacob from Los Angeles told us,

> I definitely felt like I belonged. School was what they call a home away from home for me. I really felt their support. I always did well in my classes and I always felt like my teachers were there for me. It was comfortable, you know. Like, supportive. I know this is not the experience of a lot of other students, but I really credit my teachers for all of their help and assistance.

However, as Jacob's comments importantly point out, whereas some respondents benefitted from supportive school environments others were not as fortunate. Even those who were placed into better classes found themselves lost in the academic process due in part to teachers and counselors who could not provide them with the resources they needed. Rosa from Los Angeles explained the disconnect she experienced:

> I was in a [small learning community] and there were good advisors that knew about my status, and to all the teachers, I felt comfortable telling them. I knew they will support me and they have ways to support me. It's a great support because nobody judged you. I knew I could go to them and they will have my back 100%, but they didn't know a lot about my situation, or like, they knew about me being undocumented but they didn't know how to help me. The rest of my classmates ended up applying [to college] and it just didn't happen for me.

Although Rosa developed a positive sense of self through the help of her counselors and teachers, they were unable to support her through her college application process. In the end Rosa graduated high school and began working to help support her family.

Many of our respondents were placed in general track classes or spent much of their schooling in English as a Second Language (ESL) classes. Respondents in the general track sat in much larger classes, had very little contact with other school personnel, and were hard-pressed to come up with positive examples of their school experiences. For Gino from East Los Angeles, a bad relationship with a teacher spelled overall difficulty in school.

> High school was a very difficult time for me. It seemed as though everyone there had a problem with me. I had this one teacher, my math teacher, who, I think he was having some kind of family problems. He was always yelling at me, picking on me for no reason. He made life very difficult. One day he decided that I had stoled [sic] his calculator. He made a big deal out of it. A lot of drama. I was suspended for three

days. He later found the calculator in his desk. It was too late. After that, I kind of had a reputation at school and all the teachers treated me like a criminal. I never had a chance to do anything about it. It was already decided. Really sucked.

Our respondents who were in ESL classes reported a different kind of problem. They expressed feeling overwhelmed by the additional barriers they faced because of their immigration status and their classes. Blanca from South Los Angeles conveyed the pressure she felt due to these barriers.

I know that college is important but right now I have to focus on helping my family. Without papers there's not much I can do. And it's not the focus of our teachers. They just want us to learn English and so they don't talk to us about how to apply to college. I think it's best if I work and help my family.[6]

Other students were generally happy with their teachers, but many felt disconnected from the larger school body and cut off from important resources. Orquidia, from Fullerton, California, provides an example.

All of my ESL teachers were really nice. I could really feel that they cared. It's just that, it was more of a kind of party environment, not really academics. A lot of us were undocumented and it was like they kind of felt sorry for us. But there was never anyone coming in [to the classroom] to tell us, "even though you don't have papers you can do this, you can go to college". No, I just felt like we weren't really dealing with reality. It was kind of like a handicap, in the end.

Whereas they were generally happy with their teachers, many felt disconnected from the larger school body and cut off from important resources.

However, being part of the general school body held other types of problems. Respondents from general track classes were exposed to fights and disruptive classrooms that had old and outdated materials. Lupita, from Tacoma, WA, told us that her parents actually pulled her out of school.

It got to the point where there were, there were fights every week. My parents tried to talk to my teacher about it, but it was kind of hard. They don't really speak much English and my teacher wasn't much of a help either. She cancelled a couple meetings with them and, you know, they were taking time off work to go, so they felt bad, like she wasn't respecting their time. When they finally met she really scared them with stories about teachers being attacked by students and that she didn't feel safe there. They ended up taking me out of school a couple weeks later.

Instead of comforting Lupita's parents or providing them some reassurance that she was safe at school, her teacher fed their fears about school not being a good place for their daughter.

Whereas not all of respondents' school experiences were overtly negative, many struggled to find illuminated pathways to resources. Respondents noted a disconnect between what they thought school should be and their actual experiences. Only a small number of them could actually name a teacher or other school official who they felt cared about them. Take Fatima, also from Tacoma:

> my experience at school was not terrible. I mean, I graduated with my class and I got okay grades. A few Cs here and there, but otherwise ok. It's just that I didn't relate to any of my teachers and I didn't know anyone else [at school].

Like Fatima, many of these respondents drifted through their high school years without having any significant conversations with school personnel about their hopes for the future, their career aspirations, or their postsecondary options. Many felt as though the school system let them fall through the cracks. This rang true for Alfonso, from Long Beach.

> I didn't know a lot about college. My older sister was 17 when we came, and she started working like right away. So, I didn't really have anyone at home who knew too much about college . . . I remember I saw a counselor, like a guidance counselor, during my senior year of high school. He told me that I wasn't eligible for college because of my status. He recommended that I should ask my parents to help me find a job. So, that was it. I didn't find out that I could actually go to college until about three years later.

The school experiences of our respondents provide ample evidence to support arguments that school cultures are critical in assisting students to make successful postsecondary transitions. Respondents in general track classes had less individualized attention from teachers and fewer opportunities to form positive relationships with other school personnel. As a result, many of these students fell through the cracks.

As our higher-achieving respondents' experiences demonstrate, the benefits of school-based resources are several. As a result of their relationships with teachers and counselors, many received assistance with their college applications. Their lesser-achieving counterparts did not experience the same kind of assistance. Take George, for example. After a series of misunderstandings and suspensions from school, George tried to turn his life around. After his older sister did some Internet research and found out that George could legally go to college, he committed to going to school every day and promised to raise his grades. However, he was unsure of what he needed to do in order to go about making the kinds of changes that would put him on the right path to college. In his efforts to reach out to school staff he faced dead ends and resistance.

> Even though I had a bad background, I really tried to turn myself around. Teachers didn't care about me. The Assistant Principal didn't like me. . . . The counselor wasn't there for me. I didn't know what to do. I tried to go back to regular high school, but they wouldn't let me. They said that due to "my kind", I had to be at the continuation school. I even tried to go to the district, but they gave me the run-around.

George could not find anyone at school who wanted to help him. Eventually, he grew frustrated and dropped out. He was viewed as a "troublemaker" and, as a result, was not afforded the benefit of caring and school support staff eager to help him out.

Without special attention and strong support from their schools, undocumented immigrant students face barriers that considerably undercut their ability to make successful transitions from high school to a life after that preserves some of the protections and inclusions they enjoy in K–12 schools. Indeed, other marginal student populations share many of the same questions of access. However, undocumented students' exclusions from federal and state aid create added layers of need that require support and assistance so they can navigate the difficult terrain of college applications and private scholarships. In addition, as we will see in the next section, undocumented status places additional stresses on students that create additional needs.

Contending with the Transition to Illegality

On November 25, 2011, Joaquin Luna Jr. of Mission, Texas took his life. Joaquin had hoped to become the first in his family to pursue college. But as an undocumented immigrant student he faced challenges many of his other peers never confronted. As he "transitioned to illegality" (Gonzales 2011), the exclusions, pressures, stigma, and difficulties of everyday life became too much for him. Although nothing Joaquin left behind indicted his school or his teachers, his suicide draws important attention to the confluence of unfavorable circumstances that make adolescence a difficult time for undocumented youngsters. In the previous section we examined the ways in which schools structure relationships that can foster academic success. In this section, we take a deeper look at the ways in which these relationships frame trust and help-seeking behavior.

Over the last several years, research on undocumented immigrant students has explored the tensions produced by integrated school lives and legal exclusions. For many undocumented children, participation in K–12 schools provides important opportunities to receive an education, prepare for their futures, and participate in the social and cultural worlds of their legal peers. Legally integrated into this defining institution, undocumented immigrant students are allowed to "suspend" many of the negative consequences attached to unauthorized status while accumulating Americanizing experiences. Their childhoods are experienced with few restrictions: they develop a self-image and related expectations for the future in parallel fashion with their legal peers. But as these youngsters come of age, they find that they are not able to join their friends in applying for driver's licenses, taking a first job, and receiving financial aid for college (Abrego 2006; Gonzales 2010, 2011). This powerful "awakening" has tremendous consequences for their ability to stay positive and continue to progress in school. Their identity as undocumented immigrants becomes a powerful stigma, causing most to remove themselves from important peer networks and activities for fear of being found out (Abrego 2008; Gonzales 2011). Moreover, their precarious circumstances engender additional sources of stress, such as fear of deportation and peer rejection (Gonzales and Chavez 2012).

Seeing friends move forward punctuated our respondents' own immobility. Confusion about the future constrained their decisions regarding the present. Ruben, from Seattle, explained to us that his entire future was turned upside down.

> You know, you grew up thinking, dreaming of your future. Like, "I'm going to be a firefighter when I grow up". You know, like that. I thought I could be something more. It's hard to swallow realizing that you're just an immigrant. How do you say? Undocumented? It really stopped me in my tracks.

Other respondents noted a particular fear towards facing an unprotected environment after they left school and transitioned into legal adulthood. Roberto, from Hollywood, expressed this anxiety.

> Realizing I'm undocumented I knew I'd be limited to privileges other people had. It's just a big deal, after high school you grow up, what can you do after that, like, with being illegal it's kinda hard for you after high school because you are all by yourself. And you need that support from the government or financial aid and you don't have it. And I need to think about that now in order to survive, or make it.

For many, this discovery had especially detrimental effects on school progress. Realizing the changes they were experiencing in the present would adversely affect their remaining adult lives, respondents began to view and define themselves differently. For example, Laura, from Boyle Heights, felt so deflated she gave up on school.

I just figured, "what's the point"? Why should I try anymore? What does it matter? I started skipping school. I got involved in the wrong crowd. I was really down.

For many of those we spoke to, externally conceived stereotypes came into sharper focus as fears and insecurities framed their relationships and their choices about participation in school or peer activities. This "transition to illegality" happened during a corresponding period in which American-born peers are making similar, albeit legally unrestricted, transitions into adulthood. As their peers transitioned into adulthood, undocumented students were limited by their own transition. Alejandro, from Hollywood, described the anxiety he faced with his peers.

Sometimes when I talk about the situation I feel like I'm lower than everybody else. Or, that's why sometimes I feel uncomfortable talking about it. People that don't know I'm undocumented and they ask me, I'm scared to tell them because they might think of me as being lower than them, and my confidence is hurt.

During childhood there are not typically any noticeable differences among similarly tracked peers. However, as the world of adulthood was opening up to their peers, a succession of doors was being shut on them. Jaime, from Seattle, also feared that his friends would begin to see him differently. "I was scared", Jaime stated, "I didn't know what my friends would think. What they would do. I thought it was just better to keep it a secret". For many respondents, the prospect of being found out was debilitating. They were afraid of being cast out from social circles and ostracized. They became distant from friends. Withdrawal from once regular activities and patterns took them away from environments where they could spend time with friends and peers.

Their falling off from regular activities was paired with the beginning of a chain of activities and roles for which they could not take part. Judith, from Anaheim, described a world narrowly circumscribed by her avoidance.

I figured if I was just not around it would be okay. Like if I wasn't showing up to places on the bus when everyone was driving there or why I never had any money. I thought it might let me off the hook. But what I ended up doing was, I was pushing everyone away. Like, I ended up creating this very small world.

For most American youth, the adolescent years can be difficult and full of uncertainty. Piling on top of these difficulties, exclusions from defining rites of passage, separation from peer group activities, and a debilitating stigma coming of age as an undocumented immigrant is a harrowing experience

(Gonzales, Suarez-Orozco, and Dedios-Sanguineti 2013). Trying to do it alone can be frightening.

Many of our respondents were instructed by parents and family members not to disclose their undocumented status. The everyday survival strategies of migrant parents include avoiding apprehension by immigration officials. They also avoid institutions and try to minimize their contact with institutional agents (Yoshikawa 2011). For their children, acts of self-preservation make rational sense. However, by concealing their undocumented status and not seeking help from teachers or other school personnel, they risk even greater problems.

Many of those respondents, however, who were concentrated in the advanced curriculum tracks in high school—with smaller and more supportive learning environments that gave them access to key school personnel—drew upon relationships with teachers and counselors to disclose their status and to seek out help. These respondents told us that they felt comfortable talking about their problems with school personnel because the trust was already there. Take Claudia, from Spokane:

Miss H. has always been there for me. Of course I was scared. A little embarrassed. I just knew that if anyone could help she would be the one. So I told her everything. I remember that first time she brought out a box of tissues and we had a good cry together. That's what I mean, she got it, and after that she told me that I had to pick myself up and keep going. That year she really helped me a lot. She really got me through.

Many high achievers who found teachers or counselors they could trust received important emotional support and academic guidance. These trusted figures helped them find answers to difficult questions about their futures and sought out others who could assist them. At critical times when the students' motivations were low, these relationships buoyed their hopes and aspirations.

Although many high-achieving respondents benefited from school environments that facilitated relationships of trust they could leverage to receive support at critical times, their experiences stand in direct contrast to our more modestly tracked respondents. These young people responded to the transition with similar degrees of confusion, fear, and anxiety about their futures. They similarly curtailed activities and relationships. However, their withdrawal was particularly costly, precisely because they were less integrated in their school communities. When reflecting on her high school years, Judith's memories are filled with regret and a longing for a caring adult in her life.

In a way I guess it didn't do me any good to keep so quiet. I'm not so sure, though. It's kinda both ways, like, yeah I was afraid of what the school would do. It's kind of vulnerable, you know, the situation. But then I had no one to help me. I wish someone was there to cradle me and give me advice. I think it would have helped.

As the previous section illustrated, respondents' positioning in the school hierarchy was important for accessing critical forms of support and capital. Placement in honors and AP classes strongly shaped college-going students' sense of belonging. It gave them solid claims to other identities—good student, high achiever, class president, valedictorian—that could provide a bulwark against pressures to leave school.

However, placement in middle and lower tracks typically eliminated special relationships with teachers and classroom visits from counselors. As a result, these young people were disadvantaged by structures that limited their abilities to form relationships with school personnel. Their large class sizes limited any one-on-one time with their teachers, and many of them had scarce access to counselors. Ruben expressed frustration with the limitations imposed by school and family.

This is what gets to me. I don't think any of my teachers knew my name. I was not causing trouble in class, so I wasn't known like that. And I'd always have to go straight home after school, so there wasn't really any ways to make a personal connection.

Whereas Ruben's quiet behavior did not garner him any negative attention from teachers, many other respondents were disadvantaged by teachers and administrators' perceptions of them as troublemakers. In some cases, their disruptive school behavior was rooted in frustrations tied directly to the barriers erected by their newly consequential, but still secret, undocumented status. This was true for George.

I probably missed more than 20 days during my junior year. It was like the world was caving in on me and I was having a hard, I was having a lot of troubles dealing with it. And on top of it, I was always in trouble at school. How could I talk to anyone about my problems, my situation? They assumed I was getting high or something. I just couldn't catch a break.

Whether they were assumed troublemakers or simply invisible to teachers, these respondents were unable to build important school-based social capital that would allow them to develop relationships of trust and support. Many of these problems stem from their large, overcrowded, and underresourced schools. Large classes and high student to counselor ratios mitigated opportunities for meaningful interaction with adults. Perhaps more responsible were school stratification practices that directed some students to smaller environments while funneling a larger student body to underresourced and understaffed classes. Many respondents were contending with a host of problems regarding their uncertain futures, alienation, and blocked access. Unfortunately, for most of those in middle or lower tracks, their troubles went unaddressed because their status within their schools provided no basis for forming relationships of trust or for eliciting the attention of sympathetic school personnel.

CONCLUSION

Making the transition from adolescence to adulthood is perhaps one of the most anxiety-provoking periods in the life course. Often marked by dramatic changes and uncertainty, this change entails taking on greater levels of responsibility and adult roles. This is the first time for many where choices about their futures are not automatically determined by the school cycle. For young adults who have tarnished academic records, prior trouble with the law, or circumstances that stall their advancement, future prospects are limited. As the U.S. economy has shifted from one in which high school-educated young adults could secure manufacturing employment with job security and good wages to one in which good jobs require advanced levels of education, so have traditional routes to adulthood. Without advanced degrees, many young Americans experience the transition to adulthood as one replete with barriers.

Getting a driver's license, securing a first job, starting college, going to bars and clubs, and voting mark one's entry into the legal world of adulthood. However, for those who have grown up in the U.S. but do not have legal status, these very ideals they have grown up believing in become increasingly out of their reach, thus leaving them vulnerable to the consequences of their "illegality". As undocumented immigrant students reach these important American milestones, they must learn the hard lessons of what it means to be undocumented. Equally important, they must deal with the stress and stigma that accompanies their new status. Negotiating separation among their community of peers, friends, and classmates is all the more difficult, as undocumented immigrant youth must make decisions about whether to reveal or conceal their status.

The school context—an already protected environment for undocumented students—provides an array of potential mentors in the education and development of its students. Adolescents are at a learning stage where they are gaining independence, but still require additional guidance in opening doors. Schools provide the opportunities to form these relationships. However, student positioning within school curriculum hierarchies can determine their access to resources and can facilitate relationship building. Far too often, students in general track classes face unfair disadvantages in accessing teaching and counselor time. For undocumented students, not having positive relationships with helpful and trusting adults can lead to disastrous outcomes.

Our study is largely based on the experiences of undocumented young adults who have already made high school transitions. Because of increased levels of immigration enforcement today's immigrant youth face arguably greater difficulties. Addressing their needs should be paramount among educators' concerns. Whereas most of our respondents did not have access to deferred action for childhood arrivals (DACA) while they were in high school, it has undoubtedly changed the landscape for undocumented immigrant youngsters across the country. DACA beneficiaries have obtained new jobs, increased their earnings, and now have access to driver's licenses in most states (Gonzales, Terriquez, and Ruszczyk 2014). These new forms of access have also likely widened postsecondary options for these young people. But because of the recent implementation of the program, it is still too early to discern their impact on high school-aged youth. However, in light of recent analysis of DACA applications (Singer and Svajlenka 2013) that suggest a large segment of eligible youth have not applied to the program, we suspect that those with the biggest resource challenges in schools may continue to face significant barriers to receiving DACA and accessing its benefits. Those who lack meaningful connections to school personnel or community services will continue to be disadvantaged.

What would be most beneficial for the successful transitions of undocumented immigrant students are school structures and cultures that facilitate positive interactions between students, teachers, and staff, allowing those at all levels to develop school-based social capital and build relationships of trust so critical to their success. By investing in a baseline of support for all students, schools could develop support structures necessary to facilitate more targeted outreach to undocumented students. This is not only a social justice issue, but an economic imperative for the nation.

NOTES

1. We borrow from previously published material of the first author (see Gonzales 2010 and Gonzales 2011).
2. There are presently only four states that allow undocumented students to compete for state aid. See discussion below.
3. In 1965, under Title IV of the Higher Education Act, Congress established TRIO to assist in the matriculation, retention, and graduation of low-income students.
4. Respondents for these studies were recruited from various community-based settings, including continuation schools, community organizations, college campuses, and churches. Members of research teams accompanied respondents throughout their school and work days, volunteered at local schools and community organizations, and sat in on numerous community meetings. Interviews ranged from one hour and 40 minutes to three hours and 20 minutes, and focused on questions regarding respondents' pasts and their present lives, as well as their future expectations and aspirations. Transcripts of interviews were analyzed using open coding techniques. After analyzing all interviews, responses were examined for common metathemes across all interviews. And, the names of the respondents are pseudonyms to ensure confidentiality.

5. California schools struggle to meet the needs of their students. The state ranks last in the nation in its ratio of students per counselor, at 945 to one. The national average is 477 to one. See California Department of Education, Research on School Counseling Effectiveness, http://www.cde.ca.gov/ls/cg/rh/counseffective.asp.
6. Yo entiendo que la universidad es importante, pero en este momento me tengo que enfocar en ayudar a mi familia. Sin documentos no ay mucho que pueda yo hacer. Y tampoco es el enfoque de mis maestros. Ellos quieren que aprenda ingles y entonces no nos platican sobre como aplicar a la Universidad. Yo creo que mejor trabajo y ayudo a mi familia.

REFERENCES

Abrego, L. J. 2006. "'I Can't Go to College Because I Don't Have Papers': Incorporation Patterns of Latino Undocumented Youth." *Latino Studies* 4 (3): 212–231.
Abrego, L. J. 2008. "Legitimacy, Social Identity, and the Mobilization of Law: The Effects of Assembly Bill 540 on Undocumented Students in California." *Law and Social Inquiry* 33 (3): 709–734.
Bourdieu, P. 1986. "The Forms of Capital." In *Handbook of Theory and Research for the Sociology of Education*, edited by J. Richardson, 241–258. New York: Greenwood Press.
Chavez, L. R. 1998. *Shadowed Lives: Undocumented Immigrants in American Society*. Fort Worth, TX: Harcourt Brace College Publishers.
Conchas, G. Q. 2001. "Structuring Failure and Success: Understanding the Variability in Latino School Engagement." *Harvard Educational Review* 71: 475–504.
Conchas, G. Q. 2006. *The Color of Success: Race and High-Achieving Urban Youth*. New York: Teachers College Press.
Contreras, F. 2009. "Sin Papeles and Rompiendo Barreras: Latino College Students and the Challenges in Persisting in College." *Harvard Educational Review* 79: 610–632.
Croninger, R. G., and V. E. Lee. 2001. "Social Capital and Dropping Out of High School: Benefits to At-Risk Students of Teachers' Support and Guidance." *Teachers College Record* 103 (4): 548–581.
Faist, T. 2000. "Transnationalization in International Migration: Implications for the Study of Citizenship and Culture." *Ethnic and Racial Studies* 23 (2): 189–222.
Gibson, M. A., P. Gándara, and J. Peterson-Koyama. 2004. *School Connections: U.S. Mexican Youth, Peers, and School Achievement*. New York: Teachers College Press.
Gonzales, R. G. 2010. "On the Wrong Side of the Tracks: The Consequences of School Stratification Systems for Unauthorized Mexican Students." *Peabody Journal of Education* 85 (4): 469.
Gonzales, R. G. 2011. "Learning to be Illegal: Undocumented Youth and Shifting Legal Contexts in the Transition to Adulthood." *American Sociological Review* 76 (4): 602–619.
Gonzales, R. G., and L. R. Chavez. 2012. "'Awakening to a Nightmare': Abjectivity and Illegality in the Lives of Undocumented 1.5 Generation Latino Immigrants in the United States." *Current Anthropology* 53 (3): 255–281.
Gonzales, R. G., C. Suárez-Orozco, and M. C. Dedios-Sanguineti. 2013. "No Place to Belong: Contextualizing Concepts of Mental Health Among Undocumented Immigrant Youth in the United States." *American Behavioral Scientist* 57 (8): 1174–1199.
Gonzales, R. G., V. Terriquez, and S. P. Ruszczyk. 2014. "Becoming DACAmented: Assessing the Short-Term Benefits of Deferred Action for Childhood Arrivals (DACA)." *American Behavioral Scientist* 58 (14): 1852–1872.

Hallinan, M. T. 1994. "Tracking: From Theory to Practice." *Sociology of Education* 67: 79–84.

Heyman, J. 1999. *States and Illegal Practices*. London: Bloomsbury Academic Press.

Hoefer, M., N. Rytina, and B. Baker. 2012. Estimates of the Unauthorized Immigrant Population Residing in the United States: January 2011. Washington, DC: Department of Homeland Security. Retrieved from http://www.dhs.gov/xlibrary/assets/statistics/publications/ois_ill_pe_2011.pdf.

Kilgore, S. B. 1991. "The Organizational Context of Tracking in Schools." *American Sociological Review* 56: 189–203.

Massey, D. S., J. Durand, and N. J. Molone. 2002. *Beyond Smoke and Mirrors: Mexican Immigration in an Era of Economic Integration*. New York: Russell Sage Foundation.

Oakes, J. 1985. *Keeping Track: How Schools Structure Inequality*. New Haven, CT: Yale University Press.

Olivas, M. A. 1986. "Plyler v. Doe, Toll v. Moreno and Postsecondary Education: Undocumented Adults and Enduring Disability." *Journal of Law & Education* 15: 19–55.

Olivas, M. A. 2005. "The Story of *Plyler v. Doe*, the Education of Undocumented Children, and the Polity." In *Immigration Stories*, edited by D. Martin and P. Schuck, 197–220. New York: Foundation Press.

Olivas, M. A. 2012. *No Undocumented Child Left Behind: Plyler v. Doe and the Education of Undocumented Schoolchildren*. New York: New York University Press.

Perez, W., R. Espinoza, K. Ramos, H. M. Coronado, and R. Cortes. 2009. "Academic Resilience among Undocumented Latino Students." *Hispanic Journal of Behavioral Sciences* 31: 149–181.

Pizarro, M. 2005. *Chicanas and Chicanos in School: Racial Profiling, Identity Battles, and Empowerment*. Austin: University of Texas Press.

Salsbury, J. 2003. "Evading Residence: Undocumented Students, Higher Education, and the States." *American University Law Review* 53: 459.

Schafer, W. E., and C. Olexa. 1971. *Tracking and Opportunity: The Locking-Out Process and Beyond*. Scranton, PA: Chandler.

Singer, A., and N. P. Svajlenka. 2013. *Immigration Facts: Deferred Action for Childhood Arrivals (DACA)*. Washington, DC: The Brookings Institution.

Suarez-Orozco, C., M. M. Suarez-Orozco, and I. Todarova. 2008. *Learning in a New Land: Immigrant Students in American Society*. Cambridge, MA: Harvard University Press.

Yoshikawa, H. 2011. *Immigrants Raising Citizens: Undocumented Parents and Their Young Children*. New York: Russell Sage Foundation.

9 The Diaspora Speaks Back
Youth of Migration Speaking Back to Discourses of Power and Empire

Anne Ríos-Rojas

> ¡Soy de aquí . . . Tendré sangre [de ahí] pero soy de aqui!
>
> —(Samara, Spanish youth of Moroccan
> and Pakistani descent)

> The range of contemporary critical theories suggests that it is from those who have suffered the sentence of history—subjugation, domination, diaspora, displacement—that we learn our most enduring lessons for living and thinking.
>
> —(Homi Bhaba)

The manner in which immigrant youth were involved in contests and claims over belonging and identity was poignantly marked out for me by Samara, one of many vibrant 15- and 16-year-old students I met during my initial visits to a public high school in downtown Barcelona—one of the field sites where I was conducting a yearlong ethnographic project on the politics of belonging and immigrant youth identities. Samara, confident and quick with her words, was a child of immigration growing up and going to school in one of Barcelona's bustling immigrant neighborhoods. On the first day that I met her, Samara was in a boisterous classroom with peers from as far away as Ecuador, Colombia, Bolivia, Pakistan, Morocco, and China and as near as the southern regions of Spain. During that visit I took careful note of the fluidity and multiplicity of youth immigrant identities represented within the classroom—the diversity of dress styles, linguistic registers, hues in skin tones, and performed ethnic identities.

As the anthropologist of education interested in discourses of immigration and immigrant identity, I could not resist asking Samara the seemingly innocent and, perhaps for some, straightforward question: "where are you from"? Such a question, one that was inherently about belonging, was, however, far from being straightforward for the youth interlocutors in this classroom. Rather, it was a question that was subject to contestation by Samara and her peers. Samara's immediate and firm response—"*soy de aqui*" [I'm from here]—soon caught the attention of one of her peers, Ruben, a young man from Ecuador who was sitting in the desk across the way. Aiming to correct and re-place Samara, Ruben interjected, *"mentira, que es de Pakistan"* [(that's a) lie, she's from Pakistan].

Samara, quickly jumping from her seat and defiantly planting her petite yet powerful frame in front of her accuser to challenge him, responded, *"idiota! Que soy de aqui!"* [idiot! I'm from here!]. Ruben, looking past Samara, who was by then clenching her fists and teeth in frustration, repeated to me with a grin, *"te esta mintiendo. Su padre es de Pakistan y su madre Marroqui"* [she's lying to you. Her father is from Pakistan and her mother Moroccan]. This last statement appeared to have been the final insult for Samara, whose voice then escalated several octaves to declare, *"tendre sangre, pero que soy de aqui, imbecil!"* [I might have blood from there, but I'm from here, imbecile!]. That final retort quieted Ruben, who appeared to be momentarily dumbfounded by the wrath and power of Samara's scathing critique. The silence was finally pierced by the laughter reverberating throughout the classroom, at which point the teacher needed to intervene, telling Samara to calm down and watch her language.

Questions related to belonging and identity are arguably mired in contradiction and complexity for most teenagers. However, for many transnational youth such as Samara, there is oftentimes the added burden of having one's belonging either called into question or defined for them through dominant discourses that produce and position them as "immigrants". Whether these contentions come by way of their peers, media images, political discourses, or teacher narratives, immigrant youth needed to negotiate confusing and conflicting messages about their place within their "host" society—a place many youth, like Samara, claimed as their home and their place of belonging, despite the wide range of discourses and images oftentimes complicating such claims. In Samara's quick retort—"I might have blood from there, but I'm from here"—is a possible challenge to essentialized ethnic identities as fixed and bound by origin.

I share the example here to touch on how, in this brief and animated interaction between Samara and Ruben, there are allusions to the inherent contests and tensions surrounding claims of authenticity, belonging, and rights with which immigrant youth must grapple. Later, in listening to other immigrant youth talk about why they felt they could or could not claim an identity as "Spaniard", "Catalan", "Latino", or "Moroccan", or even desired to, I would hear echoes of Samara and Ruben's spirited exchange. In their remarks we gain insight into the contradictory ways in which questions of belonging and citizenship for the young people I worked with in Barcelona were repeatedly redefined and negotiated at the intersections of ambivalence, solidarity, and resistance.

BEYOND "ORIGIN" AND "DESTINATION": CRAFTING DIASPORIC IDENTITIES

Pertinent to this analytical project is my framing of the youth in this study— young women and men of migration living within an increasingly multilingual and multiethnic society such as Catalonia, Spain. I borrow the descriptor, "youth of immigration", from Keaton's (2006) work with second-generation Muslim youth in France and from Suarez-Orozco and Suarez-Orozco's (2001) longitudinal study with "children and youth of immigration". My preference for this term comes from my dissatisfaction with what I see as the limitations of classical frameworks applied within immigration studies and the field of immigrant students and education (both in the U.S. and Spain). The term "immigrant", as DeGenova (2002) and others have argued, is often posited from the perspective of the immigrant-receiving society or nation-state. Such a vantage point is thus one already laden with particular political orientations and interests that do not necessarily coincide with those of the actors doing the migrating. "Immigrants", operating within the logic of nation-states, references the traditional push/pull, origin/destination, assimilation/acculturation tropes common in immigration studies. That is, the term builds upon the classic story of immigration whereby "outsiders" or "foreigners" hail "to the promised land" and must assimilate or reconcile the practices of their "cultures of origin" with those of their "destination".

These traditional tropes circumscribe the lives and realities of transnational youth, particularly within the context of a globalized present where youths' social realities and locations are increasingly subject to forces that extend beyond the national boundaries of their countries of origin and destination. As several scholars argue, the traditional frameworks of adaptation, assimilation, and cultural differences, although illuminating, prove insufficient for the study of immigrant youth identities within the present context of globalization and transnational migration (Abu El-Haj 2007; Abu El-Haj and Bonet 2011; Hall 2004; Lukose 2007).

Lukose (2007), for example, argues that such concepts take for granted the privileged status of the nation-state and continue to rest on the assumption that unilinear assimilation—or its contemporary counterpart, integration— is a process that actually occurs (408). The analyses and arguments in this chapter thus reflect these concerns.

Although the youth in this study were not born in Spain and thereby could be defined, in classical terms, as immigrant youth, the "immigrant" part of their selves represented but one layer of their multiple and hyphenated identities. The transnational youth in this study did not usually construct their identities in relation to immigration, despite the insistence of some of the adults in their lives, their teachers and myself included. In fact, the youth in this study repeatedly asserted that they were, first and foremost, "kids" or "persons", as well as "friends", "sons", "sisters", and "students", amongst other social identities. As Daniel, a student from Ecuador, explained when I first asked him what sort of identity he would assign to himself, "antes de nada, soy una person" [before anything, I'm a person]. Throughout my other conversations with other youth, I would hear them preface their answers to such a question with a similar claim ("I'm a person"), a subtle clue into the ways in which youth claimed a personhood and place that afforded them more space for maneuver. If anything "immigrant" was a social location from which many of the youth in this study attempted to distance themselves, having understood it to be an identity stigmatized in media and political discourses. Other less-contested reasons that these youth quite simply did not cozy up to the identifier of immigrant are possible. Apart from its apparent negative implications, youths' inability to relate to such an identity might have had more to do with the reality that the term "immigrant" was an empty signifier, one that failed to capture the transnational realities of their lives.

These young people, in working to define themselves against the backdrop of rapid globalization and competing discourses, were engaging questions that also extended far beyond their individual identities as "immigrant kids". As "transmigrants" and diasporic subjects, these young persons' lives cut across national boundaries, and their multifarious identities were configured in relationship to more than one nation-state (Miron, Inda, and Aguirre 1998). For some, their identity performances were acted out on the increasingly global/transnational stage of music and technology. When not spending their time with the inquisitive "researcher from California", as I came to be known, these youth enjoyed listening to rap, hip-hop, reggaeton, and bachata, visiting one another's Myspace and Facebook pages, holding virtual chat sessions with other youth from across the globe, and participating in other diasporic youth culture production and consumption practices.

And yet, youth collided against an inherent paradox of belonging. Within what cultural theorists are calling a "postnational" moment, where the erosion of nations and borders are making way for new, more expansive forms of postnational memberships (see Soysal 1998), borders continue to be erected rather than collapsed in the lives of some youth. Therein lies the contradiction. As Abu El-Haj and Bonet (2011) observe, "even as the everyday experiences of belonging is becoming more complex for [transnational] young people who live their lives both imaginatively and physically across borders, nation-states remain intractable, powerful forces in their lives" (Abu El-Haj and Bonet 2011, 33). In other words, whereas these global youth defined themselves in ways that stretched their identities beyond that of "immigrant", many of them nevertheless found themselves unable to escape the confining clutches of such an identity. This is the paradox of diasporic belonging. That is, when entangled with gendering and racializing processes, immigration admittedly figured as an important force—at moments a binding one—in some of these youths' self-understandings and experiences.

For some, being identified and positioned as an immigrant implied living with a series of contradictions and conditional forms of belonging. It also required learning how to maneuver through dense webs of discourses and processes of surveillance that at times worked to place limits on their dreams for the future and policed their sense of belonging, rendering their citizenship both suspect and "delinquent" (Ramos-Zayas 2007). The challenge is thus articulating a framework that situates youth *beyond origin and destination* and recognizes their own imaginings of belonging and citizenship that emerge from youths' "glocalized" (simultaneous global and local) locations (Anderson-Leavitt 2003) and from their various social locations as youth, as immigrants, and as diasporic and racialized subjects "produced through difference, a difference situated between the 'here' of the host country and the 'there' of origin, between the 'us' of a dominant community and the 'them' of multiple forms of racialized identification" (Lukose 2007, 410). Today's young people are "global youth", self-positioning and positioned within "plural worlds", their subjectivities constituted within a range of salient discourses that require careful accounting for (Nilan and Feixa 2006, 2).

The youth in this study found themselves located at the center of a range of ideological discourses that alternately glorified immigrants as the poster children of a cosmopolitan and tolerant society and denigrated them through other authoritative discourses that confirmed their inherent "otherness". Employing the concept of diaspora to frame youths' performed identities therefore helps to locate youths' presentations of self within the nexus of such opposing dynamics in ways that move beyond the simple questions of traditional vs. modern "culture", origin vs. destination, host vs. receiving societies, and recognizes instead the manner in which identities are entrenched in relations of power that exist between individuals and institutions (Keaton 1999). Furthermore, the lens of diaspora creates analytical openings for disruption, challenge, and parody with regards to traditional nationalist narratives, the space of diapora being borne out of the "return" of "immigrants" from former colonies to the postcolonial/imperial center (Lowe 1996). Such a space offers opportunities for cultural change and critique—for an "unwitting and unintended cultural challenge" to the totalizing project of empire, or what Juan Flores (2009) names as "the diaspora strikes back" (4). Within the context of this chapter, the concept of diaspora thus also directs our analytical gaze to that inherently disruptive space and subject location that transnational youth occupy. I argue that youths' responses can be read as important diasporic critiques of empire and as challenges to normative notions of belonging and citizenship.

CHARTING DIASPORIC FORMATIONS IN SPAIN

Over the course of the last decades Spain has undergone dramatic political, economic, and social transformations as consequences of globalization that have presented Spain with new opportunities while also generating new sets of political challenges and social problems. The end of the roughly 40-year Franco authoritarian regime in the mid-1970s followed by Spain's incorporation into the European Union, positioned Spain to make its "delicate transition from dictatorship to democracy" and emerge as a modern, economically advanced society (Aram 1995; Cartea and Gomez 1997). Spain's thriving and expanding economy at the time and its newfound role as competitive player in the European arena and the global market, gave rise to an unprecedented increase in the number of migrants from the Third Word, namely from Morocco, Ecuador, Romania, and Colombia (Chacón Rodriguez 2003), that arrived to fulfill Spain's need for an adaptable, industrious, cheap, and flexible workforce. By 2005, Spain had become the second country in the world after the United States in the overall number of immigrants received annually, with the immigrant share of the population increasing from 1.6% in 1998 to 11.3% by 2008 (Lanzieri and Corsini 2006). The largest non-EU immigrant groups (as of December 2010) were composed of migrants from Morocco, followed by Ecuador and Colombia.

Spain's shift from a country of emigration to one of immigration, as others have noted, has been both an "unexpected" and "uneasy" one (Arocena 2011; Colectivo IOE 2002; Cornelius 1994; Izquierdo 1996), this uneasiness perhaps most evident in opinion surveys that categorize immigration as a major national "problem". The social unease generated by these more contemporary migration flows are also palpable in popular metaphors eliciting images of chaos and disaster, all of which prey on the vulnerability of citizens (Zapato-Barrero and van Dijk 2007). The immigrants most likely to elicit a sense of anxiety among Spaniards are those that hail from Africa, Asia, Eastern Europe, and Latin America (Martín Muñoz et al. 2003, 17), *suspect subjects* who find themselves located within a contested social space intersected by a range of contradictory discourses—narratives that at once frame immigrants as "contributing" or "not contributing" and make bounded distinctions between "citizens" and "intruders" and "us" (framed as positive) and "them" (framed as negative), while communicating the broader (more tacit) message that immigrants defy normative behavior required for legitimate national belonging (Terrén 2003; Zapata-Barrero and van Dijk 2007).

During these global times and shifting landscapes, the "native" or *autoctono* population must make sense of its new neighbors, and immigrants need to negotiate their "host" society's conceptions about them while also developing their own narratives of belonging. As Mortimer, Wortham, and Allard (2010) point out, the social lenses through which immigrants are viewed and how they view themselves have important implications for their future prospects—particularly in social institutions such as schools where students are commonly measured against normative models of (national) identity and success.

This chapter directs attention to the varied ways that youth in Spain crafted and negotiated their multiple diasporic identities within these conditions of large-scale mobility, rupture, and possibility. Analytical attention is specifically focused on the multiple, fluid, and at times contradictory ways in which immigrant youth negotiate dual processes of "self-making and being-made" in their quest for cultural citizenship (Ong 1999). I examine the ways in which youth, as knowing subjects and producers of knowledge, negotiated, performed, and played with multiple, intersecting, hyphenated selves within particular ideological and material constraints (Fine and Sirin 2007; Goffman 1959; Yuval-Davis 2010).

THE DIASPORA SPEAKS BACK IN CASE STUDY FORM: ARE WE LISTENING?

Immigrant youth stand at the intersection of competing ideologies and must learn to straddle multiple worlds. As cultural mediators and innovators, young immigrant people embody a transnational sensibility, working and melding new understandings in their travels across borders of language and place (Blommaert et al. 2005). These cross-border journeys, however, are not without their border checkpoints. In their journeying across multiple spheres, youth are also subject to the surveillance of ethnicizing and racializing discourses that constitute "white public spaces" (Hill 1999; Faulstich-Orellana and Reynolds 2009). Surveillance emerged as a dominant theme in the lives of the immigrant youth I spoke with during my time as a researcher in a high school in Barcelona (2007–2008), their alleged differences disproportionately inviting the scrutinizing and racializing gaze of the police, the community, their teachers, and their peers. According to Foucault (1977), surveillance works as a powerful strategy for disciplining the conduct of others. I witnessed and have written elsewhere about the ways in which the surveillance of youth did not stop at the school's front gates; rather, the gaze entered a "welcoming" school—moving through its corridors and classrooms and attaching to the bodies of immigrant students (Ríos-Rojas 2011). For example, in their everyday maneuverings through school, youth encountered both implicit and explicit messages that they were somehow "matter out of place"—subjects whose "cultural differences" were either sources of (exoticized) admiration (i.e., the "good" kind of diversity) or the objects of careful "management" and surveillance (i.e., the "bad" kind of diversity), so as not to lead to any "integration problems" within school and broader society (Ríos-Rojas 2014). This surveillance can have enduring effects for youths' sense of belonging and flexible enactments of citizenship. As the experiences of the immigrant youth I worked with confirmed, "[y]oung people's ability to freely enjoy the physical spaces of their communities is compromised when they are treated primarily with suspicion" (Ruck et al. 2008, 27). That is, the very sort of flexible, mobile, deterritorialized practices that have come to be celebrated as a defining feature of our current era of globalization are ones that also render transnational youth as *suspect subjects*; this is the inherent paradox that immigrant youth must tenuously straddle. In this chapter, I theorize the various and unequal positionalities of immigrant youth as they navigated such a paradox and negotiated surveillance and everyday processes of (un)belonging.

Contests and struggles over diasporic modes of belonging are specifically examined through the narratives of Nadia, at the time of the study a young teen from Morocco.[1] In narrating and performing her belonging, Nadia serves as a case study example for the multiplex ways in which young immigrant people make sense of, and claim a sense of, place within an ever-shifting cultural landscape—how youth manage the complexities of belonging in a complex world and engage with, reproduce, and challenge the dominant discourses of immigration and hegemonic notions of belonging and difference swirling through and around them. Nadia's tellings of belonging provide a stepping-off point for arriving at a deeper understanding of the tensions, struggles, possibilities, and questions that immigrant youth oftentimes must encounter, illuminating the ways in which belonging is not given, but rather narrated and performed within a series of situated constraints and power relations (Foucault 1977).

The findings in this chapter are embedded in a larger ethnographic study devoted to examining the everyday politics of belonging for im/migrant youth in a small secondary school located in the greater Barcelona metropolitan area. The work was also situated within a broader, multi-sited comparative study charting the barriers and bridges in the education of the children of immigrants in the U.S. and Europe (Alba and Holdaway 2013). As an ethnography, the work draws from extended periods of participant observation within the school and the surrounding community; I spent the initial months taking stock of the nuanced norms of conduct and the everyday ebbs and flows of institutional life within the school. When I was not attending classes or participating in a range of school-related activities, I shadowed and conducted repeated in-depth interviews with a group of eight focal students, each of them diverse in terms of their ages of arrival and countries "of origin" (namely Morocco, Ecuador, Bolivia, and Colombia). Nadia, the student highlighted throughout this chapter, was one such student. Throughout the field work, I also conducted audio-recorded, semi-structured interviews with the majority of teachers, school administrators, families, and various directors of local youth organization. Additionally, a series of focus group interviews exploring themes related to perceptions and experiences of immigrant students in schools and broader society were conducted with both "native" Catalan/Spanish and other immigrant students.

Methodologically, this chapter centers the voices and experiences of youth as a legitimate and productive site for knowledge-making, analysis, and cultural critique. Youth, as critical youth studies scholars have noted, are situated at the center of globalization, their identities and very bodies quite often figuring as the "ideological battleground in contests of immigration and citizenship" (Maira and Soep 2005, xix). An explicit focus on youth narratives and perspectives thus has much to teach us about relations of power, the unmaking and making of social identities, and the production of margins and centers. Echoing Maira and Soep (2005), youth narratives direct our attention to urgent questions concerning the politics of belonging, attuning us to "which bodies and which discourses are privileged, condemned or overlooked" (xix) within our present era of globalization. And yet youth, more often the objects of knowledge rather than knowledge producers in their own right, remain an undertheorized dimension of diaspora and migration studies. Thus, in methodological terms, the decision to (re)center youths' experiential knowledge throughout this work is both explicit and intentional. Such an approach frames youth as social theorists and cultural critics, speaking agents with the critical capacity to theorize the tangled intersections of power, race, class, and gender. As I aim to highlight in this piece, youth speak. From their various diasporic locations, youth are *speaking back* to dominant and dominating narratives in order to offer up new visions of belonging and citizenship.

My analytical gaze is thus focused on the diverse ways in which young people such as Nadia attach meaning to dominant discourses of citizenship and the manner in which they carve out small spaces within those discourses for "speak-backing" and offering new possibilities for belonging. What do Nadia's narratives of (un)belonging illuminate about the tangled intersections of identity, culture, resistance, and power? How might they be read as catalysts of change? More importantly, what does this "speaking back" call on "us"—educators, researchers, activist, policymakers—to act upon? Are we listening?

NADIA: NARRATING (UN)BELONGING

As part of a pre-interview warm-up exercise, I asked Nadia to "map out" what words or images first came to mind if she were to describe herself. Quickly sketching out a stick figure in differently colored markers, Nadia explained her representation in the following terms: "I think I'm like this. Sincere, funny, Moroccan, and fun-loving" (see figure below). Glancing at the stick figure drawing framed by Nadia's adolescent, bubbled lettering, it was easy for me to see the resemblance to the bright-eyed, wide-smiled 15-year-old that sat across the lunchroom table from me. Throughout my time knowing Nadia, I had rarely seen her without a smile. She was quick to laugh and find humor in most things, her sophisticated sense of humor manifesting in our interview sessions that were repeatedly punctuated by my periodic guffaws upon hearing Nadia's acutely sarcastic analyses of topics such as friends, teachers, family, and world politics.

From the onset of the study, Nadia was described to me by her teachers as "*una chica maja*" [a friendly, likeable girl] and as "well integrated" within the social life of the school. Socially, she appeared to be well liked amongst the small group of Catalan girlfriends that she socialized with at school—a handful of girls that would search her out after class, ask if she was going down to the cafeteria for the mid-morning break, and lingered

Figure 9.1   Nadia's Self-Sketch

after our interview sessions to walk to the train station with her. According to Nadia, making friends was easy for her, and she had never found herself alone at school. She figured this was due to her own fearless extroversion. As Nadia humorously described, "I've always found someone to hang out with. I don't know, perhaps it's because even if they won't talk to me, I'll walk right up to them and talk to them until they're forced to say 'good bye'! to me".

On most days, the identity that Nadia performed was that of a self-confident, teenage girl, sufficiently style savvy to blend in with the range of adolescent styles represented within the aesthetic hierarchy of the school (neither overly concerned with her dress so as to render her a *"pija"* or a snob, nor too disaffected to make her a fashion misfit), comfortable in shifting in linguistic registers (speaking Catalan with some of her friends, Castilian with others, and a mélange of Catalan, Castilian, and Arabic with family and friends outside of school), and embracing of her multiple and fluid identities. As Nadia described herself,

> I think I'm like a person that likes to get to know a lot of people, travel and all that and learn about other places and other languages, I don't know. I'm a person that likes a lot of things [laughing]. I want to know it all. I'm very much a *chapurrera* [know-it-all] . . . I mean, when somebody new comes [to school] I'm one of the first persons that talks to her.

Nadia was also unabashedly opinionated at times and quick to call out an injustice if she evidenced it, an aspect of herself that at times had produced some friction between Nadia and her teachers. For example, if she felt a teacher had given her an unfair grade (particularly if she felt the act discriminated against her), she was not one to stay silent. Nadia shared stories where she had approached teachers to question a grade she had received, and in one case challenged a teacher to provide her with a clear rationale for giving her a lower grade than her peers when, according to Nadia, she had received a higher scores than her peers on previous tests:

> If it's the same [test], and I've passed it and there were others that failed the [same] test, well then I think that's unfair. And later, [the teacher says] "don't raise your voice at me or I'll fail you"! And she did end up failing me. But oh well, at least I was able to keep that sense of satisfaction when I said those words.

That opportunity to occupy a speaking position, regardless of its potential academic consequences, was a theme woven throughout Nadia's stories of her encounters with peers and teachers at the school and illuminates the agential tactics subjects engage in to mediate limits in their day-to-day encounters with powerful others. For example, Nadia also narrated incidents where she felt one particular teacher was badgering her and claiming that Nadia "did not even know how to spell her own last name".

> For example, in 1ESO [Educación Secundaria Obligatoria], I had Morán [name of teacher] and well, I write my last name differently, okay? Because I write it the way that you write it in Morocco, but translated. And on the class list, she had it written differently . . . I really don't know exactly how she had it written down, no idea. So, she would always say to me, "here, instead of a 'c' it should be an 'x'", or something like that. Every time I entered the classroom she would say to me, "it's just that you don't even know how to spell your own last name"! She always came out with that. It'd make me mad and I'd respond, "that's how I spell it. I'm the one who is writing it correctly, not you. *You* need to check. It must be you that has it written incorrectly on your list", and then she [would say], "do you want to punished"? From then on I decided to ignore her and not talk back. I would say to her, "yeah, yeah. I'm going to change it [the spelling]".

The question of naming is important to note because of its links to the exercise of power. Throughout my work at the school powerful dimensions of naming and who has the power to name and un-name recycled through the experiences of immigrant youth—encounters where judgments were made about Moroccan mothers "who didn't even have their own last names" (clearly a marker of their "oppressed condition' as Muslim women); students were being renamed or renaming themselves in order to belong, and immigrant students were questioned about the veracity of their last names and the correct spelling of such. The legacy of colonial conquest and slavery has taught us about the politics and power of naming and being named. Conquered and enslaved communities have been made aware of the reality that "those who name also control and those who are named are also subjugated" (King 1990, 683). Furthermore, names are deeply tied to questions of identity. When we consider the political dimensions of naming, Nadia's challenge to her teacher—"it's my last name, not hers"—and her defense of the right to claim ownership over its spelling accrues increased saliency as it sheds light on the moment-to-moment contests over belonging that immigrant youth were engaged in.

Sarah, Nadia's older sister (18 years old at the time) noted this example as a key difference in the ways in which she and Nadia approached teachers and schooling. As Sarah stated,

> me, if they [teachers] say something to me, even though I might not like it, I ignore them. I am there to study and I try to focus on that. Why am I going to make myself all upset about it, right? But Nadia can't. She get's fed up with the teachers.

Hearing this, Nadia came back with, "it's just that I'm not like you. I know how to defend myself"! Sarah, responding in a tone I had heard many an older sister take, clarified, "I do know how to defend myself, but there are other ways that I defend myself, there are other ways to do things". As we sipped on the tea and bread drizzled with honey Nadia and Sarah's mother had brought out for us, Sarah mentioned with a wry smile that their grandmother (in Morocco) was much like Nadia: "she's like that too. A rebel".

Negotiating Multiple and Hyphenated Selves in the Diaspora

Nadia also frequently invoked a transnational subjectivity, oftentimes referencing her links to both the "here" of Catalonia and Spain and the "there" of Morocco. She had traveled from Tetuan (Morocco) to Barcelona at the age of six, along with her mother, her younger and older brothers, and her sister, to be reunited with her father. The summer months, as Nadia described, were usually devoted to taking trips to visit her grandmother and her extensive network of family in Tetuan, an experience Nadia looked forward to every year. Her wish was to eventually save up enough money to travel throughout Morocco. According to Nadia, being "multicultural" entailed "knowing about different cultures". When I posed the question to Nadia of whether she would consider herself to "be multicultural", she responded positively, noting, "yes, I think so. Because I, of course, at once know about things from my country and I also know about things from here, no"? Nadia's religious identity as a Muslim also formed part of this multicultural and transnational sense of self. Within a discursive field saturated by exoticizing images of tragically oppressed and voiceless Muslim women, Nadia vibrantly resisted these dominant narratives and embraced her identity as a Muslim youth without shame. But, as

I understood from listening to Nadia, she embraced this identity not for reasons of religiosity, but more often drew on this identity to mediate restric-
tive cultural discourses about "Muslims" and resist identity-devouring
assimilation processes. Despite some of her teachers' assumptions that
Nadia, much like her older sister, would soon be "forced by her father" to
wear the *hijab* [headscarf], Nadia contested these assumptions by defiantly
stating, "I'll wear it when I decide to wear it. That's for me to decide, not
anybody else".

Embodying this multicultural sensibility, however, was not without its
snares, as Nadia spoke of the *weight* or burden of negotiating her hyphenated identities (Zaal, Salah, and Fine 2009). For example, when I asked
Nadia if she thought this multicultural sensibility and multilingualism could
be an asset in the job market, she replied,

> of course. I think so, because, like, there's a lot of foreigners now, no?
> And if you know English, Catalan, Spanish, and Arabic, I think it will
> help you out more because they will choose you before others that only
> know Catalan. Because you will be with other people that speak other
> languages that can understand you better.

However, to my question of whether she felt being multicultural could also
have disadvantages, Nadia immediately stated, "it can be disadvantage if
you have to wear the headscarf and they don't allow you to wear it at work.
That's where it can be a disadvantage. But in general, I think it's more of an
advantage than a disadvantage". Although Nadia notes that the advantages
of being multicultural generally outweigh the disadvantages, it is interesting
to note how the headscarf emerges as source of tension, a potential barrier
to job opportunities.

Nadia shared her critical appraisals of what she understood to be unjust
treatments towards women who chose to wear the *hijab* in public institutions such as the university or schools. At the time, the story of a young
girl who wanted to go to a primary school in a small town in Catalonia
was cycling through the various newspaper headlines. Nadia was familiar with the story, as she was also aware of another incident she noted
where a young woman had been evicted from a university for wearing the
hijab. To my probing question of how she felt about these events, Nadia
responded,

> I see them, on some level, as unfair. That's what I say. [AR: Can you
> explain more?] I think that, like, I don't know, it's unfair that a person
> that wants to follow her traditions and study, well that she should have
> the opportunity to have her traditions *and* at the same time study, no?
> Because there are so few people that want to even get to that point, no?
> I don't know. To not let them, to take that opportunity from them, well
> I see it as really awful. You can also, on some level, perhaps understand

them, that they might not like that you wear it, and when you're inside the school that you take it off, no? But, I don't know. I also think it's unfair.

Threaded in Nadia's response are critiques of assimilation processes and what Modood (2007) refers to as "radical secularism", the means through which secular identities, imagined as universal and invisible, are forced upon the identities of religious minorities through illiberal means in so-called liberal democracies. Nadia poignantly noted the injustices of forcing certain individuals to choose between their religious and cultural identities and the right to an education. In her mind, those should not be exclusive choices enforced upon individuals. She seemed to also implicitly question the alleged equality of such practices.

Encounters with Surveillance and the (Ab)normalizing Gaze

Although Nadia spoke of her multiple identities and varied alliances to be resources, she also framed these as sources of tension and hardship:

I think that on the one hand they are [a resource], no? But, then on the other hand it's difficult because you, of course, have certain customs, certain traditions that you follow, no? But for others it seems like so strange, no? Like, "what do you do for Ramadan that you can't drink water or anything", that's like something really strange to them.

In Nadia's narrating of self, one notes the manner in which she is implicitly aware of the effects of social scrutiny and the ways in which others might perceive particular cultural practices as "strange". I asked Nadia to imagine how her peers and teachers would respond to a student wearing a headscarf at school. Nadia, in a very serious tone, responded,

in a very strange way. They'd react really badly. They'd stare at her, looking at her badly, but later they'd end up getting used to it, no? On the one hand this school is open, but then on the other it's not.

The *(ab)normalizing and fixed gaze of others* emerged again in Nadia's description of self when I asked her if she felt it would mostly be "immature kids" that might look upon the headscarf with suspicion. Nadia described a time when she was out shopping with her older sister (who wore *hijab*):

for example, you can pass by a person . . . for example, my sister was shopping, and whatever, and this person is just staring at her and every-thing. But then when she sees her speaking in Catalan, well then it's like, "oh, look how well you speak"! You know? It's like you're thinking, "don't look at me with that face because . . ." It's very strange. The majority [of people here] are nice, but there are some that are not, and they look at you badly for the simple fact that you are wearing a scarf on your head. It's like you say, "let's see, well in the winter, well there's a lot of them that also wear it because it's cold and that's that".

Nadia, as one reads in her words, was critical of the hypervisibility and social scrutiny directed at certain individuals "for the simple fact of wearing a scarf on your head". She questioned the unequal distribution of negative meanings attached to certain practices and identities. Nadia was critical of how a headscarf on the bodies of some could be a source of suspicion—a marker of otherness only to be dispelled by demonstrating the ability to speak in Catalan (perhaps assuring her observer that she is more integrated than wearing the *hijab* would symbolize)—whereas on other bodies wearing a scarf on one's head was deemed "normal". The act of "living on the hyphen", Nadia's self-narrating seems to say, required maneuvering this tight space between the abnormal and the normal (Fine and Sirin 2007, 19).

As Nadia also alludes to in the quote above, Muslim youth, particularly young Muslim women, were enveloped in *a politics of deservingness* as they carry the burden of needing to prove their deservingness of belonging to the nation and proximity to the dominant "us" in their everyday movements through different contexts: while shopping, on the train, and on their travels to and from school. Because the *hijab*, and thus the subject marked out by it, was taken as existing outside the normative boundaries of belonging, the struggle existed in showing or proving that one can wear the *hijab and* speak Catalan. This "burden of doubt", even if it dissipates as people learn more about youth such as Nadia's sister, represented an initial hurdle to belonging (Puwar 2004, 91). It is important to note as well that Nadia states this during a particular moment in history when Moroccan and Muslim immigrants were at the center of (ab)normalizing and racializing discourses, and articulated in relation to a surplus of images and texts communicating the "facts" about the inherently backward and inassimilable *"Moro"* and Islam as antithetical to notions of democracy, Spanishness, and Europeaness. The events surrounding the "controversy" of wearing the *hijab* in schools helped communicate to youth such as Nadia that their standing in Spanish society was suspect and provisional at best, subject to a set of constraints and conditions, and that there were aspects of their selves that were at odds with the expectations for membership in Catalan, Spanish, and European society.

Nadia was certainly not alone in her critiques of surveillance and the abnormalizing gaze that constructed her belonging as suspect and positioned her outside of the nation. Through my conversations and interactions with other youth, I learned that they too were critically aware of the manner in which they were the targets of greater social scrutiny than their "native" peers and friends, the burden of this reality at moments eroding their faith in democracy and the role that education might play in creating a more just world. For many of the youth, particularly those who had borne the greater brunt of state surveillance on their bodies, racism and prejudice showed no signs of waning in modern society. As Daniel, a youth from Ecuador, soberly put it one day, "that [racism] is always going to exist. That's never going to change, that I swear. There will always be racists. Always". Coming from a 16-year-old, these words were crushing. And yet they represent the views of an increasing number of young people within a global setting where, as Ruck et al. (2008) point out, "the long arm of surveillance" reaches across "oceans and continents" to increasingly target "youth of color" (16). In a world mired by a global recession and greater social uncertainty, the likelihood is great that we evidence a spike in surveillance practices and the possessive policing of national boundaries. The opportunities for youth to name and replace the discourses and surveillance processes that render them harm are critical for achieving a truly democratic and just society.

In her narrative, Nadia appears to allude to the tensions of "being transnational" within a social and political milieu that allows for only limited notions of *who* constitutes the transnational and cosmopolitan subject. She speaks more to these constrained and conditional forms of belonging in the following section.

Negotiating a "Conditional Belonging"

Nadia, throughout her time in Catalonia, spoke of needing to learn how to navigate and negotiate what I refer to here as a *conditional belonging*. As she narrates, the process of claiming an identity as "Moroccan" had been a gradual one, one of "becoming" rather than "being" (Hall 1997), and one negotiated in relation to palpable homogenizing pressures to conform and nationalist desires for closure. Nadia described the developmental pathway of her identity as "a Moroccan girl" (*Marroquina*) as being shaped by that initial moment of contact with the dominant other when she first arrived to Spain. Nadia's first elementary school memories were punctuated by feelings of fear and of having to perform "other" identities:

> I was afraid to show who I was, and all, and I had to pretend to be someone else. But later on, when I learned how to speak and got to know myself better, well then, that's just how I was, that's that. I could no longer change. But maybe back then I thought, "if my personality from there isn't liked by those here". So then I sought out a person and I'd be like her. I'd seek out the personality of another person, even though I don't like that very much, but that's what I did.

Nadia described the process through which she begins by "pretending to be someone else" until she finally learns who she "truly" is, a point of no return in Nadia's self-telling ("I could no longer change"). One sees Nadia, years later, trying to make sense of the processes through which she was positioned by others, noted in her recollections of feeling that her "personality from there" (Morocco) was likely not well received by "those here". To manage that split between "here" and "there", Nadia noted that she resorted to taking on the identities of others ("I sought out a person and I'd be like her").

Viewed through a Goffmanian lens, one observes Nadia performing the identities of others in ways similar to the manner in which an understudy memorizes the script of the protagonist should her/his presence ever be required on stage (Goffman 1959). Actors, however, do not perform their identities on stages divorced from broader power relations.[2] As Goffman observes, an actor can oftentimes employ a performance to vest him/her with a certain power or legitimacy and in this way influence others' readings and treatment of him/her. Goffman (1959) states,

> when an individual projects a definition of the situation and thereby makes an implicit or explicit claim to be *a person of particular kind*, he automatically exerts a moral demand upon the others, obliging them to value and treat him in the manner that persons of his kind have a right to expect. He also implicitly forgoes all claims to be things he does not appear to be and hence forgoes the treatment that would be appropriate for such individuals.
>
> (13, emphasis added)

Nadia's need to take on the personality of others can be understood as a typical example of adolescents' struggles to fit in—what is oftentimes normalized in discourse as a human desire to belong. However, adding the element of power to the analysis, one can additionally read in Nadia's identity moves an attempt to claim to be a particular "kind of person" in the Goffmanian sense—one more like the dominant them of the "here" (Spain) and less like the person from "there" (Morocco), a performance that could serve to disavow and replace a stigmatized identity "from there".[3] It is a performance, however, that does not come without taking a certain psychological toll. As Nadia self-consciously notes, it was a practice she was not proud of ("even though I don't like that very much, but that's what I did").

During later conversations, Nadia went on to describe her journey from denying her Moroccan identity towards moving into a position of defending and embracing it in the face of powerful pressures to assimilate and claim otherwise.

> I say, "I'm from Morocco" There's always people that say, "but you've lived here all your life and you speak very well", and such. But, the same, I was born there, I'm from there. And that's it. And even if I had citizenship status from here I would still say, "I'm from there", because I don't know. But there really are people that would change so that they could then say, "look, I'm from Spain", and such. But that doesn't interest me.

I think that I am like that. [AR: And have there been times when this changes or when it's changed for you? Have there been times when there is a part of who you are that you felt you needed to change?] Well, no. It depends. Well maybe before, yes, no? I mean, when I was in elementary [school], where I didn't know anyone or anything, I didn't say "Moroccan". But now I could care less what they think, since I already know the people here and how they are, and that's it. Like, I think that they already knew [that I was Moroccan], but if they asked me I wouldn't tell them. Like, that was during the first three years that I was here. But now I don't care. I could care less what people have to say. I think that you are from wherever you are from. You can be the same person without . . . I mean, I am from Morocco, Ana is from here, Diana is from Cuba, and we can all still be good friends all the same, you know? You don't have to be from here to have friends. And you don't have to be the same as them in order for them to be your friends. If people accept you for how you are, well, great, but if they don't, then you'll find other [friends]. For me, if you accept me as I am, well great. If not, goodbye!

There are several layers of belonging that Nadia narrates here. As Nadia notes, claiming an identity as Moroccan seems out of the norm, and, as she explained to me during our meetings, people seemed to be surprised that even after nine years of living in Catalonia, she continued to claim such an identity. This well-meaning questioning by others was at times exasperating to Nadia, as she once said to me: "yeah, I know. It's what everybody asks me! Everybody says the same thing, 'if you have lived your entire life here, why aren't you saying you're from here'"? Within a broader societal framework that appeared to be weary of ethnic identifications, as these might prevent integration, one can understand this to be a reasonable question.[4]

I recall one teacher stating at a conference on immigration and education at the University of Barcelona that her wish for her Moroccan-born nephew growing up in Catalonia was that he could grow up to claim an identity as a "Catalan". Why would/could Nadia not claim an identity as "Catalan", "Spanish", or "Catalan-Moroccan"? Throughout my work I heard echoes of this refusal from other youth of migration (namely, youth from Latin America) who also strategically rebuffed such an identity. Why? The tension and the struggle, I believe, laid in the *terms* or *conditions* of claiming such an identity. That is, what was demanded of youth such as Nadia in order to belong as a "Catalan" or a "Spaniard"? Life experience had seemingly communicated to Nadia that occupying such a position would ask that she deny or give up many aspects of herself that she was unwilling to part with. As Nadia later noted,

> if I have that religion, and I speak that language and all that, well then I consider myself more from there. But for people here that is not like normal, since I've like lived here all my life, I'm supposed to be from here. But then that would mean that I can't practice my religion and whatever.

As Nadia soberly states, claiming an identity "from here" implies the loss of too much—the stakes too high, as it would imply denying her the right to practice her religion, to speak her language, and perform a range of other identities. Nadia's words express the cost involved with this form of conditional belonging: "for them you would have to change your language, your religion to be accepted by them. And I think that that is so much to ask. It's too much"! As a teen, Nadia navigated these tensions related to identity within an adolescent arena where drinking and smoking were normalized. For example, during recess breaks at the high school, large groups of students (in 3ESO through *Batxillerat*) would gather near the front gates, sometimes accompanied by a teacher or two, to smoke a cigarette. (This was jarring for me, and it was a popular topic of discussion amongst the immigrant teens I spoke with, who appeared to be horrified by the young age at which, and how often, "the Spaniards" smoked.) When I asked Nadia if she might consider herself "Catalan-Moroccan", she explained these tensions further:

> no, no I don't think so. Well, it's like this. For example, my religion, it has a lot of things that I wouldn't be able to do. But for all the rest, since I've lived all my life here, they think that I should have to do them. Drinking alcohol, smoking. But they say, "but you've already been here all your life, why don't you just try it". And, well, let's see, "I've been here all my life, but I'm from there". And then we start to argue and we end up mad at each other.

Nadia, having temporarily lived through a period where she had felt a sense of loss and self-erasure (explaining, as well, how she went through a stage when she didn't speak Arabic with her brothers and sisters or in public spaces), was in the process of crafting a more confident self. In the earlier quote, Nadia alluded as well to an alternative to the more subtractive, assimilative processes she felt swirling around her, invoking more additive identities and ways of accommodating and acculturating that did not necessarily require assimilation (Gibson 1988). Nadia drew on her multicultural friendships as an example of the opportunities inherent in a more expanded form of belonging, one where "you don't have to be the same as them in order for them to be your friends". Implicit in Nadia's statement is thus a critique of conditional forms of belonging, an inclusion that was granted only through limited and narrow terms (i.e., "being more like us"). It is a form of belonging that leaves little room for maneuver for youth such as Nadia who do not want to undergo complete self-erasure. As Tariq Modood (1997) has similarly noted, equality is "not having to hide or apologize for one's origins, family, or community but requiring others to show respect for them, and adapt public attitudes and arrangements so that the heritage they represent is encouraged rather than contemptuously expect them to wither away" (358).

Questions related to belonging and identity were contradictory and con-tested for youth such as Nadia, as they were for the other youth participants in the study who felt little motivation to lay claim to a "Spanish" or "Cata-lan" identity—least of all when they understood such claims to come at the expense of their varied and multiple identities and particularly so when, for many, the ways in which that identity was being constructed already served to exclude them from belonging to it. It is, after all, difficult to claim mem-bership in a club to which you feel like you only marginally belong (if you belong at all).

Throughout my conversations with many of the immigrant teens in this study, they repeatedly expressed that they wanted nothing to do with notions of Spanishness or Catalaness. These choices speak to youths' agency in crafting their own identities ("self-making"). Nevertheless, it is also important to recognize the ways in which even what might appear as self-imposed limitations are socially and culturally, and thus powerfully, influenced ("being made"). Individuals might feel they cannot claim to belong because they anticipate the negative responses of others to such identity claims, or they may feel that, even though they would appear to have a strong prima facie claim to national identity, as one example, the way in which this identity is socially and culturally produced serves to either exclude them from belonging to it or demands painful identity contortions in order to fit the narrow molds available. It is worth noting that Nadia, despite bearing all the markers of "successful" integration—speaking the national language (i.e., Catalan), having an autochthonous (i.e., native Catalan) peer network, and, during the time of the study, not displaying any "obvious" images of "difference" or engaging in Islamic practices such as wearing *hijab*—oftentimes noted feeling out of sorts, or as she put it to me once, "feeling out of the game". During our final interview I asked Nadia point-blank if she felt like she belonged in school and in larger Cata-lan and Spanish society. Her response speaks to the ways in which, for youth of migration such as Nadia, such a question was oftentimes negoti-ated within the crevices of a liminal space—a diasporic space that Trinh Minh-ha (2010) describes as a generalized condition of being "elsewhere within here". As Nadia responded, "I think that I'm neither in nor out. I'm like in between".

SEEKING OPENINGS IN DOMINANT
AND DOMINATING DISCOURSES

Poststructural and postcolonial readings have offered important insights into the nature of identity-making within contexts of oppression and inequality, illuminating the ways in which dominant discourses of power are never fully dominating. Rather, there are fissures and critical openings in dominant discourses that yield opportunities for agency and subversive acts of resistance. For example, Nadia perceived such an opening in particular history lessons in her social studies class, where she could draw upon a discourse that positioned the Moors as superior and more civilized than the Spaniards:

I think that, I don't know, for example, for people here we're the uncouth ones, no? The filthy ones and all that. But it was us that showed them [the Spaniards] how to take showers, no? I like that this appears in the book; it makes them stay like this for bit [making a movement to signal thinking], no? And [the book] also talks about how we invented numbers; we were the ones that brought philosophy, mathematics, and all that. [AR: You like learning about this then?] Yes, so that students can learn that we're not all stupid like they think we are. It's like they [the students] go, "ah, well I didn't know about this". Well then, get with the program! [laughing]

Narratives of dirt and filth (vs. cleanliness) have historically been central to processes of racialization, the means through which the domination and disciplining of the "other" have been legitimated across societies. Oftentimes, references to dirt or lack of hygiene are used to mark out disordered bodies (Stephenson 1999). As Mary Douglas (1991) argues, dirt is "matter out of place": "where there is dirt there is system [of power]. Dirt is the by-product of a systematic ordering and classification of matter, in so far as ordering involves rejecting inappropriate elements" (35). Throughout my time in Spain it was not uncommon to hear students and adults mention "those *Moros* that didn't bathe", "that smelled bad or strange". As one Spanish student replied during a focus group conversation around the topic of discrimination, she felt that the "*Moros*" were more vulnerable to be discriminated against because they were "dirty".

Nadia offered a critical awareness of these hurtful representations of "dirty *Moros*". It is therefore significant to note the manner in which she strategically inverted the dominant discourse, restating that the "*guaros*", or "filthy ones", were not Moroccan immigrants, or the Moors for that matter (the "us"), but Spaniards (the "them") who, as Nadia stated, learned proper hygiene from the Moors. This opening in the social studies textbook discourse, however small, allowed Nadia to insert herself into the conversation and carve out a space where she could assert an alternate positioning—one temporarily vested with more knowledge and power.

THE DIASPORA SPEAKS BACK: AGENCY, IDENTITY, AND POWER

Ultimately, Nadia's narratives of (un)belonging echoing throughout this chapter serve to illuminate the ways in which subjects negotiate borders of belonging and exclusion within the asymmetries of power that are constitutive of what is being termed "the diaspora". This is, indeed, the "difference" that diaspora makes, as Lukose (2007) argues—one that directs our gaze towards the unsettled spaces where "diasporic cultural sensibilities" articulate. The need for frameworks that can help us to understand the intricate nature of the ways in which young people make and remake their hybrid selves in contexts of diapora—sometimes in spaces that leave little room for maneuver—is thus an on-going and necessary project. For youth such as Nadia, the story of inventing (and reinventing) new selves and struggling to perform hybrid identities that express their full humanity is one that was always unfolding within the context of broader, powerful, assimilating discourses, whose primary aim was not the welcoming of "difference" but rather its control through the setting of *conditions*. The larger message relayed to transnational youth is, "[f]irst assimilate, and then be different within permitted boundaries" (Minh-ha 2010). Nadia's stories spill over the molds offered up by nationalist narratives, resisting the reductive action of nationalist closures in order to reveal the inherently unsettled nature of empire. Whereas hybridity is a regular feature of our global times, that ambiguity has been accompanied by the hardening of borders and a virulent propensity for containing racialized populations. Nadia's "dissenting citizenship" (Maira 2009) helps us move beyond such an impasse, carving out an opening in what appears to be a totalizing discourse and disrupting nationalist narratives of "democracy" and "equality" so central to the maintenance of projects of empire.

Contrary to nation-centric public and political discourses overly concerned with the integration (or assimilation) of immigrants, Nadia's counternarrative can thus be read as a speaking back to some of the assumptions inherent in assimilationist discourses. As a counterscript, such a narrative unsettles the very idea of "host" and "receiving" societies such as Spain as self-evident centers of immigrant "reception" and "integration". "Dear Spain and Catalonia", youths' diasporic narratives seem to say, "we are here to stay and our differences will not disappear into an assimilated invisibility. Accept us as we are. Embrace us without preconditions and requirements that you would not require of your 'native' population". Embedded in youths' stories marked by critique, struggle, and ambiguity lies the possibility for resistance, change, and hope. Young people such as Nadia, I believe, are in the process of articulating political sensibilities and a critical consciousness of empire that have yet to be fully acknowledged and theorized.

In my conversations with Nadia and other youth, I asked them to ponder "what rights were most essential to them". Some of the youth spoke to themes that Nadia already mentioned here—of their right to belong without surveillance and without being marked out as delinquents. Those were the words of Ariana, a young girl from Ecuador, who stated, "the right to an education, the right to allow us to stay here, because we don't do anything wrong and if sometimes we do something bad, it's not *all* of us". Penelope, her best friend, added, "yeah, the right for equality. That is not just because we're immigrants that it means we're worth less". Throughout my conversations with Nadia and other youth, many referenced the right to freedom of thought, speech, and belonging—"to be able to express their ideas and emotions". As Elena, another student from Ecuador, put it, in addition to a right to her education, she expressed as well the importance of being able to author a sense of self,

> of being how I am. Of having a say in things. I mean, in that if I make a decision or if there is something I want to say, that they are open to it. Meaning, not that they have to accept it, but that they at least *listen* to it.

Elena's final words enjoin us to consider the intersections and entanglements of belonging for youth of immigration, and to explore what we might learn about more expanded forms of belonging from listening to the immigrant youth—vibrant young men and women who did not necessarily refuse belonging, but rather did not believe that it should come bound and packaged in the form that it was offered up to them. Rather than a conditional belonging, these youth demand a full belonging—an alternate vision for being human within our present era of globalization. As Elena's bold statement implies, the *diaspora is speaking back*. Are we prepared to truly listen?

NOTES

1. In order to protect the privacy of my participants, all names used throughout this chapter are pseudonyms.
2. Although Goffman's dramaturgical framework for understanding the performative nature of identities seems to pays less attention to the role of power in mediating the performances of actors, power is implicit in his analyses.
3. "Technologies of power" determine the conduct of individuals and submit them to certain ends of domination (Foucault 1988, 18). However, intersecting with these "technologies of power" are also what Foucault (1988) terms "technologies of the self", which open up avenues through which individuals are able to "effect their own means or with the help of others a certain number of operations on their own bodies and souls, thoughts, conduct, and way of being, so as to transform themselves in order to attain a certain state of happiness, purity, wisdom, perfection, or immortality" (18). This framing is also helpful for understanding the range of operations that Nadia and other immigrant youth performed on their selves to accomplish specific ends.
4. For example, similar to France, ethnic origin census data for citizens is not collected in Spain because it is believed these categorizations might work to reproduce segregation and notions of difference. Implicitly, I believe this

policy practice says something about the ways in which Spanish citizenship is imagined and constructed. The relinquishing of pre-Spanish identities and assimilation into "Spanish culture" thus appears to go hand in hand with the acceptance of Spanish citizenship.

REFERENCES

Abu El-Haj, T. 2007. "'I Was Born Here But My Home It's Not Here': Educating for Democratic Citizenship in an Era of Transnational Migration and Global Conflict." *Harvard Educational Review* 77 (3): 285–316.

Abu El-Haj, T., and S. Bonet. 2011. "Transnational Communities and the 'War on Terror' Education, Citizenship, and the Politics of Belonging: Youth From Muslim." *Review of Research in Education* 35: 29–59.

Alba, R., and J. Holdaway, eds. 2013. *The Children of Immigrants in Schools: A Comparative Look at Integration in the United States and Europe.* New York: NYU Press.

Anderson-Leavitt, K. 2003. *Local Meanings, Global Schooling: Anthropology and World Culture Theory.* New York: Palgrave Macmillan.

Aram, J. 1995. "Economic Liberalization and Social Values: Spain in the Decade of the 1980s." *Journal of Socio-Economics* 24 (1): 151–168.

Arocena, F. 2011. "From Emigrant Spain to Immigrant Spain." *Race and Class* 53 (1): 89–99.

Blommaert, J., J. Collins, and S. Slembrouck. 2005. "Spaces of Mulltilingualism." *Language and Communication* 25: 197–216.

Cartea, P.A.M., and J.A.C. Gómez. 1997. "Emigration to Immigration: Young People in a Changing Spain." In *Racism in Europe: A Challenge for Youth Policy and Youth Work*, edited by J. Laurens Hazekamp and K. Popple, 65–89. London: UCL.

Chacón-Rodríguez, L. 2003. "La Inmigración en España: Los Desafios de la Construcción de una Nueva Sociedad." *Migraciones* 14: 219–304.

Colectivo IOE. 2002. *Inmigración, Escuela y Mercado de Trabajo: Una Radiografía Actualizada.* Barcelona: Fundació "La Caixa."

Cornelius, W. 1994. "Spain: The Uneasy Transition from Labor Exporter to Labor Importer." In *Controlling Immigration: A Global Perspective*, edited by W. Cornelius, P. Martin, and J. Hollifield, 331–369. Stanford, CA: Stanford University Press.

DeGenova, N. 2002. "Migrant 'Illegality' and Deportability in Everyday Life." *Annual Review of Anthropology* 31: 419–447.

Douglas, M. 1991. *Purity and Danger: An Analysis of Concepts of Pollution and Taboo.* New York: Routledge.

Faultstich-Orellana, M., and J. Reyolds. 2009. "New Immigrant Youth Interpreting White Public Space." *American Anthropologist* 111 (2): 211–223.

Fine, M., and S. Sirin. 2007. "Theorizing Hyphenated Selves: Researching Youth Development in and Across Contentious Political Contexts." *Social and Personality Psychology Compass* 1 (1): 16–38.

Flores, J. 2009. *The Diaspora Strikes Back: Caribeño Tales of Learning and Turning.* New York: Routledge Press.

Foucault, M. 1977. *Discipline and Punish: The Birth of the Prison.* New York: Pantheon Books.

Foucault, M. 1988. "Technologies of the Self." In *Technologies of the Self*, edited by L. Martin, H. Gutman, and P. Hutton, 16–49. Amherst: The University of Massachusetts Press.

Gibson, M. 1988. *Accomodation Without Assimilation: Sikh Immigrants in an American High School.* Ithaca, NY: Cornell University Press.

Goffman, E. 1959. *The Presentation of Self in Everyday Life.* Garden City, NY: Doubleday.

Hall, K. 2004. "The Ethnography of Imagined Communities: The Cultural Production of Sikh Ethnicity in Britain." *Annals of the American Academy of Political and Social Science* 595: 108–121.

Hall, S. 1997. *Representation: Cultural Representations and Signifying Practices.* London: Open University.

Hill, J. 1999. "Language, Race, and White Public Space." *American Anthropologist* 100 (3): 680–689.

Izquierdo, A. 1996. *La Inmigración Inesperada: La Población Extranjera en España (1991–1995).* Madrid: Trotta.

Keaton, T. 1999. "Muslim Girls and the 'Other France': An Examination of Identity Construction." *Social Identities* 5 (1): 47–64.

Keaton, T. 2006. *Muslim Girls and the Other France: Race, Identity Politics, and Social Exclusion.* Bloomington: Indiana University Press.

King, S. 1990. "Naming and Power in Zora Neale Hurston's *Their Eyes Were Watching God.*" *Black American Literature Forum* 24 (4): 683–696.

Lanzieri, G., and V. Corsini. 2006. *Eurostat: First demographic estimates 2005.* Luxembourg: European Communities.

Lowe, L. 1996. *Immigrant Acts: On Asian American Cultural Politics.* Durham, NC: Duke University Press.

Lukose, R. 2007. "The Difference That Diaspora Makes: Thinking Through the Anthropology of Immigrant Education in the United States." *Anthropology and Education Quarterly* 38 (4): 405–418.

Maira, S. 2009. *Missing: Youth, Citizenship, and Empire after 9/11.* Durham, NC: Duke University Press.

Maira, S., and E. Soep. 2005. "Introduction." In *Youthscapes: The Popular, the National, and the Global,* edited by S. Maira and E. Soep, xv–xxxv. Philadelphia: University of Pennsylvania Press.

Martin-Muñoz, G., J. García-Castaño, A. López-Sala, and R. Crespo, eds. 2003. *Marroquíes en España: Estudio Sobre su Integración.* Madrid: Fundación Repsol.

Minh-ha, T. 2010. *Elsewhere, Within Here: Immigration, Refugeeism, and the Boundary Event.* New York: Routledge.

Miron, L. F., X. J. Inda, and J. Aguirre. 1998. "Transnational Migrants, Cultural Citizenship, and the Politics of Language in California." *Educational Policy* 12 (6): 659–681.

Modood, T. 1997. *Church, State, and Religious Minorities: PSI Research Report.* London: Policy Studies Institute.

Modood, T. 2007. *Multiculturalism: A Civic Idea.* Malden, MA: Polity Press.

Mortimer, K., S. Wortham, and E. Allard. 2010. "Helping Immigrants Identify as 'University-Bound Students': Unexpected Difficulties in Teaching the Hidden Curriculum." *Revista de Educación* 353: 107–128.

Nilan, P., and C. Feixa. 2006. "Introduction: Youth Hybridity and Plural Worlds." In *Global Youth? Hybrid Identities, Plural Worlds,* edited by P. Nilan and C. Feixa, 1–13. London: Routledge.

Ong, A. 1999. *Flexible Citizenship: The Cultural Logics of Transnationality.* Durham, NC: Duke University Press.

Puwar, N. 2004. *Space Invaders: Race, Gender and Bodies Out of Place.* Oxford: Berg.

Ramos-Zayas, A. Y. 2007. "Becoming American, Becoming Black? Urban Competency, Racialized Spaces, and the Politics of Citizenship among Brazilian and Puerto Rican Youth in Newark." *Identities: Global Studies in Culture and Power* 69 (14): 85–109.

Ríos-Rojas, A. 2011. "Beyond Delinquent Citizenships: Immigrant Youth's (Re)visions of Citizenship and Belonging in a Globalized World." *Harvard Educational Review* 81 (1): 64–93.

Ríos-Rojas, A. 2014. "Managing and Disciplining Diversity: The Politics of Conditional Belonging in a Catalonian Institut." *Anthropology and Education Quarterly* 45 (1): 2–21.

Ruck, M., A. Harris, M. Fine, and N. Freudenberg. 2008. "Youth Experiences of Surveillance: A Cross-National Analysis." In *Globalizing the Streets: Cross-cultural Perspectives on Youth, Social Control, and Empowerment*, edited by M. K. Flynn and D. C. Brotherton, 15–30. New York: Colombia University Press.

Soysal, Y. N. 1998. "Towards a Postnational Model of Membership." In *The Citizenship Debates: A Reader*, edited by G. Shafir, 189–217. Minneapolis: University of Minnesota Press.

Stephenson, M. 1999. *Gender and Modernity in Andean Bolivia*. Austin: University of Texas Press.

Suarez-Orozco, M. 2001. "Globalization, Immigration, and Education: The Research Agenda." *Harvard Educational Review* 77 (3): 345–365.

Terrén, E. 2003. "La ironía de la solidaridad: cultura, sociedad civil y discursos sobre el conflicto racial de El Ejido." *Reis. Revista Española de Investigaciones Sociológicas* 71 (102), 125–146.

Yuval-Davis, N. 2010. "Theorizing Identity: Beyond the 'Us' and 'Them' Dichotomy." *Patterns of Prejudice* 44 (3): 261–280.

Zaal, M., T. Salah, and M. Fine. 2009. "The Weight Of The Hyphen: Freedom, Fusion And Responsibility Embodied By Young Muslim-American Women During A Time Of Surveillance." *Applied Developmental Science* 11 (3): 164–177.

Zapata-Barrero, R., and T. van Dijk, eds. 2007. *Discursos Sobre la Inmigración en España: Los Medios de Comunicación, los Parlamentos y las Administraciones*. Barcelona: Fundació CIDOB.

10 Global Urban Youth Culture
Peer Status and Orientations toward School among Children of Immigrants in New York and London[1]

Natasha K. Warikoo

Dominant explanations for the low socioeconomic outcomes of some ethnic groups in the United States suggest that low-skilled minority, immigrant families living among other disadvantaged minorities will assimilate into the urban underclass, and as a consequence their children will demonstrate "reactive ethnicity" (Gans 1992), adopting the "adversarial subculture" of the "values and norms" of the inner city's "outlooks and cultural ways", leading to poor outcomes in school and beyond (Portes and Zhou 1993, 81). This "downward assimilation" trajectory is one of three possibilities outlined by segmented assimilation theory (Portes, Fernandez-Kelly, and Haller 2009; Portes, Fernández-Kelly, and Haller 2005; Portes and Zhou 1993).[2] An early example of segmented assimilation theory, Alex Stepick's (1998) ethnography of 1980s Miami shows how academically successful Haitian Americans in Miami maintain ethnic identities, whereas their low-achieving counterparts identify as African American and reject Haitian identity in their styles, dress, and attitudes. Stepick suggests that this cultural assimilation leads low achievers to downward assimilation. Modood (2004) has suggested that segmented assimilation theory is applicable in the British context, as well, and can explain the higher levels of university enrollment among Indians and Pakistanis, compared to Afro-Caribbeans, in Britain.

Researchers in the U.S. have suggested four elements to culture among the immigrant second generation who downwardly assimilate: (1) an *oppositional peer culture* that rebels against authority, rejects academic achievement, and sanctions high achievers; (2) beliefs that *racial discrimination limits future options*; (3) *low aspirations*; and (4) *consumption and taste preferences* linked to urban African American culture—for example, rap music (Portes et al. 2005; Portes and Rumbaut 2001; Portes and Zhou 1993; Stepick 1998; Zhou and Bankston 1998). In Britain, scholars link ethnic minority oppositional cultures to taste preferences (Majors, Gillborn, and Sewell 2001; Modood 2004; Sewell 1997). For example, Modood (2004) suggests that downward assimilating Afro-Caribbeans in Britain have adopted the "working class, popular culture, often American-derived . . . of Hollywood, soap-operas, music, clothes fashion", whereas South Asians have maintained their ethnic identities and, as a result, have had more educational success (102).

Whereas the literature on assimilation has analyzed demographic and structural influences on assimilation pathways, there has been less analysis of the role of culture in those pathways, even while culture is used to explain outcomes. Hence, in the case study that follows I focus on three key questions related to cultural incorporation. First, do second-generation youth in Queens, New York attending a low-performing school exhibit oppositional cultures, as expected by downward assimilation theory? In order to answer this question, I analyze youth cultures[3] in terms of attitudes, taste preferences in music and style, and behaviors in the face of conflict. I compare the cultural orientations and styles of two second-generation groups, one high-achieving in the U.S. and Britain (Indians) and one lower-achieving (Afro-Caribbeans), evaluating whether the cultural orientations of second-generation, Afro-Caribbean youth, who are sometimes thought to embody oppositional cultures (Modood 2004; Stepick 1998; Waters 1999), are substantively different from second-generation Indians, who are thought to embody positive cultural orientations (Gibson 1988; Modood 2004). Second, how does second-generation youth culture compare between New York and London? This question addresses whether the presence of an oppositional culture among disadvantaged African American peers makes a difference in the cultural lives of children of immigrants in the United States. If, as some have suggested, downward assimilation is related to the influence of an African American-influenced peer culture and U.S.-style urban poverty, then second-generation youth cultures should look different in London, where the native poor are Whites and there is not as much class and race segregation. Third, if not oppositional peer culture, what *does* explain second-generation cultural practices in low-achieving urban schools? I employ 80 in-depth interviews with one-and-a-half- and second-generation[4] Indians and Afro-Caribbeans in both cities; ethnographic field work from one multiethnic, low-income school in both cities; and a survey of one-and-a-half- and second-generation teens in both schools (*n* = 125).

I found that oppositional peer cultures do not explain downward assimilation in the New York or London high schools. The findings were consistent across the two ethnic groups, in spite of Indians in both cities having higher overall academic achievement than Afro-Caribbeans (Portes and Rumbaut 2001; UK Department for Education and Skills 2005), and in spite of New York students' proximity to American ghetto poverty. African American-rooted hip-hop music and style dominated taste preferences in both cities, but this was largely a global influence rather than the local cultures suggested by downward assimilation theory; hence the similar findings in London where there are no African Americans. Similar taste preferences in both cities suggest a *global urban youth culture* with respect to taste. Nonetheless, there were poor academic outcomes in both school contexts—evidence for downward assimilation. *Peer status* considerations better explain the youth cultures I encountered in both cities. That is, I found that second-generation teens used cultural cues—including, but not limited to, cultural consumption—to vie for status within the peer status hierarchies. This included demonstrating hipness among peers— wearing stylish clothing, listening to music popular among peers (in the case of contemporary New York and London, hip-hop), and defending one's pride when provoked. Crucially, this peer culture was not opposed to adult expectations and culture by design. The peer status analysis explains the apparent paradox of teens' participation in styles and behaviors that adults read as delinquent or rebellious while expressing positive attitudes toward school, achievement, and opportunities for success. It also explains seem-ingly anti-school forms of conflict resolution (fighting in class, talking back to teachers, and more) among teenagers in school—rather than rebellion, these behaviors stem from the struggle to maintain pride and peer status. Academic achievement, then, had little bearing on peer status. Rather, it was the accoutrements of hipness that mattered to second-generation teens and that determined peer status. This finding suggests a shift in understand-ing the cultural mechanism by which some second-generation minority youth fail to achieve academically; my findings show that it is not for want of aspirations or to express resistance to schooling.

These findings resonate with recent research critiquing oppositional culture explanations of school orientation among African American (Ainsworth-Darnell and Downey 1998; Carter 2003, 2005; Cook and Ludwig 1998; Tyson, Darity, and Castellino 2005), Latino (Conchas 2001), and working-class youth (Davies 1994, 1995), and among high school dropouts (Tanner 1990). They extend previous research on the importance of peer status in the American high school experience (Brown 1990; Coleman 1961; Milner 2004; Rigsby and McDill 1975) by showing how children of immigrants adopt and engage peer status hierarchies in high school. In doing so I speak to an older debate on whether there is an "adolescent soci-ety" (Coleman 1961), and if so, whether or not it is opposed to academic achievement (McDill and Rigsby 1973; Rigsby and McDill 1975). James Coleman (1961), in his classic *The Adolescent Society* (1961), suggested that American adolescents had begun to form a distinct culture that is ori-ented away from adult culture and has its own status system, norms, and goals. Although Coleman suggested that adolescent culture's cultural scripts were not necessarily those that lead to high academic achievement, it was scholars in the tradition of subcultural studies, both in the U.S. and Britain, who suggested that adolescent subcultures explicitly *oppose* school norms (Cohen 1997[1972]; Hall and Jefferson 1976; Willis 1977). Arguments in the subcultural theory tradition suggested that academic achievement has a negative effect on peer status, rather than Coleman's (and this study's) implications that academic achievement has a *very weak, positive* effect on peer status.

METHODS AND CONTEXT

A multi-method approach triangulates this research: ethnographic observations at multiethnic high schools, a survey with 125 teenagers at the
schools, and 80 in-depth interviews. Two schools, one in each city, were
chosen for this research with four criteria in mind: (1) evidence of downward assimilation in terms of low academic performance, in order to
understand the cultural practices that might influence that downward trajectory;[5] (2) multiethnicity, with no majority group and significant numbers of second-generation Indians and Afro-Caribbeans (the largest groups
common to both cities, for comparability); (3) class comparability across
the two sites; and (4) traditional school structure for the city.

I spent four months at York High School[6] in New York, attending every
day, and six months in Long Meadow Community School in London,
attending three to four days per week. In both schools I shadowed teachers
and students and wrote detailed field notes. I took on the role of observer
rather than teacher's aide, to minimize the degree to which students censored
themselves and their behaviors around me. Ethnographic data allowed a
comparison of what students *said* with what they *did*.

Surveys were conducted with mixed groups of students during four here-
togeneous classes (by ethnicity/race, gender, skills) in each site; they gave
a sense of overall interests, attitudes, identities, and backgrounds in the
schools. All students present were surveyed, but only one-and-a-half- and
second-generation students are included in results presented in this chapter.[7]
Although students could opt out of the survey, none in either city chose to
do so. Survey responses provided an overview of student backgrounds and
attitudes in each school, facilitating the New York-London comparison.

In-depth interviews determined whether and how cultural choices sig-
naled particular ways of being, and the manifestations of these meanings in
teenagers' daily lives. Interview topics included ethnic background, activities outside of school (sports, time with friends, and more), family and
friend influences, tastes in music and style, identity, friends, school groups
and status, future plans, and experiences with discrimination. There were
20 students of each ethnic group in each city (half girls and half boys), for
a total of 80 in-depth interviews (see Table 10.2). Because of York High
School's greater diversity, I had some difficulty finding enough Indian and
Afro-Caribbean students. Eventually I went to a neighboring school to
complete interviews with Afro-Caribbean students. Although not ideal, the
descriptions below suggest that the schools are in fact very similar. In both
cities, interviews lasted from 40 minutes to 90 minutes (sometimes in multiple sittings), and were subsequently transcribed. They took place in school,
most often in the library, or in an open classroom. Transcripts were coded
using Atlas.ti, and then analyzed by reviewing the quotes listed under different codes and by using the matrix method of Miles and Huberman (1984)
to examine gender, ethnic, and national differences in the interview data.

Table 10.1 Survey Respondents*

	New York		London	
Mean age	15.8 years		15.1 years	
Gender	*Number*	*Percentage*	*Number*	*Percentage*
Boys	33	42%	64	58%
Girls	46	58%	46	42%
Mother's birthplace				
West Indies	30	38%	12	11%
India	4	5%	27	24%
East Africa (Kenya, Uganda)	0		7	6%
Dominican Republic, Puerto Rico	10	13%	0	
Morocco	0		7	6%
Pakistan	0		7	6%
U.S./Britain	14	18%	31	28%
Other	17	21%	19	17%
No Answer	5	6%	1	1%
Second Generation**		48%		65%
First or 1.5 Generation***		33%		7%
Total	80		111	

*The data in this table reflect overall survey data, before non-second- and one-and-a-half-generation respondents were removed. Gender percentages and mean age were similar for one-and-a-half/second-generation respondents.
**Second generation defined as U.S./UK-born children with foreign-born mothers, or foreign-born children who arrived at or before age five.
***First or one-and-a-half generation defined as foreign-born children arriving after age five.

Table 10.2 In-Depth Interview Subjects

		London	New York
2nd Generation			
Indians	Boys	10	10
	Girls	10	10
Afro-Caribbeans	Boys	10	10
	Girls	10	10
Total: 80 Interviews		*40*	*40*

The Schools

The New York school, York High School, lies on the border of Brooklyn and Queens. As with many urban areas (and the London school's neighborhood), the better-off population of the neighborhood generally sends its children to parochial, private, and specialized public schools, and students from neighboring, more disadvantaged neighborhoods commonly come by bus or subway to attend the school, usually by assignment by the New York City Department of Education. Two-thirds of one-and-a-half- and second-generation students surveyed reported that their fathers had had less than a high school education, and another 15% reported that their fathers ended formal education after high school.

York High is diverse. 81% of students have foreign-born mothers, and nearly half are second generation (based on survey data). Hispanics (42%) and Asians (about 37%)[8] are the largest groups at the school, but the statistics mask the internal diversity of the groups (NYC Department of Education 2004).[9] Black students make up 14% of the school population, and this includes both African Americans and Afro-Caribbeans (NYC Department of Education School Report Card 2004). Lastly, Whites are 7% of the school population (NYC Department of Education School Report Card 2004). The school was home to over 3,000 students at the time of my research. 34% of students were eligible for free student lunches during the time of this research, although the actual percentage of families living in poverty was likely to be much higher.[10] In terms of academic achievement, the school's official graduation rate was 44% (compared to 58% for New York city), although a group of 1,100 ninth grade students in 2002 dwindled to 430 12th grade students by 2005[11] (see Table 10.3) (NYC Department of Education School Report Cards 2004, 2005). I focused my research on grades nine through 11, ages 14–17.

I completed interviews with Afro-Caribbeans in New York at Harrison High School, which lies less than two miles from York High School, and no other high schools lie between the two. Harrison High School's student body in 2003–2004 was quite similar to York High School's in terms of ethnicity and race and eligibility for free or reduced school meals. A school administrator at York High called Harrison its "sister school". Many students at Harrison reported having friends at York, and vice versa. 15 of the 20 interviews with Afro-Caribbeans in New York were with students at Harrison. A comparison of interview responses between the Afro-Caribbean students at York and those at Harrison revealed no major differences.

The London school, Long Meadow Comprehensive School, sits in the northwest borough of Brent. Over 60% of Brent's population is of non-British origin, which is the highest percentage of minorities in all of Britain's boroughs (Office for National Statistics 2001). Brent ranks 81st out of 354 Local Authorities in England (with one being the most deprived

Table 10.3 The Schools in Comparison

	London: Long Meadow Community School		New York: York High School	
Free Lunch Eligibility		33%		34%
Racial Makeup	Afro-Caribbean	15%	Black (includes Afro-Caribbean, African American)	14%
	Indian	16%	Asian and Others (includes Indian, Indo-Caribbean, other Asians, Mixed, Native American)	37%
	White	17%	White (non-Hispanic)	7%
	Mixed, Other, or Unspecified	25%	Hispanic	42%
Number of Students		1,180		3,100
Exam/Graduation Results	At least 5 A-C GCSEs	43%	Graduation Rate	44%

Sources: UK Office of Standards in Education School Reports, 1998, 2004; NYC Department of Education School Report Card, 2003–2004 School Year.

Local Authority in England) (Neighbourhood Renewal Unit 2004). Long Meadow lies in the more deprived south Brent, marked off from north Brent by a major highway.

Long Meadow's 1,100 students reflect the ethnic and racial diversity of the borough. The largest ethnoracial groups are White British students (17%), Indians (16%), and Afro-Caribbeans (15%); still, these groups together comprise less than half of the student population. One-third of Long Meadow's students are eligible for free student lunches (24% of London's secondary public school students overall are eligible for free lunches). In terms of educational outcomes, in 2003, 43% of Long Meadow 11th grade students attained five grades of C or above on the General Certificate of Secondary Education (GCSE) exams (the national average is 52%) (OFSTED 2003) (see Table 10.3).[12] Although Long Meadow hosts students from ages 11–18 (including a Sixth Form for ages 16–18), I focused my research on Years 10–11 and the Lower Sixth Form, which included ages 14–17, in order to coincide with the ages of my New York research. The measures above suggest that students in both schools are somewhat below average for their respective cities in terms of social class and academic achievement, although not the worst off in the two cities.

FINDINGS

In order to analyze whether students exhibit oppositional cultures, I first present data on their attitudes and beliefs about school, which are mostly positive. Second, I present data on taste preferences, comparing youth in London and New York. I find that most youth in both cities engage a *global* youth taste culture, rather than locally influenced taste cultures. The lack of oppositional attitudes and beliefs suggests that a better explanation for seemingly oppositional behaviors is in order. Hence, the third section analyzes teen responses to conflict and interactional styles among youth in the study, to understand seemingly oppositional behaviors. I show how teenagers emphasize self-pride and maintaining respect among peers and teachers, which can impede educational achievement, despite students' best intentions.

Attitudes: Little Evidence of Oppositional Cultures

Downward assimilation theory suggests three aspects of the cultures of second-generation youth who do not achieve in school, which are that: (1) they share a disinterest in education with peers through a peer culture that doesn't value academic achievement, (2) they believe that racism and discrimination negatively affect the life chances and school achievement of their ethnic/racial group, and (3) they lack ambitions for academic achievement, and don't believe that working hard will lead to future success. In this section I assess students' views in these three domains.

Attitudes Within Peer Culture

Second-generation teens did not seem to experience peer pressure to demonstrate low academic achievement. First, respondents felt their friends valued education: on the survey conducted, 80% of students in New York and 96% of students in London agreed with the statement "among my friends, doing well in school is important", and a majority strongly agreed. Second, students who did well did not experience low social status as a result of their academic performance—84% of youth in New York and 85% in London *disagreed* with the statement "among my peers, it is not cool to do well in school", and a majority strongly disagreed. Interview data resonated with these findings. Ajay, an Indian[13] student in London, explained that even when students misbehave in class, they prefer to get good grades:

> N: *Would you say it's not cool to do well in school here?*
> R: *No I wouldn't say that.*

N: *Or is it cool to misbehave?*
R: *Maybe like joke on the teachers yeah, but . . . they may mess around here, but they want to get good grades really.*

Many students in fact expressed annoyance at peers who disrupted classes for no reason. Sophie, an Afro-Caribbean student in London, explained:

N: *Would you say that it's cool to misbehave a little bit or, say, talk back to teachers? Does that make you popular?*
R: *It don't make you popular, sometimes it makes you stupid. Some students do [misbehave] and people will be like, "why you doing that? Why are you being stupid"?!*

Sophie's response resonates with the responses of many Indians and Afro-Caribbeans in both cities.

Not only was misbehavior often disliked by peers, but most youth preferred to give appearances of doing well academically. Joe, an Afro-Caribbean student in New York, said that high-achieving students don't get bullied, and he further accused popular peers of suggesting that they do well, when they really don't:

N: *How do popular kids tend to do in school in terms of grades?*
R: *They—majority, I saw they're fronters, because they put up a front like they are doing well in school. Majority of them are doing bad! Like the ones you don't expect to see in like Saturday school [make-up and remedial classes], they are the ones going!*

Joe was a self-described popular, but low-achieving, student. He points out that rather than masking *high* achievement, some students actually masked *low* achievement. I observed many instances of bragging about academic skills in both New York and London.

Individual Beliefs about Racism and Discrimination
A set of survey questions asked students to agree or disagree (strongly or weakly) with, among others, statements on racism and discrimination. Students generally thought teachers were fair. 73% of New York students surveyed and 77% of London students surveyed agreed that "teachers in this school are fair to students, regardless of their race". When I asked students in interviews a more generic question about whether teachers in their school are fair, not specifying race, less than 10% made reference to race. Lastly, survey respondents didn't perceive unequal opportunities for different race groups: 89% of survey respondents in New York and 84% in London agreed that "young people of my race have a chance of making it if we do well in school", and the majority strongly agreed.

Perceptions of Opportunities and Aspirations

Finally, I found little evidence to support the suggestion that, in reaction to the racism they observe, second-generation teens will not believe in mainstream routes to success. Students in both cities expressed strong agreement with the statement "I would like to complete college/university": 100% in New York and 93% in London agreed. Students also generally believed that they would indeed do so: 94% in New York and 91% in London agreed that "I believe I will complete college/university". Furthermore, students believed that working hard in school would lead them to success in school and in life, with over 95% of students in both cities agreeing that "if you work hard in school, you will do well", and almost all agreeing that "doing well in school and getting an education is important to getting ahead in life". These data show that the vast majority of students believed that their hard work could pay off, and that they planned to go on to college. The overall findings resonate with recent research finding little evidence of African American and working-class oppositional attitudes (Ainsworth-Darnell and Downey 1998; Carter 2005; Davies 1995; Tanner 1990; Tyson et al. 2005); here I extend this growing literature to the immigrant second generation.

The small percentage of students who *did* express oppositional beliefs cannot account for the overall low achievement in both schools; recall that less than half of students are graduating high school in both sites. Still, was there a minority for whom perceptions of bias and peer culture lead to low aspirations? To answer the question, I compared the educational expectations of the minority who did express so-called oppositional beliefs with the educational expectations of those with positive beliefs. I found that the minority who expressed negative beliefs had similar educational expectations to those with positive beliefs. For example, of students who agreed that "among my friends, it is not cool to do well in school", 94% believed they would complete college/university, compared to 92% of those who disagreed with the statement and believed they would complete college/university. Similarly, in terms of perceptions of discrimination, 88% of those who disagreed that "young people of my race have a chance of making it if we do well in school" believed that they would complete college; this compares to 93% of those who agreed with the statement, a statistically insignificant difference. Results were similar for other attitudinal measures. Hence, the minority who did perceive a negative peer culture or discrimination didn't seem to let these perceptions affect their beliefs about educational achievement (see Table 10.4). These findings run counter to the suggestion that disadvantaged youths' perceptions of blocked opportunities for mobility and achievement lead to stunted educational aspirations. Even when students *did* feel that their peer culture required poor school performance or *did* perceive racial inequality in opportunities, these perceptions did not lead to low educational aspirations.

Table 10.4 Influence of Perceptions of Disadvantage on Desire for Higher Education

	I believe I will complete university/college	
Among my friends, it is not cool to do well in school.	Agree (*n* = 18)	94% (*n* = 17)
	Disagree (*n* = 97)	92% (*n* = 89)
Young people of my race have a chance of making it if we do well in school.	Agree (*n* = 103)	93% (*n* = 96)
	Disagree (*n* = 16)	88% (*n* = 14)

Source: Survey data, *n* = 125.

These findings resonate with research showing that some minority youth are able to both recognize discrimination and racism while still maintaining high aspirations and the belief that they are able to achieve if they put their minds to it (López 2002; Mehan, Hubbard, and Villanueva 1994; Ramos-Zayas 2003).

Tastes: Music, Clothing, and Sneakers

I found that style rooted in African American street music—hip-hop—has become mainstream urban popular culture, both in the U.S. and UK, and not just among Black youth (see also Cutler 1999; Maira 2002). This suggests that, today, hip-hop is a *global* urban youth culture, rather than something based on neighborhood and proximity to African American peers, as suggested by downward assimilation theory. Below, I highlight students' taste preferences.

Music

Both interview and survey responses demonstrated the widespread popularity of hip-hop music among the second generation in both cities. When I asked students during interviews what kinds of music they regularly listen to, 84% told me some form of hip-hop—hip-hop, rap, R&B, or UK garage.[14] On surveys, when asked to name their three favorite music artists or songs with artists, students in both cities also showed a strong favor for hip-hop, indicating that the interview findings were not limited to the ethnic groups I interviewed. Of the top 10 artists named in both cities on the survey (either as favorites, or as singers/rappers of favorite songs), six are African American rappers or R&B singers, two are Caribbean singers of reggae (Sean Paul) and soca (Kevin Lyttle) who were played regularly on mainstream hip-hop radio in New York and London at the time of the research, one is the controversial White American rapper Eminem, and one is a Spanish *bachata* band (Aventura) that describes itself as interweaving hip-hop and R&B into its music and dresses in the style of hip-hop artists

(Aventura 2008). These data were quite similar in London and New York, and by ethnic group. Indeed, even when students consumed ethnic-identified music like *reggaeton* (music sung and rapped in Spanish, mixing Latin American styles and reggae with hip-hop and rap) and *bhangra* (Punjabi folk music, often remixed with hip-hop), often it was remixed with, or in the style of, hip-hop.

In these contexts, White-identified music—rock, punk, grunge—was perceived as rebellious, rather than hip-hop or rap music. For example, Nicole, an Afro-Caribbean rock fan I met in London, told me that her peers chastised her for her taste for rock.

> N: *What kind of music do you listen to?*
> R: *All kinds of music, but . . . Well, I don't buy CDs . . . but if I had money, I would go and buy Evanescence and Linkin Park [rock bands] and stuff like that . . . My peers, they are all like "why do you listen to White music"? But just because White people sing it doesn't mean it's for White people.*

Nicole questions her peers' expectation that she listen to "Black" music.

Demonstrating the expected music tastes led to peer status and, conversely, other tastes were frowned upon. For example, Niko, an Afro-Caribbean student in London, was introduced to rock music by his cousin. He grew to like it, and now listens to a variety of styles of music regularly. Niko told me that his three favorite artists or groups are The Darkness (a rock group), 50 Cent (hip-hop), and Justin Timberlake (pop). When I asked Niko if the music he listens to relates to his identity, he replied that he keeps his appreciation for rock to himself.

> R: *I would never, ever tell you [a peer] what I like. I am afraid I might get laughed at or something like that. I try to cover it up—no, not cover up, but I try to hide some of it because I feel that most of it is unnecessary to tell to other people.*
> N: *What do you try to hide, what part?*
> R: *The rock, because most of them [peers] will laugh at that . . .*

Niko, a social student who played soccer with his classmates at lunchtime, explains the importance of demonstrating the "right" music taste for maintaining symbolic status. Among his peers, a taste for hip-hop and rap, not rock music, was part of mainstream peer culture. Hence, peer sanctioning had a conforming influence on youth, as youth used signals of conformity to mainstream tastes in order to gain status among peers (Adler and Adler 1995). This evidence suggests that hip-hop has become a global, mainstream genre rather than local, neighborhood-influenced and race-influenced music.

Style

Hip-hop had a strong influence on style. In the survey I asked students to choose one or more words from a list to best describe their style of clothing. The most common choice in London was casual, followed by stylish and then hip-hop. In New York, *hip-hop* was the most frequently chosen descriptor (see Figure 10.1). Of those in both cities who ticked *casual*, 29% also ticked hip-hop; similarly, of those who ticked *stylish*, 39% also ticked hip-hop.

Style mattered a lot to most teens. For example, Terry, an Afro-Caribbean boy in London, told me he prefers branded sneakers so that he can keep up with peers and be seen as hip: "you gotta mind what you wear because people might diss [disrespect] you . . . for not wearing what they are wearing. . . . You can't wear something too cheap, you know. You will probably get dissed. That's how it is these days". Terry, like most of his peers in London, as well as youth in New York, recognized the low peer status that could result from unstylish clothing.

When I compared the attitudes of students with hip-hop style and a taste for rap music with other students' attitudes, I didn't find significant differences (see also Tanner, Asbridge, and Wortley 2008).[15] Of those with hip-hop style, 90% believed they would complete university, compared to 93% of those who didn't identify with hip-hop style. In addition, 81% of those with hip-hop style disagreed with the statement "among my friends, it is not cool to do well in school"; similarly, 86% of those with non-hip-hop style disagreed. In terms of perceptions of discrimination, for the statement "young people of my race have a chance of making it if we do well in

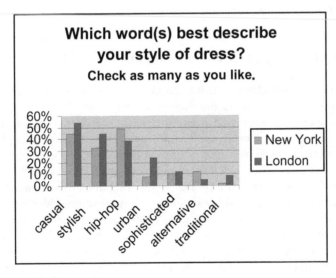

Figure 10.1   Clothing Style

Table 10.5   Influence of Hip-Hop Style on Perceptions and Aspirations

	Hip-hop style	Other styles
I believe I will complete college/university.	90% Agree	93% Agree
Among my friends, it is not cool to do well in school.	81% Disagree	86% Disagree
Young people of my race have a chance of making it if we do well in school.	87% Agree	85% Agree

Source: Survey data, *n* = 125.

school", 87% of those with hip-hop style and 85% of those with non-hip-hop style agreed (see Table 10.5). All of these differences are statistically insignificant.

Furthermore, students interviewed in both cities were much more likely to cite media influences than peer influences on their styles of dress; this was especially true of Afro-Caribbean students, who were more than twice as likely to mention media influences compared to peer influences on their style. This suggests that local African American peer influences are not the primary determinant of their styles.

The data on music and style illustrate two important points: (1) urban African American–rooted hip-hop style and music dominate the tastes of second-generation youth in both New York and London, and hip-hop's influence is global rather than via neighborhood peers; and (2) tastes for hip-hop style are not associated with greater anti-school attitudes or perceptions of discrimination.

BEHAVIORS AND INTERACTIONAL STYLES

Although their attitudes and tastes do not show evidence for oppositional orientations, many students did engage in behaviors detrimental to their academic success. I witnessed many instances of students talking back to teachers and wearing clothes such as do-rags against school rules. In addition, in interviews well over half of boys in both cities reported having been in a physical fight in high school, as did one-third of girls in both cities. These are the behaviors that have led previous scholars to conclude that students are engaging in oppositional cultures. If oppositional identities cannot explain these behaviors, then what can? I turn next to the behavioral aspects of peer cultures in these two schools to understand what's driving them. Self-reported explanations give priority in meaning to the actors themselves (Ewick and Silbey 1995). In this case, teens' narratives on conflicts in school counter the common explanation that they signify a lack of value in education (see also Morrill, Yalda, Adelman, Musheno, and Bejarano 2000).

I focus on conflicts between students and between students and teachers, because this is where schooling and youth behaviors often clash—for example, through conflicts with teachers, or in physical fights between students that lead to school suspension. In this section I describe three types of interactions and responses to conflict among youth: (1) instrumental or rational responses, enacted in order to prevent future teasing or bullying, (2) more intuitive responses that defend self-pride and gain symbolic status among peers, and (3) responses defending self-pride with teachers, which also gain symbolic status in front of peers. These responses represent parts of the "tool-kit" (Swidler 1986) of conflict resolution behaviors available to the second-generation youth in my study. The data suggest a high concern with maintaining status among peers.

Instrumental responses were common in both cities. Robert, an Afro-Caribbean and African American New Yorker in ninth grade, explained to me that he engaged in a fight in order to stop harassment at his school in Queens. He only fought, however, after attempting to resolve the conflict peacefully and reporting the harassment to his teacher:

N: *Have you ever been in a fight?*
R: *Yeah, last year . . . Because the kids here were picking on me. I told the teacher, and the teacher didn't do anything . . . The next day [the bully] was hitting me in class, so then after school he was like, "oh, we gonna fight right now". . . . And then . . . I didn't do anything at first, I waited. He hit me and then I got up and I punched him in his face and his mouth was bleeding . . . I would never hit anybody just for hitting people sake. . . . I would only do it to defend myself. . . . The result of that was he stopped picking on me. Because when you stand up to a bully, then they stop picking on you. That's what I think.*

Robert describes a situation in which he first attempts to resolve the conflict using all the other techniques he can think of, including the right behavior according to school rules. However, when he hasn't been able to stop his harassment, he does fight, and he learns the hard way that "standing up to a bully"—that is, defending oneself—can prevent harassment from peers. This skill was crucial given the context in which most urban minority youth attend school. The respect associated with defending one's pride does not always represent what youth aspire to, but rather serves as a cultural resource for survival.

Many boys told me about similar instrumental fights in junior high or ninth grade, which "proved" to peers that they were tough, and prevented future harassment and hence future need to fight. The threat alone that one is willing to fight when necessary—as demonstrated by a ninth grade fight—was enough to prevent future conflicts. Elijah Anderson (1999) recounts similar behaviors among young men in inner-city Philadephia. Robert's experience points to the physical, not just symbolic, threats that youth in the schools contended with. The pressure to defend oneself to the point of physical fighting was stronger in New York compared to London, perhaps due to the much larger gang presence there. Toughness and sometimes physical fights were cultural resources that allowed teens to survive and maintain respect in their peer social worlds. Still, London-born Anish, and others like him, clarified that not engaging in the expected response to provocation, rather than academic achievement, was what led to teasing from peers.

N: *Do kids get made fun of because they are doing well in school?*
R: *Not really. It's not by doing well in school, it's just those that are quiet—that's why some people take the piss out [make fun of them]. They just sit there instead of saying something.*

Academic achievement was much less relevant than style and comportment in the social sphere of youth and status hierarchy.

There was a fine line between instrumental narratives that described a student engaging in peer conflict to prevent further bullying, and narratives that more explicitly referenced the need to demonstrate toughness and maintain self-pride in front of peers. Pradeep's story is one example of this. 16-year-old Pradeep came to New York from India and got involved with local gangs soon after he arrived, which was just three years before I met him. He told me that he did not engage in "all that bad stuff" in India. I asked him to explain why he changed when he came to the U.S. He told me this:

I had to get involved. Because if you don't they tease you for no reason, like the big boys. Yeah, anyone—like big boys. . . . He's gonna be like, "you're this and that. You cannot fight". You know, I used to be like that in middle school, but when I came [to high school] I met boys like him [points to friend], big boys, and that's all.

A tall and brawny boy himself, Pradeep later emphasized,

there is no other option; you have to fight, because if you don't fight you get insulted. You get beaten up by other kids. If you want to stay alive over here, you have to fight.

Pradeep's earnest explanations for his fights demonstrate his perception of the necessity of fights to prevent real, physical violence from peers; it is an instrumental explanation. However, in response to his middle school experience, Pradeep got involved with local gangs as a means for protection. Far from simply preventing further violence and attacks from peers, Pradeep now seemed to enjoy his new life in which he had the respect of peers, and because now others at school wouldn't attack him. Pradeep wore a bandana over his long hair (not cutting one's hair is a tenet of Sikhism, Pradeep's faith) rather than the traditional turban—the bandana looked somewhat like the do-rags that many of his peers wore. He went from a victim of bullying in junior high school to being a member of a gang that could bully others. During his interview he described with excitement an instance of rivalry between his gang and another, in which he was shot in the leg at a distant park late at night. His reason for involvement with gangs went from personal safety—instrumental reasons—to gaining respect and status among peers, or symbolic status.[16]

Gang involvement didn't prevent Pradeep from high aspirations, though. He told me that he planned to go to college and to become an engineer or work in biotechnology after high school; he earnestly told me that when he got older he would change his ways.

> N: *And if you look to your life 10 years from now. What does it look like?*
>
> R: *I'm going to be a gentleman. . . . I'm going to leave everything after high school, like all that stuff that I am doing right now. I'm going to get a nice job, you know. I'm going to go to college. Study hard. . . . Because all that stuff I'm doing right now, it's not going to help me after college or you know after high school. . . . Like I see my boys, they are all in jail. . . . And I don't want that. . . . In like, in a year or like after high school that's it.*
>
> N: *And so why do you say that you're going to do it in a year or after high school, as opposed to, say, right now?*
>
> R: *Not right now. Because I know that's my age.*

Pradeep expresses high aspirations and beliefs that he will live the American dream, in spite of gang involvement and apparently anti-school behaviors. He sees his delinquent behaviors as part of the norms for his age—at this age, peer respect matters a lot. Unfortunately, his current school behaviors—he told me he often cuts school and has low grades—are likely to prevent him from achieving his goals.

Others more single-mindedly described their conflicts with peers as means for defending symbolic status, rather than in response to fears of physical violence. When I asked John, an Afro-Caribbean boy in London, whether it makes a student cool to misbehave in class, he replied,

> *it's normally just sticking up for yourself, that's all. . . . Like, if someone tries something on you, tries to beat you up or something, you stick up for yourself. That's what people normally would respect.*

John clarifies misbehavior as having to do with "sticking up for yourself" and maintaining respect, or status, in the eyes of peers. Knowing how to behave and interact with peers in ways to maintain peer respect was an important part of youth culture in both cities. I then asked John how academic achievement affects peer status.

> N: *What about, if you do well in school. Do people not like you if you*
>   *do well in school?*
> R: *No, they don't really mind that, if you do well or not, really.*

John confirms that not maintaining pride rather than academic achievement (high or low) leads to low peer status.

The need to defend one's pride and maintain respect was not unique to boys. I asked Ranjit, an Indian ninth grade student in New York, whether she had ever been in a fight:

> R: *I've been in two fights, last year and this year, because girls, they*
>   *like to say something. But when you say something to them, they*
>   *don't say nothing . . . If you got something to say, say it to my face!*
>   *It's better than saying it behind my back; and I don't like liars.*
> N: *So girls were talking behind your back?*
> R: *Yeah, and then my best friend told me . . . and I went up to her [the*
>   *girl talking about Ranjit] face and she goes, "oh I didn't say that".*
>   *She was mad [very] nervous! And I said "why you being nervous?*
>   *You tell me right now that you said that"! And that's just how we*
>   *started fighting.*

To resolve the affront to her pride and respect among peers (especially those who were told negative things about her), Ranjit had to confront the source of the rumors aggressively. She later explained her perception of the difference between immigrants from India and Indians "born here" (like herself): second-generation kids stick up for themselves and respond to challenges and attacks, unlike the recently arrived immigrants, who ignore affronts. The implication was that she commanded respect, and soon enough immigrants would learn that they, too, needed to demonstrate their willingness to fight back. Just as many boys reported fights in ninth grade that established their respect, many girls—like Ranjit—reported major conflicts in ninth grade, as well, even if these did not always escalate into physical fights. Indeed, although boys more commonly engaged in physical fights, girls, too, had a fair number of fights in high school—half as many girls as boys reported having been in a physical fight in high school.

Finally, conflicts with teachers were another way for teens to demonstrate their self-pride in front of peers, and hence to gain status among peers. Afro-Caribbean Terry, who lived in London, explained,

> *to me, everyone is the same. If you don't give me respect I won't give*
> *you respect. That's how it is. I won't treat a boy different from a teacher.*

*They are both the same—what's the difference? I ain't gonna actually
act rude, because [teachers] are actually older—respect your elders
and everything. But if they are actually disrespecting you, you just
gotta talk.*

Terry was raised in London by his mother, who is from Jamaica, and he
is not in touch with his African father. His emphasis on respect suggests its
importance among students in his school. His understanding that to maintain respect he had to respond when others were rude or disrespectful—even
teachers—demonstrates an important behavioral element of the youth culture I encountered in both cities. Again, these behaviors were not unique to
boys. Michelle, a 16-year-old, Afro-Caribbean student in New York, told
me: "I respect my teacher only if they respect me. They want to get loud,
I get loud". In other words, if an opponent raises the level of a conflict to
shouting, in order to maintain respect in the eyes of peers Michelle must
shout back, or "get loud". But the motivation for speaking up is respect
in the eyes of peers and self-respect, rather than defiance of the teacher
or school authorities. Unfortunately, standing one's ground in this manner
will likely be interpreted as defiance and disinterest in the eyes of school
authorities.

The youth described above responded to conflict for two related reasons: first, for the instrumental purpose of preventing harassment and
physical violence, and second, to maintain respect among peers, which led
to symbolic status among their peers. The sometimes unconscious nature
of the escalation of these conflicts, seemingly natural events, are similar
to the ways in which cultural capital's *habitus* seems natural and not
constructed or deliberately chosen by those who embody it. The "right"
responses to conflicts with both peers and teachers in class can lead to
symbolic status among peers. The line between these two goals was sometimes unclear. For example, recall Pradeep's explanation of joining a gang
in high school to end the common harassment he faced in junior high
school. Joining the gang, however, probably led to its own symbolic status
for Pradeep. Similarly, Willis, in a study of British youth, describes this
as fighting for "maintaining honor and reputation whilst escaping intimidation and 'being picked on'" (Willis 1990, 103). Other scholars also
have documented the importance of respect and pride among poor and
working-class youth and men (Anderson 1999; Bourgois 1995; Duneier
1992; Lamont 2000; Willis 1990). Although it may be heightened in disadvantaged environments, the importance placed on respect may be common to all youth. In his landmark study of adolescent youth cultures,
James Coleman (1961) suggested that "the fundamental competition in a
high school is neither for grades, nor for athletic achievements, nor any
other such activity. It is a competition for recognition and respect" (143;
see also Milner 2004).

PEER STATUS AND THE BALANCING ACT

The second-generation youth in this study expressed positive orientations toward mainstream success, a taste for African American-identified hip-hop music and style, and a need to maintain self-pride in confrontations with peers and teachers. At the same time, both schools exhibit low academic achievement overall. How can a theory of second-generation youth culture reconcile these findings? Downward assimilation theory's suggestion of oppositional cultures, influenced by African American peers, does not resonate with the findings on attitudes. Furthermore, the finding that second-generation youth in London, too, prefer African American-rooted music and style suggests that hip-hop is now a globalized taste culture for urban youth, rather than something unique to disadvantaged neighborhoods in urban America. Finally, the finding that in spite of positive school orientations many second-generation teens still engage in physical fights and other confrontations detrimental to academic success suggests that teenagers are quite concerned about maintaining pride and status in front of their peers.

Rather than an oppositional youth culture, the social world described above is one in which the quest for *peer status* has a strong influence. That is, teen behaviors can better be explained by their desires to gain status— being "cool"—among their peers. James Coleman, in *The Adolescent Society* (1961), documented the shift in post-war American society that led to an autonomous social field of youth, with its own status system. More recently, Murray Milner (2004) has analyzed peer status among college-bound students from diverse high schools in the United States, concluding that teens are so preoccupied with peer status because they spend the vast majority of their waking hours with other teens, not adults, and because they have little power or say in the other domains of their lives. Children engage in their own status hierarchy, based on their own social world and a distinct set of status considerations.

What does it take to gain peer status? Wearing stylish clothing, listening to popular music, and defending one's pride all lead to peer status; and conversely, "nerdy" clothing and lack of toughness in conflicts lead to low peer status and, sometimes, bullying. In the most disadvantaged neighborhoods, maintaining pride can prevent not just symbolic sanctioning but real, physical violence—having "streetsmarts" is a matter of survival (Anderson 1999; Conchas and Vigil 2012). Prudence Carter (2005) identifies the resources that leads to status among a disadvantaged group as *nondominant cultural capital*: "a set of tastes, appreciations, and understandings, such as preferences for particular linguistic, musical, and dress styles, and physical gestures used by lower-status group members to gain 'authentic' cultural status positions in their respective communities" (50). In other words, nondominant cultural capital buys status in a nondominant social world, such as regards Black youth or second-generation youth. Carter's formulation takes off from Bourdieu's (1986) definition of (mainstream) cultural capital and the ways in which knowledge about high-status culture can lead higher-class children to higher academic achievement through an unwritten set of skills, including ways of speaking and interacting with teachers, comportment, and certain taste preferences. Whereas Bourdieu shows how there is an upper-class culture expected at school that serves to maintain the status quo and to prevent disadvantaged children from achieving academically, Carter's analysis shows that there is also an unwritten set of cultural rules for behavior that lead to status among minority youth. Crucially, nondominant culture is not in opposition to mainstream culture but rather places different emphasis on academic success vs. success among peers.

The findings of this case study similarly show that academic achievement has little bearing on peer status (see also Eder and Kinney 1995). Rather, it is the accoutrements of hipness that matter to peers. Also, responding to provocation in the expected manner among peers also affects peer status. This finding resonates with Jackson's (2001) research on African American youth in Harlem. He found that the phrase "acting White" was used not to describe academic behaviors, but rather to describe "microbehaviors" at school, such as how a student carries himself and his speech patterns (also see Carter 2005; Tyson et al. 2005). This finding and theoretical understanding of youth culture suggests a shift in understanding the mechanism by which some second-generation minority youth fail to achieve academically and experience "downward assimilation"; it is not for want of aspirations, as these findings show, but rather it results when the quest for peer status comes into conflict with academic achievement by, for example, responding to provocation by fighting to defend one's pride. Teens thus are attempting to succeed in two distinct social worlds—the world of conventional school success, and their peer social world. These findings also diverge from the tradition of subcultural theory in Britain and the U.S., which suggested that working-class youth reacted against their limited opportunities by forming countercultural identities (Cohen 1955; Cohen 1997[1972]; Hall and Jefferson 1976; Hebdige 1979; Tanner 1978; Willis 1977), perhaps due to the different era in which that research was conducted. Finally, the findings diverge from the narrative of oppositional culture theory (Ogbu 1990, 1991, 2004), and cultural explanations given for downward assimilation among children of immigrants (Portes et al. 2005; Portes and Rumbaut 2001; Portes and Zhou 1993) (see Table 10.6).

The above discussion demonstrates that cultural markers and status are quite important to teenagers, but the cultural codes they employ are different from mainstream cultural capital. The peers they encounter are a powerful force in their lives, and the main source of social interaction. Hence, it is no surprise that their influence is quite powerful.

Thus, schools have two social fields operating simultaneously. One is the official school culture, put forth and reinforced by adults—administrators, teachers, and security guards. This culture has its own status system and

Table 10.6 Explaining Downward Assimilation

	Oppositional Culture Explanation	Peer Status Explanation
Rejection of mainstream goals and norms	Yes	No
Values academic success	No	Yes
Relationship between peer social world and adult social world	Oppositional by design, conflictual	Distinct, but not by design
Source of taste culture	Neighborhood, African American peers	Global, media
Source of low peer status	Academic achievement	Fashion, music, not responding when provoked
Source of ethnic/racial inequality (culture)	African American peer influence	Emphasis on peer culture (fashion, music, respect)

expectations, according to grades, positive relationships with teachers, and cooperation with authority. It expects students to defer to authority, deal with peer conflict through adult intervention, and don non-hip-hop styles. Mainstream cultural capital leads to success in this social world. The other social world in schools is that of youth, which pays little attention to grades and relationships with teachers (either in the positive or negative sense) and instead emphasizes coolness, popularity, and familiarity with what is hip among youth. This social world expects teens to maintain self-respect, deal with peer conflict by responding when provoked, and consume hip-hop music and style. *Nondominant* cultural capital leads to success in *this* social world (see Figure 10.2).

These two sets of cultural expectations are different cultural tool-kits aimed at different goals. That is, they are different kinds of status, earned through different cultural practices. Some students, like Robert, were more successful than others in this balancing act, talking explicitly about changing their behaviors, ways of speaking, and styles in different situations to promote the perceptions they wanted people to take away about them:

> *I do speak slang, but, like, I will know how to talk around people. Like how I am talking right now to you, I won't talk like this to my friends. I will be like, "oh wassup".*

Others prioritized one social world over the other, some by emphasizing peer status to the detriment of cultural tools necessary for school success,

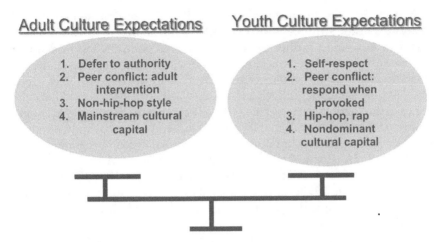

Adult Culture Expectations

1. Defer to authority
2. Peer conflict: adult intervention
3. Non-hip-hop style
4. Mainstream cultural capital

Youth Culture Expectations

1. Self-respect
2. Peer conflict: respond when provoked
3. Hip-hop, rap
4. Nondominant cultural capital

Figure 10.2   Balancing Acts

and others by emphasizing adherence to adult cultural expectations in school to the detriment of peer status. What students wanted most was to be successful in the balancing act between peer status *and* mainstream success in terms of work, education, and material well-being.

CONCLUSION

Through a careful consideration and emphasis on culture, I have demonstrated that the cultural explanation of proximity to inner-city culture leading to adversarial cultures is a weak explanation for the downward assimilation trajectory of segmented assimilation theory. This finding for children of immigrants resonates with research showing the lack of utility of oppositional culture arguments among White youth (McDill and Rigsby 1973; Rigsby and McDill 1975), working-class youth (Davies 1994, 1995), African American youth (Ainsworth-Darnell and Downey 1998; Carter 2003, 2005; Cook and Ludwig 1998; Tyson et al. 2005);, and even school dropouts (Tanner 1990). The comparative element of the research allowed me to distill what is unique to the U.S. context, and what is similar among youth living in globalized, multicultural cities. The lack of major differences in youth cultures between London and New York suggests that the presence of African Americans in urban America cannot explain the behaviors of the urban, disadvantaged second generation, as downward assimilation theory suggests; it further suggests that hip-hop has become a global currency for status among urban youth of all ethnic and racial backgrounds, rather than being a localized, predominantly African American-favored genre.[17] The findings diverge from Stepick's findings among Haitian Americans in Miami, perhaps due to the time of study (this research was conducted almost 20 years after Stepick's). Indeed, 10 years after Stepick's research was done he found a greater emphasis on Haitain pride and less evidence of downward assimilation coinciding with African American cultural identity (Stepick 1998,72). In contemporary urban America, ethnic pride is strong (Kasinitz, Mollenkopf, and Waters 2002; Warikoo 2004). It could also be the case that only in very specific types of schools—high-poverty, predominantly African American schools, such as those in Stepick's study—is there evidence for negative cultural assimilation among second-generation Afro-Caribbeans. However, the recent studies questioning African American oppositional cultures (Ainsworth-Darnell and Downey 1998; Carter 2005; Cook and Ludwig 1998; Tyson et al. 2005) suggest that there may not actually be an oppositional African American culture into which children of immigrants can assimilate.

Youth culture sometimes conflicted with academic success not via oppositional intentions, but as an unintended consequence of balancing nondominant culture with dominant school norms. This finding, along with new theoretical understanding of youth culture, suggests that the mechanism by which some second-generation minority youth find themselves in low-achieving, predominantly minority schools is not for want of aspirations, as these findings suggest, but rather results when, among other things, the quest for peer status comes into conflict with academic achievement. Some students are able to balance the two social fields and achieve success in both; others find this balance more difficult.

In addition to the cultural components described above, Portes, Rumbaut, Zhou, and their colleagues have shown how important *structural* influences can lead to downward assimilation. Indeed, these may have the most impact on downward assimilation. Recent formulations of segmented assimilation theory suggest, in fact, that structural factors are the predominant factors in determining outcomes for the second generation: "downward assimilation [emerges] as an outgrowth of a web of constraints, bad luck, and limited opportunities. . . . Results [from the CLIS study] are almost frightening in revealing the power of structural factors—family human capital, family composition, and modes of incorporation—in shaping the lives of these young men and women" (Portes et al. 2005, 1031–1032). School structural factors can also lead to downward assimilation, through organizational structures, assessment, tracking, and disciplinary systems that disadvantage second-generation minority youth (Conchas 2001; Flores-González 2002; Gillborn 2005; Gillborn and Youdell 2005; López 2002; Valenzuela 1999).[18]

The findings presented in this chapter suggest that theories of assimilation should reconsider the role of global urban youth *culture* in the assimilation process for children of immigrants. By culture I mean specifically tastes, interactional styles, and attitudes among youth, not simply parents' ethnic cultures. Studies comparing disadvantaged and advantaged groups will more easily answer the question regarding what is unique to disadvantaged urban, ethnic minority youth, and what they share with more middle-class youth. Finally, and perhaps most significantly, efforts on school reform ought to emphasize engagement with youths' peer-oriented worlds in order to aid disadvantaged students in balancing their peer and school social worlds.

NOTES

1. Adapted from R. Saran and R. Diaz, eds. 2010. *Beyond Stereotype: Minority Children of Immigrants in Urban Schools.* Rotterdam: Sense.
2. Segmented assimilation theory incorporates cultural *and* structural explanations; in this chapter, I focus on the cultural explanation.
3. By culture I mean systems of shared practices and meanings that include attitudes, ways of understanding the world (beliefs), tastes (expressive symbols), and "tool-kits" or "cultural scripts" for behavior (Lamont 2000; Swidler 1986).
4. I define the second generation as those born in the U.S. or UK with foreign-born parents, as well as the foreign born who arrived before age five. I call individuals born abroad but arriving between the ages of five and 10 one-and-a-half generation.
5. I consider schools' underachievement as a whole, rather than individual students' academic achievement, as evidence for downward assimilation in those schools.
6. Throughout this article I have changed the names of the schools, students, and teachers in the interest of confidentiality.
7. The survey was administered in four Personal, Social, and Health Education (PSHE) classes in London, and in four English classes in New York. PSHE is taught to Form Classes, which are deliberately mixed in terms of gender, ethnicity, and skill level, according to a school administrator. The English classes in New York were: one "remedial" ninth grade English class (15 of the 19 ninth grade English classes were remedial), one general English 10th grade class, and two mixed 10th/11th grade classes serving medium-achieving students. The highest achievers are not in the New York survey, because of the classes I surveyed. This should not matter, because the data are used to test the hypothesis of *downward* assimilation, more evident in low achievers rather than high achievers. One limitation of the survey, however, is the absence of school dropouts from the survey. Also, students who were absent on the day of the survey were not included in the data; this likely slightly skews the data to exclude the lowest achievers who do not attend class regularly.
8. Because school statistics count Asians together with those in the "other" category, this figure may be slightly high.
9. Official school data do not disaggregate students beyond the categories Asian, Black, Hispanic, Native American, and White.
10. When the school did a drive to get all students to return application forms for free school meals soon after my research, 87% of students became eligible for free school lunches.
11. The number of ninth grade students is much higher than the number of students entering the school each year, because those who don't pass enough classes remain as ninth graders, sometimes for three or even more years. Still, reported graduation rates are often inflated (Orfield 2004).

12. The GCSE exams are the exit exams for schooling in the UK, taken at age 16. Five C or above GCSE grades (one grade is awarded for each subject) is the minimum requirement for entering most British universities, and five A–G grades is the minimum standard for saying one has finished school "with qualifications".

13. In this article, because most interviews were with second-generation youth, students described as "Indian" or "Afro-Caribbean" are all second generation, unless otherwise indicated.

14. UK garage is a British form of rap music, generally with much faster beats and rapping than American rap.

15. Tanner and his colleagues (2008) found that a taste for heavy metal, hard rock, alternative, punk, and grunge music together led to less agreement with the statement "education is an important part of life", but the same was not true for a taste for Black-origin styles of music.

16. Similarly, Zukin and Maguire (2004) find that working-class mothers feel conflicted between "shopping by necessity"—similar to Pradeep's fighting to prevent physical violence—and "shopping for status"—similar to Pradeep's later gang membership.

17. Of course, myriad differences distinguish the second-generation experience in London and New York. Afro-Caribbeans in Britain are more integrated at home and at school than their U.S. counterparts, and they intermarry with Whites at much higher rates (Burgess and Wilson 2004; Model and Fisher 2002; Peach 1996). Also, patterns of migration are different, Afro-Caribbeans and Indians traditionally coming to Britain as colonial subjects, in contrast to Afro-Caribbean and Indian migration to the United States, which sees itself as a nation of immigrants (Foner 2005).

18. Some have questioned the notion of downward assimilation altogether, suggesting that, in fact, children of immigrants thought to downwardly assimilate are actually doing better than their parents, and are assimilating in similar patterns to the turn-of-century wave of immigration (Kasinitz, Mollenkopf, Waters, and Holdaway 2008; Perlmann and Waldinger 1997; Waldinger and Feliciano 2004).

REFERENCES

Adler, P. A., and P. Adler. 1995. "Dynamics of Inclusion and Exclusion in Preadolescent Cliques." *Social Psychology Quarterly* 58 (3): 145–162.

Ainsworth-Darnell, J. W., and D. B. Downey. 1998. "Assessing the Oppositional Culture Explanation for Racial/Ethnic Differences in School Performance." *American Sociological Review* 63 (4): 536–554.

Anderson, E. 1999. *Code of the Street: Decency, Violence, and the Moral Life of the Inner City.* New York: W. W. Norton.

Aventura. 2008. Retrieved February 5, 2015, from www.aventuraworldwide.com.

Bourdieu, P. 1986. *Distinction: A Social Critique of the Judgement of Taste.* London: Routledge and Kegan Paul.

Bourgois, P. I. 1995. *In Search of Respect: Selling Crack in El Barrio.* Cambridge: Cambridge University Press.

Brown, B. B. 1990. "Peer Groups and Peer Cultures." In *At the Threshold: The Developing Adolescent,* edited by S. S. Feldman and G. R. Elliot, 171–196. Cambridge, MA: Harvard University Press.

Burgess, S., and D. Wilson. 2004. *Ethnic Segregation in England's Schools.* London: CASE Paper Centre for the Analysis of Social Exclusion, London School of Economics.

Carter, P. 2003. "'Black' Cultural Capital, Status Positioning, and Schooling Conflicts." *Social Problems* 50 (1): 136–155.

Carter, P. 2005. *Keepin' It Real: School Success Beyond Black and White.* New York: Oxford University Press.

Cohen, A. K. 1955. *Delinquent Boys: The Culture of the Gang.* Glencoe, IL: Free Press.

Cohen, P. 1997[1972]. "Subcultural Conflict and Working-Class Community." In *The Subcultures Reader,* edited by K. Gelder and S. Thornton, 90–99. London: Routledge.

Coleman, J. S. 1961. *The Adolescent Society: The Social Life of the Teenager and Its Impact on Education.* New York: Free Press of Glencoe.

Conchas, G. Q. 2001. "Structuring Failure and Success: Understanding the Variability in Latino School Engagement." *Harvard Educational Review* 71 (4): 475–504.

Conchas, G. Q., and J. D. Vigil. 2012. *Streetsmart Schoolsmart: Urban Poverty and the Education of Adolescent Boys.* New York: Teachers College Press.

Cook, P. J., and J. Ludwig. 1998. "The Burden of 'Acting White': Do Black Adolescents Disparage Academic Achievement?" In *The Black-White Test Score Gap,* edited by C. Jencks and M. Phillips, 375–393. Washington, DC: Brookings Institution Press.

Cutler, C. A. 1999. "Yorkville Crossing: White Teens, Hip Hop and African American English." *Journal of Sociolinguistics* 3 (4): 428.

Davies, S. 1994. "Class Dismissed? Student Opposition in Ontario." *Canadian Review of Sociology and Anthropology* 31 (4): 422–445.

Davies, S. 1995. "Reproduction and Resistance in Canadian High Schools: An Empirical Examination of the Willis Thesis." *The British Journal of Sociology* 46 (4): 662–687.

Duneier, M. 1992. *Slim's Table: Race, Respectability, and Masculinity.* Chicago: University of Chicago Press.

Eder, D., and D. A. Kinney. 1995. "The Effect of Middle School Extracurricular Activities on Adolescents' Popularity and Peer Status." *Youth and Society* 26 (3): 298–324.

Ewick, P., and S. S. Silbey. 1995. "Subversive Stories and Hegemonic Tales: Toward a Sociology of Narrative." *Law and Society Review* 29 (2): 197–226.

Flores-González, N. 2002. *School Kids/Street Kids: Identity Development in Latino Students.* New York: Teachers College Press.

Foner, N. 2005. *In a New Land: A Comparative View of Immigration.* New York: New York University Press.

Gans, H. J. 1992. "Second-Generation Decline: Scenarios for the Economic and Ethnic Futures of the Post-1965 American Immigrants." *Ethnic and Racial Studies* 15 (2): 173.

Gibson, M. A. 1988. *Accomodation Without Assimilation: Sikh Immigrants in an American High School.* Ithaca, NY: Cornell University Press.

Gillborn, D. 2005. "Education Policy as an Act of White Supremacy: Whiteness, Critical Race Theory and Education Reform." *Journal of Education Policy* 20 (4): 485.

Gillborn, D., and D. Youdell. 2005. *Whose Children Left Behind? The Impact of Institutional Arrangements and Practices on Pathways through Education.* Paper presented at the Educating Immigrant Youth: Mobility and Citizenship in International Perspective, London.

Hall, S., and T. Jefferson. 1976. *Resistance Through Rituals: Youth Subcultures in Post-war Britain.* London: Hutchinson.

Hebdige, D. 1979. *Subculture: The Meaning of Style.* London: Routledge.

Jackson, J. L. 2001. *Harlemworld: Doing Race and Class in Contemporary Black America.* Chicago: University of Chicago Press.

Kasinitz, P., J. H. Mollenkopf, and M. C. Waters. 2002. "Becoming American/ Becoming New Yorkers: Immigrant Incorporation in a Majority Minority City." *International Migration Review* 36 (4): 1020–1137.

Kasinitz, P., J. H. Mollenkopf, M. C. Waters, and J. Holdaway. 2008. *Inheriting the City: The Children of Immigrants Come of Age.* Cambridge, MA: Harvard University Press.

Lamont, M. 2000. *The Dignity of Working Men: Morality and the Boundaries of Race, Class, and Immigration.* New York: Russell Sage Foundation and Harvard University Press.

López, N. 2002. *Hopeful Girls, Troubled Boys: Race and Gender Disparity in Urban Education.* New York: Routledge.

Maira, S. 2002. *Desis in the House: Indian American Youth Culture in New York City.* Philadelphia: Temple University Press.

Majors, R., D. Gillborn, and T. Sewell. 2001. "The Exclusion of Black Children: Implications for a Racialised Perspective." In *Educating our Black Children: New Directions and Radical Approaches,* edited by R. Majors, 105–109. London: Routledge.

McDill, E. L., and L. C. Rigsby. 1973. *Structure and Process in Secondary Schools: The Academic Impact of Educational Climates.* Baltimore: Johns Hopkins University Press.

Mehan, H., L. Hubbard, and I. Villanueva. 1994. "Forming Academic Identities: Accommodation Without Assimilation Among Involuntary Minorities." *Anthropology and Education Quarterly* 25 (2): 91–117.

Miles, M. B., and A. M. Huberman. 1984. *Qualitative Data Analysis: A Sourcebook of New Methods.* Beverly Hills, CA: Sage Publications.

Milner, M. 2004. *Freaks, Geeks, and Cool Kids: American Teenagers, Schools, and the Culture of Consumption.* New York: Routledge.

Model, S., and G. Fisher. 2002. "Unions Between Blacks and Whites: England and the US Compared." *Ethnic and Racial Studies* 25 (5): 728–754.

Modood, T. 2004. "Capitals, Ethnic Identity and Educational Qualifications." *Cultural Trends* 13 (2): 87–105.

Morrill, C., C. Yalda, M. Adelman, M. Musheno, and C. Bejarano. 2000. "Telling Tales in School: Youth Culture and Conflict Narratives." *Law and Society Review* 34 (3): 521–565.

Neighbourhood Renewal Unit. 2004. *Indices of Deprivation 2004: Local Authority Summaries.* Office of the Deputy Prime Minister.

New York City Department of Education. 2004, 2005. *School Report Cards.* New York.

Office for National Statistics. 2001. Census 2001: Key Statistics. People and Society: Population and Migration, Table KS06.

OFSTED (Office for Standards in Education, Children's Services, and Skills). 2003. *School Inspection Report.*

Ogbu, J. 1990. "Minority Education in Comparative Perspective." *Journal of Negro Education* 59 (1): 45–57.

Ogbu, J. 1991. "Immigrant and Involuntary Minorities in Comparative Perspective." In *A Comparative Study of immigrant and Involuntary Minorities,* edited by J. Ogbu and M. Gibson, 3–33. New York: Garland Publishing.

Ogbu, J. 2004. "Collective Identity and the Burden of 'Acting White' in Black History, Community, and Education." *The Urban Review* 36 (1): 1–35.

Orfield, G. 2004. *Dropouts in America: Confronting the Graduation Rate Crisis.* Cambridge, MA: Harvard Education Press.

Peach, C. 1996. "Does Britain have Ghettos?" *Transactions of the Institute of British Geographers* 21 (1): 216–235.

Perlmann, J., and R. Waldinger. 1997. "Second Generation Decline? Children of Immigrants, Past and Present—A Reconsideration." *International Migration Review* 31 (4): 893–922.

Portes, A., P. Fernández-Kelly, and W. Haller. 2005. "Segmented Assimilation on the Ground: The New Second Generation in Early Adulthood." *Ethnic and Racial Studies* 28 (6): 1000–1040.

Portes, A., P. Fernandez-Kelly, and W. Haller. 2009. "The Adaptation of the Immigrant Second Generation in America: A Theoretical Overview and Recent Evidence." *Journal of Ethnic and Migration Studies* 35 (7): 1077–1104.

Portes, A., and R. G. Rumbaut. 2001. *Legacies: The Story of the Immigrant Second Generation.* Berkeley: University of California Press and Russell Sage Foundation.

Portes, A., and M. Zhou. 1993. "The New Second Generation: Segmented Assimilation and its Variants." *The Annals of the American Academy* 530: 74–96.

Ramos-Zayas, A.Y. 2003. *National Performances: The Politics of Class, Race, and Space in Puerto Rican Chicago.* Chicago: University of Chicago Press.

Rigsby, L.C., and E. L. McDill. 1975. "Value Orientations of High School Students." In *The Sociology of Education: A Sourcebook,* edited by H.R. Stub, 53–75. Homewood, IL: The Dorsey Press.

Sewell, T. 1997. *Black Masculinities and Schooling: How Black Boys Survive Modern Schooling.* Stoke on Trent, UK: Trentham Books.

Stepick, A. 1998. *Pride Against Prejudice: Haitians in the United States.* Boston: Allyn and Bacon.

Swidler, A. 1986. "Culture in Action: Symbols and Strategies." *American Sociological Review* 51 (2): 273–286.

Tanner, J. 1978. "New Directions for Subcultural Theory." *Youth and Society* 9 (4): 343.

Tanner, J. 1990. "Reluctant Rebels: A Case Study of Edmonton High School Dropouts." *Canadian Review of Sociology and Anthropology* 27 (1): 74–94.

Tanner, J., M. Asbridge, and S. Wortley. 2008. "Our Favourite Melodies: Musical Consumption and Teenage Lifestyles." *British Journal of Sociology* 59 (1): 117–144.

Tyson, K., J. W. Darity, and D. Castellino. 205. "It's Not 'a Black Thing': Understanding the Burden of Acting White and Other Dilemmas of High Achievement." *American Sociological Review* 70 (4): 582–605.

UK Department for Education and Skills. 2005. *Ethnicity and Education: The Evidence on Minority Ethnic Pupils.* Research Topic Paper: RTP01–05.

Valenzuela, A. 1999. *Subtractive Schooling: Issues of Caring in Education of U.S.-Mexican Youth.* Albany: State University of New York Press.

Waldinger, R., and C. Feliciano. 2004. "Will the New Second Generation Experience 'Downward Assimilation?' Segmented Assimilation Re-assessed." *Ethnic and Racial Studies* 27 (3): 376–403.

Warikoo, N. 2004. "Cosmopolitan Ethnicity: Second Generation Indo-Caribbean Identities." In *Becoming New Yorkers: Ethnographies of a New Second Generation,* edited by P. Kasinitz, J.H. Mollenkopf, and M.C. Waters, 361–392. New York: Russell Sage Foundation.

Waters, M.C. 1999. *Black Identities: West Indian Immigrant Dreams and American Realities.* New York: Russell Sage Foundation and Harvard University Press.

Willis, P.E. 1977. *Learning to Labour: How Working Class Kids Get Working Class Jobs.* Farnborough, UK: Saxon House.

Willis, P.E. 1990. *Common Culture: Symbolic Work at Play in the Everyday Cultures of the Young.* Boulder, CO: Westview Press.

Zhou, M., and C. L. Bankston. 1998. *Growing Up American: How Vietnamese Children Adapt to Life in the United States.* New York: Russell Sage Foundation.

Zukin, S., and J. S. Maguire. 2004. "Consumers and Consumption." *Annual Review of Sociology* 30 (1): 173–198.

Contributors

Cynthia N. Carvajal is completing her master's degree in sociology and education policy at Teachers College, Columbia University. Her research explores the impact of the Deferred Action for Childhood Arrivals (DACA) program on students' educational, social, and developmental experiences in K–12 institutions. She is a scholarship recipient of The East Los Angeles Committee Union (TELACU), a University of California, Los Angeles (UCLA) alumni scholar, and a Congressional Hispanic Caucus Institute (CHCI) alumnus. She was born in Guadalajara, Mexico and immigrated to East Los Angeles, California at the age of five. She received her BA at the University of California, Los Angeles, where she double majored in political science and Chicana/o studies and double minored in education and public policy.

Vichet Chhuon, PhD, is an assistant professor of culture and teaching and Asian American studies at the University of Minnesota, Twin Cities. His research examines how race, identity, and institutional opportunities shape academic engagement and youth development for young people, particularly students of color.

Gilberto Q. Conchas is professor of education policy and social context at the University of California, Irvine. He obtained a PhD in sociology from the University of Michigan, Ann Arbor and a BA in sociology from the University of California, Berkeley. Conchas' research focuses on inequality, with an emphasis on urban communities and schools. He is the author of *The Color of Success: Race and High-Achieving Urban Youth* (2006), co-author of *Small Schools and Urban Youth: Using the Power of School Culture to Engage Youth* (2008), and co-author of *StreetSmart SchoolSmart: Urban Poverty and the Education of Boys of Color* (2012). Conchas has been a visiting professor at the University of Southern California, San Francisco State University, University of Washington, the University of Barcelona, Spain, and the University of California, Berkeley.

Sean Drake is a PhD candidate in sociology at the University of California, Irvine. Sean earned a BA in psychology (with honors) from Stanford University. His research interests include race/ethnicity, education, immigration, and athletics. His research on the academic engagement and achievement of Black male youth was recently published in the journal *Urban Education*, and he has presented his work at the Yale Urban Ethnography Project Conference. Sean is currently working on an ethnographic project that investigates how the racial/ethnic diversity and academic culture in high schools affect racial meanings, identities, and group boundaries in an era of steady immigration from Asia and Latin America.

Glenda M. Flores specializes on Latina/o sociology, Latina professionals, gender and work, and the sociology of education. Her primary research agenda focuses on the mobility pathways of the children of Latino immigrants and their workplace experiences in the white-collar world. In particular, she examines why college-educated Latinas enter the teaching profession and their impact on school climate in immigrant and multiracial schools. Her work on the scarcity of Latinos/as in the STEM (science, technology, engineering, and math) fields appears in the *Latino Studies* journal. The National Science Foundation, Myra Sadker Foundation, Ford Foundation, and the Spencer Foundation have supported her research.

Roberto G. Gonzales is assistant professor of education at Harvard University. His research focuses on the ways in which legal and educational institutions shape the everyday experiences of poor, minority, and immigrant youth along the life course. Over the last decade professor Gonzales has been engaged in critical inquiry regarding what happens to undocumented immigrant children as they make transitions to adolescence and young adulthood. His work has been published in top social science journals and policy reports, and has been featured in most of the major media outlets. It has also helped policymakers, educators, and community practitioners better understand contemporary immigration at the level of everyday, lived experience.

Michael A. Gottfried is an associate professor of education policy and the economics of education at the University of California, Santa Barbara. He holds a PhD and MA in applied economics from the University of Pennsylvania and a BA in economics from Stanford University. Gottfried's research focuses on addressing a range of educational policy issues, with a particular interest in improving educational equity and outcomes for students from high-needs groups. His work has won national-level awards, including several from the American Educational Research Association.

Briana M. Hinga is a postdoctoral researcher and lecturer at the University of California, Irvine. She completed her PhD in education at the University of California, Irvine (UCI), with specializations in educational context and social policy and learning, cognition, and development. Her research illuminates how history, social structure, schooling practices, policies, perceptions, and actions interact to shape educational opportunity. She focuses on partnerships with communities, students, and schools to design and evaluate learning environments that foster possibility and social justice.

Alex Romeo Lin is a postdoctoral research fellow in the T. Denny Sanford School of Social and Family Dynamics. He received his PhD in educational policy and social context from the University of California, Irvine. He has longstanding interest in three research areas: (1) positive youth development: studying the development of values and civic engagement across adolescence and young adulthood, (2) school- and family-based interventions: improving the design, delivery, and evaluation of interventions directed towards adolescents, and (3) inequality: addressing sociocultural processes within school contexts for low-income immigrant and U.S.-born Latino, Asian American, and African American youth.

Kelly Nielsen is a doctoral candidate in the department of sociology at the University of California, San Diego. His research focuses on the narrative constructions of social life and the intersections of biography and social structures in higher education. Relying on longitudinal qualitative methods, his work explores postsecondary educational institutions and the diverse trajectories of college students. In particular, his work seeks to understand the community college experience and the specific role that community colleges play in student outcomes. His research pays particular attention to the race, class, and gender dimensions of postsecondary experiences and how they intersect in specific urban contexts. He has also published in the area of international migration, specifically the family dynamics of migration between Mexico and the United States.

Gilda L. Ochoa is professor of sociology and Chicana/o-Latina/o studies at Pomona College, where she teaches and writes on Latinas/os, education, and race/ethnicity. Her newest book, *Academic Profiling: Latinos, Asian Americans, and the Achievement Gap* (2013), has received awards for its focus on eradicating racism. It was also named as one of 35 books that all educators of African American and Latino students must read. Ochoa's other books include *Becoming Neighbors in a Mexican American Community* (2004), *Learning from Latino Teachers* (2007), and *Latina/o Los Angeles* (2005), co-edited with her brother, Enrique C. Ochoa. In the classroom, she aims for interactive and transformative learning spaces. A recipient of several teaching awards from UCLA and Pomona College, she speaks regularly at high schools and colleges and collaborates with teachers on various student-centered projects. The daughter of first-generation college students who, together, taught public school in the San Gabriel Valley for over 60 years, she received her BA in sociology from the University of California, Irvine and her PhD from UCLA.

Leticia Oseguera is associate professor in education policy studies and senior research associate in the Center for the Study of Higher Education at Pennsylvania State University. Her research focuses on understanding college access and educational opportunities for historically underserved and underrepresented student populations, and she has secured funding for her work from various foundations, policy centers, and state departments of education. Dr. Oseguera's research has been published in *Youth and Society, Research in Higher Education, Review of Higher Education, Journal of College Student Retention,* and *Journal of Hispanic Higher Education.*

María G. Rendón is an assistant professor at University of California, Irvine (UCI) in the Department of Planning, Policy, and Design. She received her PhD in sociology and social policy from Harvard University. Her primary research interests are in the fields of urban neighborhoods, immigration, urban poverty, and social policy. Her research examines the role high poverty neighborhoods have in shaping life outcomes. She has published in several journals, including *Ethnicities, Social Problems, Housing Policy Debate* and the *Journal for Health and Social Behavior.* Professor Rendón is currently working on a book examining how the urban context impacts the social mobility trajectories of inner-city, young, Latino men, drawing on extensive field work with young, Latino, adult men and their immigrant parents conducted before and after the Great Recession. Prior to arriving at UCI, professor Rendón was a postdoctoral scholar with the Robert Wood Johnson Health Policy program at UCSF/UC Berkeley. She is originally from a working-class neighborhood, the city of Lynwood in Los Angeles, and received her BA from the University of California, Irvine.

Anne Ríos-Rojas (who also goes by Anna) grew up in the diasporic space emergent between San Francisco, California and Costa Rica. Currently, she is an assistant professor in the Department of Educational Studies at Colgate University. An anthropologist of education, her ethnographic research takes up questions related to the (bio)politics of belonging, citizenship, and nationalisms, as these are encountered and negotiated by transnational youth in Spain and beyond. Her work has appeared in *Harvard Educational Review* and *Anthropology & Education Quarterly.* Anna's other academic interests include critical race studies, Latina feminist pedagogies, and artistic activism.

Natasha K. Warikoo is associate professor at Harvard Graduate School of Education. Warikoo studies race, ethnicity, and education, using the tools of the sociology of culture to reveal social and cultural processes in schools and universities. Her book, *Balancing Acts: Youth Culture in the Global City* (University of California Press, 2011), analyses how youth cultures among children of immigrants are related to their orientations toward schooling through ethnographic, interview, and survey data in diverse New York and London high schools. *Balancing Acts* won the Thomas and Znaneicki Best Book Award from the American Sociological Association's International Migration Section. Warikoo spent the 2013–2014 year at the Russell Sage Foundation, where she worked on a project about the perspectives of students attending elite British and American universities on merit in admissions, inequality, and race. This project compares how national contexts, university practices, and race shape students' meaning-making related to diversity and excellence. She is currently writing a book, *What Merit Means: Admissions, Race, and Inequality at Elite Universities in the United States and Britain.* Warikoo completed her PhD in sociology at Harvard University, and previously was on the faculty at University of London's School of Advanced Study. Prior to completing her PhD Warikoo was a teacher in New York City's public schools for four years.

Index

CPSIA information can be obtained
at www.ICGtesting.com
Printed in the USA
FSHW02n2052070918
51945FS